R. G. Collingwood and
the Second World War

R. G. Collingwood and the Second World War

Facing Barbarism

Peter Johnson

BLOOMSBURY ACADEMIC
LONDON • NEW YORK • OXFORD • NEW DELHI • SYDNEY

BLOOMSBURY ACADEMIC
Bloomsbury Publishing Plc
50 Bedford Square, London, WC1B 3DP, UK
1385 Broadway, New York, NY 10018, USA

BLOOMSBURY, BLOOMSBURY ACADEMIC and the Diana logo are
trademarks of Bloomsbury Publishing Plc

First published in Great Britain 2021
Paperback edition published 2022

Copyright © Peter Johnson, 2021

Peter Johnson has asserted his right under the Copyright, Designs and Patents Act, 1988, to be identified as Author of this work.

For legal purposes the Acknowledgements on p. xiv constitute an extension of this copyright page.

Cover image: Bomb damage on a Maltese street, World War II, 1942. Photo by The Print Collector/Getty Images.

All rights reserved. No part of this publication may be reproduced or transmitted in any form or by any means, electronic or mechanical, including photocopying, recording, or any information storage or retrieval system, without prior permission in writing from the publishers.

Bloomsbury Publishing Plc does not have any control over, or responsibility for, any third-party websites referred to or in this book. All internet addresses given in this book were correct at the time of going to press. The author and publisher regret any inconvenience caused if addresses have changed or sites have ceased to exist, but can accept no responsibility for any such changes.

A catalogue record for this book is available from the British Library.

Library of Congress Cataloging-in-Publication Data
Names: Johnson, Peter, 1943– author.
Title: R.G. Collingwood and the Second World War: facing barbarism / Peter Johnson.
Description: London ; New York : Bloomsbury Academic, 2021. | Includes bibliographical references and index. |
Summary: "As one of the few philosophers to subject civilisation and barbarism to close analysis, Collingwood was acutely aware of the interrelationship between philosophy and history. This book combines historical, biographical and philosophical discussion in order to illuminate Collingwood's thinking and create the first in-depth analysis of Collingwood's responses to the Second World War"– Provided by publisher.
Identifiers: LCCN 2020035937 (print) | LCCN 2020035938 (ebook) |
ISBN 9781350160644 (hardback) | ISBN 9781350203013 (paperback) |
ISBN 9781350162952 (ebook) | ISBN 9781350162969 (epub)
Subjects: LCSH: Collingwood, R. G. (Robin George), 1889-1943–Political and social views. | Collingwood, R. G. (Robin George), 1889–1943. New Leviathan. | Philosophers–Great Britain–Biography. | War and civilization. | World War, 1939-1945–Causes. | History–Philosophy. | Political science–Philosophy.
Classification: LCC B1618.C74 J645 2021 (print) | LCC B1618.C74 (ebook) |
DDC 192–dc23
LC record available at https://lccn.loc.gov/2020035937
LC ebook record available at https://lccn.loc.gov/2020035938

ISBN: HB: 978-1-3501-6064-4
PB: 978-1-3502-0301-3
ePDF: 978-1-3501-6295-2
eBook: 978-1-3501-6296-9

Typeset by Newgen KnowledgeWorks Pvt. Ltd., Chennai, India

To find out more about our authors and books visit www.bloomsbury.com and sign up for our newsletters.

For Sue – the one and only

Contents

Preface	ix
Acknowledgements	xiv
Chronology	xv
Works by R. G. Collingwood (with Abbreviations Used in the Text)	xviii
Introduction	1
Part I Prelude	11
1. Appeasement, war and the enemy within	13
2. One cheer for Marx	37
3. A philosopher at Delphi	55
4. Talking with Yahoos	71
Part II Engagement	87
5. Why are we at war?	89
6. Fighting back	99
7. *The New Leviathan* and the impact of events	115
8. *The New Leviathan* in 1940	125
9. Two cheers for Vansittartism: R. G. Collingwood and Germany	143
Part III A new beginning	173
10. Civility and the claims of justice	175
11. Civility and economic licentiousness	203
Afterword	217
References	223
Index	233

Preface

R. G. Collingwood's *The New Leviathan* is a remarkable book. There has been nothing quite like it in philosophy before or since. Like all books it speaks for the author, but unlike many books it also speaks directly to us. The reason for this comes from its author's cast of mind as much as his way of doing philosophy. Collingwood's subject is the modern state, society, civilization and barbarism. But this is only half the story. None of these forbidding ideas would mean anything very much apart from the humanity that formulated them. Collingwood puts us – humanity – first. To understand our politics, our culture, our ways of life, we must understand the sensations, feelings, emotions, will and thoughts which feed them. The state is the product of the ways we feel and think. Civilization is expressed in its artefacts but it belongs primarily to the minds which bring them alive.

In Frith's great painting The Derby Day the day belongs to the crowd. Horses and jockeys, even the race itself, are background to an occasion which is made by all. In the same way Collingwood puts humanity centre stage. What counts is that which makes a civilized existence possible and that is to be found in us. Equally, and it is a thought which some have wanted to resist, what defies civilization is found there, too. Collingwood's interest is not in us as a collection of individuals. His concern is not with mine or yours, as if these were always mutually exclusive. While he is often tempted to use the imperious 'we' his overriding concern is with ours, with what hopes, fears and anxieties we share in a world in which we all happen to have been born and learn to speak, and in the location where history and the accidents of social circumstance have placed us. Like its great predecessor, the Leviathan of Thomas Hobbes, Collingwood's book has a universal voice as well as a particular one. It talks therefore to all societies which find their basic moral and political principles under attack and who are made to call on resources which are deeper than social and legal rules and institutions.

The New Leviathan owes a large debt to Hobbes and to the quite different tradition of philosophical idealism which forms the background to much of Collingwood's thinking. It also owes a great deal to history in the shape of the situation in which he and his country found themselves in 1939. In this way

Collingwood found himself living through the philosophical subject his book was about, an experience of civilization under threat, which brings it much closer to events than has been supposed. Each day's writing brought news of the war which had the potential to disturb the plan for the book its writer had in mind. It was an experience which strained the powers of authorship as well as the ability to distil principles of civilization from a context in which barbarism had to be faced and in which the nature of the responsibility to face it belonged to everyone. This is the subject of my book. The years Collingwood lived through when *The New Leviathan* was gestating in his mind and then when it was written were the years in which the future of civilization was in the balance. On 18 June 1940, with France conquered, the French writer Paul Valery reflected 'In the space of several days, we have lost all certainty. We are on a terrifying and irresistible slope. Nothing that we could fear is impossible; we can fear and imagine absolutely anything' (Paxton, 1972, 3). France's fate might well have been Britain's, too. Collingwood knew that to counter this feeling in thought he would have to dig deep into philosophy and history as well as the anxieties that the British people were experiencing. Topics which informed the book were those which worried people at the time: whether Hitler could be appeased, whether a future civilized life would be possible at all, who Britain was at war with – the German people or Nazism, and justice in British society for those who had borne the burdens of war. These were the issues which poured in on Collingwood as writing progressed. These were the years through which Collingwood lived – day by day, week by week, interrupted at times by prolonged illness – years in which he articulated his thoughts about the times in philosophical terms. This approach widens his book's scope and also reflects Collingwood's determination that the intellectual battle against barbarism has to be joined and that philosophy must be at the heart of it.

Few studies have addressed *The New Leviathan* from an historical point of view as well as a philosophical one. My aim is to make good this deficiency by showing how Collingwood changes his focus, as the book proceeds, from the defence of civilization to the unenviable actions of a liberal state when forced to set aside its principles to preserve its existence and to the role of civilization and its offspring, civility, in the reconstruction of a liberal society. The argument of *The New Leviathan* is intended to reach beyond its particular time, but history in the shape of the vicissitudes of life, in this case the twists and turns of a war against a vicious barbarism, together with the uncertainties of its outcome when Collingwood was writing the book during much of 1940 and 1941, is ever present.

Collingwood's hope was to make it clear to his readers just why Britain was fighting a war which was proving hugely costly in both human life and resources. Here was an opportunity to forge the rapprochements between philosophy and history and theory and practice which were his lifelong concerns. It was he who showed us how history, together with the distinctive work of the historian, should be understood and why history mattered to philosophers who, in his opinion, generally carried on their activities in stern disregard of it. *The New Leviathan* was the book Collingwood gave up his work on the philosophy of history to write. When we realize the importance of that subject to him we see just how demanding he must have found the choice which forced him to change tack. Moreover, when we appreciate the seriousness of the illness which all but overwhelmed him during the writing of the book we see also the degree of personal courage which he needed to find to bring the project to completion.

It can reasonably be said that Collingwood died before his time. Since Collingwood's death at least three generations of readers have ensured that most of his books have remained permanently in print. References to him and his work across the academic spectrum have never been more numerous and pretty much all his oeuvre is now available to be read, something which was not true in the years immediately following his death and for some time afterwards. Subjects of philosophical discussion such as aesthetics and the philosophy of history – in each of which Collingwood published ground-changing work – were very much in cold storage during Collingwood's lifetime and during subsequent years have been given the lease of life they deserved.

Collingwood's was a voice in the history of philosophy that was stilled too early. Importantly, what Collingwood left uncompleted was the manuscript of the work he gave up to write *The New Leviathan*. That work was *The Principles of History*, an undertaking that can reasonably be called his magnum opus, left unfinished at his death but now published in its original state (along with other pieces which for many different reasons were unpublished in Collingwood's lifetime). Such is his sympathy, breadth of interest and the inclusiveness of his understanding of civilization that new generations should have little difficulty in adapting his thoughts to their world. Had he lived Collingwood, never short of pugnacity when he thought it was needed, would certainly have wanted to say more about central themes to do with the ways of life of human beings in the late twentieth century and early twenty-first century. Governments generally dislike being told what to do and in the main Collingwood as a philosopher refrained from telling them, although there are passages in *The New Leviathan* where readers might easily be forgiven for thinking that is precisely what he is doing. Collingwood's official view was that the divide between philosophy and politics was conceptual. And it is this which ensures the permanent value of Collingwood's basic arguments. *The New Leviathan* is not a blank cheque in which future readers fill in the amount which takes their fancy, but Collingwood does readily admit that the pattern of ideas he expounds will never be totally exhaustive of alternative possibilities. History is not like that. When a liberal state faces a crisis from within or without, especially one where it is required to undermine or weaken its own principles in order to survive, then in these circumstances individuals are thrown back on their own moral resources to decide what to do. This is exactly how the first readers of Collingwood's book reacted: as happened in quite a few instances they covered their copies with annotations and comments, even on one occasion supplying their own index (for the first edition of the book, reprinted in 1944, and for many later impressions, there was none).

History, as Collingwood well knew, has its own logic. *The New Leviathan* was published in the summer of 1942 (Collingwood received his copy from Oxford University Press on 2 June of that year). In the following month after heavy house to house fighting the German army took control of Rostov, the gateway to the Caucasus. At that point the triumph of barbarism looked assured. German forces were then split, with one group heading to Stalingrad, the other to the Caucasus itself. The consequences of this decision were to prove disastrous. Early next year, on 9 January 1943, Collingwood died at his old home at Lanehead in the Lake District. The following day, trapped at Stalingrad, the German commander, Field Marshal Friedrich von Paulus, refused to surrender and a new, to the German army ultimately devastating, Soviet offensive began. The next weeks and months marked the German retreat as the tide of battle slowly turned in favour of the Allies. Civilization did have a future, even though it was at this time little more than a weakling child. In these new circumstances the relevance to readers of *The New Leviathan* changed from being a defence of civilization to the nature of its role in post-war reconstruction, together with the principles and politics which should govern it. Talking of the spirit of agreement as the mainspring of a way of life Collingwood's words would then surely have struck a chord: '*Being civilised* means *living, so far as possible, dialectically*, that is, in constant endeavour to convert every occasion of non-agreement into an occasion of agreement. A degree of force is inevitable in human life; but being civilized means cutting it down, and becoming more civilized means cutting it down still further' (NL 39.15; italics in original). In this preface, I have indicated why the subject of this book is of such significance to anyone who wishes to understand how our view of the Second World War can be deepened through the philosophical perspective on those events that Collingwood provides. Collingwood's ideas did not die with him. Indeed, in an article for *Prospect Magazine* in 2019 my old friend and colleague Ray Monk makes precisely this point.

> RG Collingwood [was] one of the most remarkable, open and eclectic minds of the 20th century … His intellectual range was astonishing. In philosophy itself, Collingwood made important contributions to aesthetics, the philosophy of history, metaphysics, the philosophy of language, and the understanding of philosophical method. He had important things to say about how each of these contributes to our understanding of ourselves … Astonishingly, Collingwood achieved everything he did despite dying at the age of just 53 in 1943 … [T]he question of what course post-war philosophy in Britain might have taken if Collingwood had not succumbed to a series of strokes at this relatively early age must rank as one of the great 'what ifs' of intellectual history.
>
> (Monk, 2019)

Acknowledgements

Special thanks are owed to Abigail Lane, editorial assistant at Bloomsbury, for her help in seeing this book through to completion at a particularly difficult time.

For permission to use material which, in its original versions, appeared first in the following journals I would like to thank the editorial staff at the *History of Political Thought*, *British Journal for the History of Philosophy*, *Collingwood and British Idealism Studies* and the *International Journal of Social Economics*.

Chronology

Year	Event	R. G. Collingwood
1938		
Autumn		*The Principles of Art* published
28–9 September	Munich Agreement	
2 October		Preface *An Autobiography* written
3 October	House of Commons Munich debate	
22 October		Recuperative voyage to the Dutch East Indies: during outward and return voyages worked on *An Essay on Metaphysics*, *The Principles of History* and revised proofs of *An Autobiography*
9 November	Kristallnacht	
1939		
27 February	Britain and France recognize Franco government; Negrin stripped of power	
15 March	Germany occupies Czechoslovakia	
31 March	Britain and France give security guarantees to Poland	
7 April		Returns from Dutch East Indies
Trinity Term		Lectures on 'Metaphysics'
22 May	Military alliance between Germany and Italy	
27 June		Left from Antibes for sailing trip around Greek islands
17 August		Begins journey back to England leaving Naples 20 August
23 August	Nazi-Soviet non-aggression pact	

Year	Event	R. G. Collingwood
1 September	German invasion of Poland	
September		*An Autobiography* published
3 September	British declaration of war on Germany	
30 November	Soviet invasion of Finland	
Michaelmas term		Lectures on 'Nature and Mind'
November/ December		Preliminary work on *The New Leviathan*, including the Preface
1940		
January		Writes 'Fascism and Nazism'
From January		Writing *The New Leviathan*
Hilary term		Lectures on Moral Philosophy Lectures on 'The Idea of Nature in Modern Science'
7 March		*An Essay on Metaphysics* and *The First Mate's Log* published
Trinity term		Lectures on 'The Idea of History'
10 May	Churchill becomes prime minister	
11/12 May	Germany invades low countries	
24/30 May	Dunkirk evacuation	
May/June	Internment introduced in Britain	
4 June	Churchill's post-Dunkirk speech in House of Commons	
14 June	German troops enter Paris	
11 July		Writes letter to *The Times* on internment
15 August	Battle of Britain	
7 September	German blitz on London and other cities	
7 October		Collingwood in London during the Blitz
Michaelmas term		Lectures on 'Philosophical Theory of Society and Politics'

Year	Event	R. G. Collingwood
1941		
26 January		Reaches the mid-way point of writing *The New Leviathan*; suffers severe stroke
1 March		Resigns as Delegate to the Clarendon Press
6 March	Churchill's Battle of the Atlantic Directive	
26 March		Resigns his professorship
6 April	German forces invade Greece	
April		Moves to South Hayes Streatley
7 May		*The Three Laws of Politics:* Lecture delivered at Cambridge on Collingwood's behalf
22 June	Germany invades the Soviet Union	
6 August		Final manuscript of *The New Leviathan* reaches Clarendon Press
7 December	Japan attacks Pearl Harbour	
8 December	USA declares war	
1942		
16 January		Preface to *The New Leviathan* written
20 January	Wannsee Conference	
15 February	Fall of Singapore	
2 June		Writes to the Clarendon Press to thank them for an advance copy of *The New Leviathan*
Summer		Seriously ill, returns to Lanehead near Coniston
1943		
9 January		Death of R. G. Collingwood

Works by R. G. Collingwood
(with Abbreviations Used in the Text)

AA	*An Autobiography* (1939), Oxford, Oxford University Press.
AWOW	*R. G. Collingwood's An Autobiography and Other Writings with Essays on Collingwood's Life and Work* (2013), edited by David Boucher and Teresa Smith, Oxford, Oxford University Press.
D	'The Devil' (1916) in *Concerning Prayer*, London, Macmillan, 449–75.
EM	*An Essay on Metaphysics* (1940), Oxford, Clarendon Press, Revised edition with an Introduction and Notes by Rex Martin (1998), Oxford, Clarendon Press.
EPS	'Economics as a Philosophical Science' (1925), *International Journal of Ethics*, XXXV: 162–85, as reprinted in *Essays in Political Philosophy, R. G. Collingwood* (1989), edited with an introduction by David Boucher, Oxford, Clarendon Press, 58–77 (EPP).
FML	*The First Mate's Log of a Voyage to Greece in the Schooner Yacht Fleur De Lys in 1939* (1940), London, Oxford University Press.
FN	'Fascism and Nazism' (1940), *Philosophy*, 15: 168–76, as reprinted in EPP 187–96.
FT	'Fairy Tales' (1936–7), as reprinted in PE 115–288.
	'Goodness, Rightness, Utility', Lectures 1940, reprinted as Appendix 1, NL
IH	*The Idea of History* (1946), edited by T. M. Knox, Oxford, Clarendon Press, Revised edition, edited with an introduction by Jan Van Der Dussen (1993), Oxford, Clarendon Press.
IN	*The Idea of Nature* (1945), edited by T. M. Knox, Oxford, Clarendon Press.
MGM	'Man Goes Mad' (1936), as reprinted in *The Philosophy of Enchantment, Studies in Folktale, Cultural Criticism, and Anthropology* (2005), edited by David Boucher, Wendy James and Philip Smallwood, Oxford, Clarendon Press, 305–35 (PE).
MM	'Money and Morals' (1919), Lecture to the Student Movement, London Branch, 27 May 1919, Bodleian Library, Oxford, Dep.Collingwood 5, 7.
NAPH	'The Nature and Aims of a Philosophy of History' (1925), *Proceedings of the Aristotelian Society*, 25: 151–74, as reprinted in *Essays in the Philosophy of History*, edited with an introduction by William Debbins, Austin, 1965, 34–56 (EPH).
OPH	'Outlines of a Philosophy of History' (1928), as reprinted in IH 426–81.
NL	*The New Leviathan* (1942), Oxford, Clarendon Press, revised edition (1992), edited and introduced by David Boucher, Oxford, Clarendon Press.

PA	*The Principles of Art* (1938), Oxford, Clarendon Press.
PAE	'The Place of Art in Education' (1926), *The Hibbert Journal*, XXIV: 434–48, as reprinted in *R. G. Collingwood Essays in the Philosophy of Art* (1964), edited by Alan Donagan, Bloomington, Indiana University Press, 187–207 (EPA).
PH	*The Principles of History and Other Writings in the Philosophy of History* (1999) edited with an Introduction by W. H. Dray and W. J. van der Dussen, Oxford, Oxford University Press.
PNP	'The Present Need of a Philosophy' (1934), Philosophy, IX: 262–5, as reprinted in EPP 166–70.
POLA	'Political Action' (1928), *Proceedings of the Aristotelian Society*, XXIX: 155–76, as reprinted in EPP 92–109.
RP	*Religion and Philosophy* (1916), London, Macmillan.
R's P	*Ruskin's Philosophy: An Address Delivered at the Ruskin Centenary Conference, Coniston, August 8th, 1919* (1922), Kendal, Titus Wilson, as reprinted in EPA 5–41.
SM	*Speculum Mentis* (1924), Oxford, Clarendon Press.
TLP	*The Three Laws of Politics* (1941), London, Oxford University Press, Humphrey Milford, as reprinted in EPP 207–23.
WCM	'What "Civilization" Means', as reprinted as Appendix 2 of NL 480–511.

Introduction

During the worried, brittle period before the outbreak of the Second World War it was the Anschluss, the German annexation of Austria in March 1938, which first brought home the ordeal that would have to be faced if Hitler's Germany were to dominate Europe. The philosopher R. G. Collingwood began writing his intellectual life story, which he called *An Autobiography*, only a few weeks after Austria was forced into the Third Reich. He continued working on it throughout the summer of that year when Czechoslovakia's fate hung in the balance and, prior to the Munich agreement when a false peace was reached, he would have known with absolute certainty what Nazism represented and why appeasement merely lent encouragement to German political outrage and ambition. Collingwood does not mention the Anschluss in *An Autobiography*, but in a letter to his close friend Tom Hopkinson, written some five months or so into the Second World War, with the gestation of *The New Leviathan* complete and its composition proceeding with urgency, he repeats the message of the famous headline used by *The Times* in its issue of 15 March 1938 to describe the event (R.G. Collingwood to Tom Hopkinson, letter dated 21 January 1940, RC: 139). 'The Rape of Austria' signified what Hitler stood for. Like *The Times* Collingwood laid much of the blame for German restlessness on the Versailles settlement, but nothing could permit the violation of legal and constitutional order which the Anschluss involved and nothing could tolerate the brutal anti-Semitism which followed it.

Collingwood's purpose in writing *The New Leviathan* (1942) arose in this context. So it is important to note the connection between *An Autobiography* (1939) in which philosophy is seen as operating in intimate conjunction with history and *The New Leviathan* in its concern to find a political philosophy appropriate to its age and in its more specific aim of rejuvenating liberalism. Minimally Collingwood is committed to the view that moral concepts come to life in history. One implication of this belief is clear. A moral concept which has a definable sense in one period might find itself transformed, undermined or even lost in another. Appeasement is a case in point. To a Christian and a liberal such as Collingwood the key political virtues were the ability to moderate in the face of differences of opinion and to pacify where there is a potential conflict. Had appeasement worked, as it might have done if Hitler had been satisfied with bringing Austria and the Sudetenland within the Greater German Reich and made to stop his expansion at that point, then the appeasers might well have been remembered as peacemakers. It can be argued that even in this scenario appeasement still had a price, one moreover which was not paid by the appeasers themselves. In practice, however, few ideals are costless and as Collingwood remarks himself the job of an ideal is not to make political life painless but to mark the distance between the ideal and the compromises that sometimes have to be made.

In fact, the Anschluss proved a nail in the coffin of appeasement. Its failure was a function of history. The abhorrent behaviour of a dictator compelled bad consequences from good intentions, with the result that a way of behaving held to be desirable in civilized relationships was made to appear a vice. Directed at a political leader who was not set on a path of domination, destruction and evil appeasement might have worked. Would Collingwood's lacerating comments on the Germans as the Fourth Barbarism then have needed saying? Taking history out by changing it, however, is not an option. *The New Leviathan* was written in response to events. Collingwood's purpose is to grasp civilization and barbarism as concepts which are historically instantiated as well as open to philosophical investigation, in the case of civilization generically as a process of approximation to an ideal state and specifically as concerning the relations between members of the same community, their relations with members of other communities and their relations with the natural world.

The union of philosophy and history which is essential to understanding *The New Leviathan* is complex, but in none of its aspects is philosophy conceived as a mirror of its age. There are good reasons for this. An age may contain ideas and practices which are of little or no use to philosophy. Equally, philosophy may argue to conclusions which are absent from or out of tune with the age. More importantly, the conceptual clarification which is philosophy's business is also at least potentially reformatory. By releasing a concept from any excrescence to which it has become attached its meaning can be made more apparent, possibly even more authentic. Collingwood follows this route in his aesthetics where he distinguishes between art proper and art so-called. A similar move is made in political philosophy where in *The New Leviathan* he separates the state as he thinks it has become – the agency of insecurity and destruction – from the state as he thinks it might be, or can be interpreted as promising to be – the agency of safety and reconciliation. Thomas Nagel makes the first of these assertions when he says that 'the great modern crimes are public crimes' (Nagel 1978: 75), but without, as Collingwood does, following it with the second, that the state can be reconstructed through philosophy so as to make its true nature clear.

The Anschluss made European governments think – about actions so reprehensible that it is likely that they would rather not have thought about them at all. For some individuals, reflection on actualities was a professional requirement. One was Sir Alexander Cadogan, a senior figure in the British Foreign Office during this crisis, who, after coming to the realization that Britain could do little to alleviate the plight of countries like Austria, wrote in his diary,

> What I wonder is, is it even now not too late to treat the Germans as human beings? Perhaps they wouldn't respond to such treatment. What I have always had in mind these last two years (and urged) is that we should ask them whether they won't let us try our hand at helping to remedy the grievances which they make so much of but which they don't make very clear
>
> (Cadogan 1971: 70; from a letter dated 22 April 1938)

Two years or so after these words were written clarity about German intentions was not a difficulty. Britain was facing the immediate impact of German military power, and Collingwood was well on the way with the composition of *The New Leviathan* which was written explicitly as a contribution to the War effort. However, 'the Germans as human beings', as Cadogan expresses it, remained acutely problematic, so creating an issue which in both theory and practice was a source of deepening concern as the War progressed.

The economic depression, rise of the dictatorships and the very real loss of confidence in liberalism which marked the inter-War period in Europe gave Collingwood a watershed experience in politics. In his own opinion, perhaps too slowly, he came to see that a gloves-off philosophy was not what his age required. Like Marx, he wanted, as he said, 'a philosophy that should be a weapon' (AA 153). During the 1930s history was politics. For the liberal intellectual that Collingwood assuredly was political commitment could no longer be delayed. When it seemed that for anyone with integrity there was no other place to be, Collingwood, with many reservations and not a little nervousness, added his voice to that of the progressive Left.

The New Leviathan was written during the early part of the Second World War and was, like its great predecessors, Hobbes's own *Leviathan* and Hegel's

Philosophy of Right, an attempt to crystallize its age in thought. Its main line of argument – grounding political philosophy in the philosophy of mind – is transparent; yet, as Collingwood intended, there is also much which is entwined with its time. Clive Bell writing in *The New Statesman* in October 1939 shared Collingwood's anxieties when he said 'It would be a poor thing if in the process of resisting barbarism we lost our own civility.' After Munich Sir Cuthbert Headlam, Conservative Member of Parliament and diarist, reflected on the Germans – 'Our only policy is to treat them as civilized human beings but to see to it that we are strong enough to stand up to them if they don't play the game – they recognize force and nothing else' (Headlam 1999: 137). The novelist J. B. Priestley's call not for victory only but for a just society to end the War sounded to some not simply unrealistic but also dangerously left wing. In a longer perspective, views like these can seem ephemeral. Collingwood's Germanophobic remarks are of their context, but there was nothing platonic about his relationship with Vansittartism, the doctrine which formed the basis for discussion of German as opposed to Nazi responsibility for the War, and his book would not have been the book he wished to write if he had excluded them.

At the start of the Second World War in Britain patriotism, if not without extensive grumbling and allocation of blame, was not in short supply. It coexisted nevertheless with anxiety, uncertainty and doubt. Was the War an event which British imperialism had brought upon itself or was it sparked solely by a barbarism without? Collingwood took the view that the primary reason for a civilization's collapse comes from within. It was not barbarian military prowess which caused the fall of the Roman Empire, but, as the historian of imperial decline, Edward Gibbon, put it, 'the stupendous fabric yielded to the pressure of its own weight' (as quoted in Porter 1988: 135). There is hyperbole in the idea of the Blitz as the judgement which capitalism merits, and Collingwood never subscribed to it. In lectures given in 1928 he did ponder 'our modern tendency to over-emphasize the value of material civilization and to regard the savage as a slave to exploit and a brute to despise' (OPH, IH 469), but in October 1940, while his liberal conscience remained intact, he saw the War as resulting not from British vices but German aggression; after experiencing British resolve at first hand he was convinced that 'Hitler could never beat us' (R.G. Collingwood to F. G. Simpson letter dated 7 October 1940, RC:178). One point in this cluster of thoughts is worth stressing. Collingwood's discussion of civilization runs parallel with his liberalism, although lacking complete identification with it. In his view the savage is not an external object over which a civilization rules, but a stage in a process, one which 'the civilized man contains within him' (FT, PE

180). Nor is this assertion necessarily psychoanalytical in character. It is known, as the central claim of Collingwood's philosophy of history makes clear, as any historical present is known, by studying the past which it contains, and thus he writes 'the problem of anthropology is a special case of the problem of self-knowledge; and history is the only way in which man can know himself' (FT, PE 180). Nor should this setting aside of naturalism surprise us since in *The New Leviathan* the defence of civilization derives from the philosophical liberal's first premise and value – 'Here, with the appearance of free will in human life, begins the process of civilization' (NL 36.84). Collingwood, like George Orwell, had seen what totalitarian power can do, and if, unlike Orwell who did, he was too ill to consider joining his Local Defence Volunteers (later to be called the Home Guard) it is difficult not to believe that if he could have done he would.

Collingwood thought of a civilization as 'a way in which people live' (EM 226). Whether a way of life has reached its fullest expression and has become jaundiced or inadequate to new needs and aspirations or even unsustainable are questions that are worked out at the level of practice, where practice is informed, not by a body of theory which is independent of the way of life itself, but a set of interrelated ideas embedded in it. Nor is the test of practicability in any sense utilitarian or pragmatic. Strains which cause such deep-lying dissonance are historical in character. By conceiving of a given way of life as a logical as well as an historical construct metaphysics is the science which, in Collingwood's view, analyses the structure of presuppositions which makes that way of life what it is. When that way of life changes then, as Collingwood says, its replacement needs 'a new science and a new civilization' (EM 227). *The New Leviathan* is relevant here because it was completed in the context of rapid and substantial global transformation and, in specific regard to Britain, before the great documents of social justice such as the Beveridge Report transformed British life.

Collingwood's purpose was breathing new life into liberalism. Like his contemporary, George Orwell, who warned of the presence of totalitarian frames of mind in all political societies, Collingwood believed that no civilization is completely divorced from barbarism. Against totalitarianism's contempt for liberal values and in the context of an impending war in which their very existence was at stake Collingwood knew that the restoration of liberalism could not be piecemeal. It would have to show why liberal values are fundamental to any human society worth the name. Justice is the first liberal value, possibly its keystone. Facing barbarism is not like facing injustice, although there are overlaps. In Collingwood's hands the difference is conceptual. It arises from the meaning of terms. Barbarism is the attempt to bring civilization to an end. Writing in her diary at the start of the Second World War Virginia Woolf confessed to her anxiety that 'Civilization had shrunk' (Woolf 1990: 460, entry dated Saturday 23 September 1939). Or, in terms of the uncivil condition as described by Thomas Hobbes in his book *Leviathan*, not only was there no amenity or embellishment in life, 'no arts, no letters, no society' (Hobbes 1651: Part I, Chapter XIII), all there was in life were disunion, quarrel, brutality and fear. Civility is Collingwood's shorthand for minimum human decency or rectitude.

The Anschluss was an event in history, but from the perspective of *The New Leviathan* it was much more. The questions it raised stamped their intransigence on Allied thinking as the nihilism at the centre of Nazism became plain. Against this background just war theory had a relatively limited field of application. Hitler's world view existed in total opposition not only to the principles of just war but also to the ethical assumptions which gave those principles sense. Collingwood knew that to face up to barbarism the depth of its intellectual assault could not be ducked. And so his defence of civilization in *The New Leviathan* reaches outside politics to start from a philosophy of mind as well as the moral and social existence which follows from it. It was a suggestive remark by Rousseau which, in addition to Hobbes and the broader philosophical influences on his thought, set Collingwood on this track. During the first winter of the War he said in a lecture 'It was Rousseau who stated the connection between political autonomy and moral autonomy: the principle that only a man morally conscious of his ability to make and break and alter rules as such can be politically conscious of his ability to make, break and alter laws' (NL 458). Or, as Isaiah Berlin makes a similar point – 'So long as there were laws men could obey, they could escape (e.g. non-Jews under Hitler) – but *arbitrary* rule leads to helplessness and therefore to malleability' (Berlin 2015: 251).

In his preface dated 16 January 1942 Collingwood tells us that he started *The New Leviathan* because 'We did not know what we were fighting for and that our leaders were unable or unwilling to tell us' (NL lx). But during the time Collingwood was referring to, namely the British declaration of war or just a little after, most people in Britain would have known what they were fighting against. This was impressed on them in the clearest possible terms by the German invasion of Poland on 1 September 1939, together with all that had gone before by way of revealing Germany's behaviour throughout the 1930s, as well as the ample evidence of Hitler's intentions and the kind of state Germany had become. What Britain was fighting for, however, was less clear cut. The protection of British sovereignty and interests were certain aims, but purposes beyond this such as the liberation of Europe were hard to express as well as deliver and were modified, in some areas forcibly, as the conflict neared its end. By 'what we were fighting for' Collingwood undoubtedly meant something wider than national self-interest, an idea which was more inclusive, possibly more abstract, but certainly closer to his diagnosis of Germany's political condition. It has been argued that for realists Britain's going to war in 1939 was 'chiefly to protect the nation's interests, to maintain its honour and to preserve the balance of power', whereas for idealists it was 'chiefly to uphold the liberties of small states to destroy the evils of militarism and aggression, and to restore international harmony and goodwill' (Kennedy 1975: 156). If a little imperfectly it can be argued that the politics of *The New Leviathan* reflects this division. Arguments over means and ends, for example, which quite obviously played a large part in the Allied discussions of winning the War, are also brought within the orbit of Collingwood's philosophical account.

It has been suggested that what is most noticeable about the question Collingwood sets himself is its tone of voice (Inglis 2009: 314). By way of illustration this is Naomi Mitchison talking about her motives in writing about politics in the late 1930s when Hitler's shadow was beginning to impress itself on Europe. She says that she rushed into it 'feeling it was essential for social democrats to have strong rocks to hold to in a hurricane' (Mitchison 1979: 171). The tone of intellectual entitlement, of earnestness and of the freedom to preach to others is hard to miss. Collingwood shares in some of this, but what rescues him is not merely lack of bookishness. He was never able to make much sense of a manual of practical activities, whether of cookery and gardening or art and politics. Rather it is his understanding of philosophy which saves him. It is the job of philosophy to clarify, not to stand above life. And so it is his philosophical purpose which makes the nature of his question plain. Given that in 1939 it was barbarism which Britain faced then no philosophical account of what Britain was fighting for could work unless it used the method, language and terminology appropriate to its subject matter. Indeed, very early in the War Collingwood made his view of the inter-relationship between civilization and barbarism very clear. He writes 'Every new advance of civilization, once achieved, has a double face. For those who wish to behave in a civilized manner it gives new opportunities for civilized behaviour; for those who wish to behave barbarously it gives opportunities to create new forms of barbarism' (NL 496–7). In other words, it is not that civilization has advanced while barbarism remains only as a static relic of some ancient animosity or retarded evolutionary stage. The two concepts are tied together such that any philosophical enquiry into a conflict between civilization and barbarism will fail if it does not recognize this fact. In this way Collingwood's philosophical arguments express a universal concern as well as responding to their historical context. And so Collingwood defended civilization as a logically necessary term in a series, one which began with body and mind and proceeded through stages to the state but did not end with it. No believer in world government Collingwood nevertheless saw the idea of civilization as a concept political philosophy could not do without.

Collingwood did not live to see the Second World War through to its conclusion. He died on 9 January 1943, some two months after the British prime minister Winston Churchill famously announced of the British victory in Egypt that 'This is not the end. It is not even the beginning of the end. But it is, perhaps, the end of the beginning.' The War Collingwood experienced and thought about was largely European in location and political focus. By the time of the illness which killed him it had become a global war, one which at an enormous cost in terms of human life and resources and in spite of the vagaries of its historical outcome led to the defeat of Germany and the Nazism which had penetrated its body politic.

I have organized this study of Collingwood and the Second World War chronologically. No life, however, is lived for the convenience of historians or biographers, nor is Collingwood's philosophy always wholly in line with the historical events which accompany it, and so I sometimes step outside the narrative of events to develop arguments or consider a particular point as it was treated by later philosophers. Collingwood's battles with appeasement, his entanglement with Marxism, the voyage to Greece and the philosophical and political manifesto which governs his reaction to events are my topics in Part I: Prelude. In Part II: Engagement, I examine Collingwood's reaction to the War in his philosophy and as he experienced it. I dispel some of the mystery surrounding the composition of *The New Leviathan* and I analyse Collingwood's treatment of the moral and political dilemmas which arose for liberals fighting such a war. In Part III: A New Beginning, I consider Collingwood's defence of civility in relation to the idea of social justice. Theories of political obligation differ from theories of social justice. They raise different questions and cover significantly different ground. In Part III, I assess Collingwood's arguments for civility in the light of this distinction and in relation to the work of later philosophers on social justice as the concept central to a liberal view of the modern state.

A longer version of Chapter 2 was published in *History of Political Thought*, XXXVIII, I, 2017, 134–66 under the title 'One Cheer for Marx: R. G. Collingwood's Defence of the "Fighting Philosopher"' and of Chapter 4 as 'Talking with Yahoos: Collingwood's Case for Civility' in the *British Journal for the History of Philosophy*, 16, 3, 2008, 595–624. A version of Chapter 6 was published in *Collingwood and British Idealism Studies*, 19, 2, 2013, 169–201 under the title 'Fighting Back: R. G. Collingwood and the Origins of Resistance in Europe during the Second World War'. A version of Chapter 10 was published in *Collingwood and British Idealism Studies*, 16, 1–2, 2010, 69–112 under the title "R.G. Collingwood and the Claims of Justice." Chapter 11 was published in the *International Journal of Social Economics*, 37, II, 2010, 839–51 under the title 'R.G. Collingwood on Civility and Economic Licentiousness'.

Part One

Prelude

1

Appeasement, war and the enemy within

It was three months or so into the Second World War when Collingwood began work on *The New Leviathan*. A year or so earlier omens for peace were in disturbingly short supply. In the summer of 1938, as Collingwood was writing his autobiography, civility in the world at large was an ideal more recognized in the breach than the observance. Along with H. G. Wells who believed that by the time of the Second World War the human mind had reached the end of its tether, Collingwood saw Europe as 'a wilderness of Yahoos' (*AA* 91). The poet Stephen Spender, in another life story, tells us why. Spender writes, 'The sense of political doom, ending in unemployment, Fascism, and the overwhelming threat of war, was by now so universal that even to ignore these things was in itself a political attitude' (Spender 1951: 249). Not to take a political stance on the issues of the time was an indication of despair. Collingwood belonged to the liberal tradition of thinking which the experience of the 1930s had done much to undermine. Spain was a symbol of hope, but when the future of parliamentary democracy in Spain was a lost cause, and after Munich in September when what seemed a betrayal sealed Czechoslovakia's fate, no liberal-minded intellectual could look on politics except in disillusionment.

Spender saw how this state of mind came about: 'the words "intervention", and its counter, "non-intervention", are better keys to the understanding of this phase even than "Republican", "Red", "Fascist" and the rest' (Spender 1951: 261–2). Intervention signified action. Where one stood on Spain, the Anschluss, and the agreement at Munich was the test of decency in politics. By this standard Collingwood judged the foreign policy of the British government a culpable failure. The appeasement of Germany had avoided war, but at a severe moral cost. Left-inclined liberals interpreted non-intervention as passivity. The blame for the rise of Nazism lay not within Germany itself but in the weakness of the liberal democracies which allowed it to happen. It was evidence that the British government's true purpose, one disguised from the British people, was to accommodate Germany, so, in effect, collaborating in the expansion of its tyranny across much of Europe. Add to this Collingwood's fear of the rise of Fascism within Britain, and it is not difficult to see why his opposition was not solely to appeasement as policy but also to the prime minister, Neville Chamberlain, himself.

The Oxford parliamentary by-election held at the end of October 1938 brought these issues to a head. It was a trial of the policy of appeasement as well as an opportunity for left-wing parties to voice their opposition to the way they believed the country was being governed. Collingwood reached his views on the issues which monopolized the election before the campaign gained its momentum, and he left England for the Far East before the poll took place. Foreign policy dominated the by-election with much of the campaign's intensity deriving from the Anschluss, the German annexation of Austria, in the spring of 1938. Fear of greater German revanchism was one consequence of this, along with recognition of the conundrum which resulted, namely the need for policies which would deter Germany and avoid war.

Yet another development was the perceived chance to bring about a realignment of political forces in Britain by broadening the anti-Fascist opposition and ending appeasement as the principle directing British foreign policy. It became possible to imagine a unity of purpose bringing together liberals and socialists with communists, possibly pacifists and other anti-war groups, to form an anti-Chamberlain mass, a Popular Front, with the potential to bring about a change if not to the government, which seemed impregnable in electoral terms, then to its policies.

For a philosopher like Collingwood who aimed to link philosophy with history and with life the Popular Front's appeal during the summer of 1938 must have been close to irresistible. In his autobiography Collingwood says that after rejecting Fascism which as a liberal democrat he was bound to do, he also rejected socialism 'on the ground that the parliamentary system was still working well enough to perform its proper function as an antiseptic against class war' (AA 159). And yet in saying this Collingwood, like many on the progressive left, was making the diminution of class warfare the test of parliamentary democracy's success. By this standard, parliamentary democracy in Britain under the National Government was a sham.

Distrust of the National Government was basic to the Popular Front's rhetoric in 1938 and concealed the Front's unwillingness to approve the rearmament policies which the government felt able to propose. Idealistic as always, Collingwood's romantic view of the Spanish imbroglio allowed him to ignore any arguments that supported the British Government's policy of non-intervention. Moreover, his defence of intervention placed him solidly on the left of the anti-Chamberlain divide since, if not entirely without hesitation, supporters of a Popular Front included in their fight against appeasement those dissident Conservatives whose disgust with any accommodation with Germany made them Chamberlain's natural opponents. Collingwood not only supported military intervention in Spain but did so without giving much consideration to where it might lead. He displayed no trust at all in Chamberlain or in his government, and in the late summer of 1938 he was so impressed by Marxism that he subjected the failures of the British parliamentary system to a class analysis which could have come straight from an Independent Labour Party pamphlet.

Collingwood's autobiography is the story of his thought, but it is also personal and political. He began writing it at the end of July 1938. Its final pages refer to the crisis over Czechoslovakia and to the prime minister's negotiations with Hitler at Berchtesgaden, Godesberg and Munich. The announcement of the visit to Munich which was made to the House of Commons on 28 September was seen by Collingwood largely as a propaganda stunt, as was the flight to Germany two days later. Collingwood's preface is dated 2 October 1938, that is one day after Chamberlain's briefly triumphant return and one day before the four-day debate over Munich which began in the Commons on 3 October.

For intellectuals in Britain during the 1930s, political attitudes could not be piecemeal. Nothing less than a body of systematically related ideas seemed able to explain events so disparate in nature and time, and Collingwood was no exception. Moreover, to commit oneself without hypocrisy no theory could be divorced from action. Collingwood's analysis of British foreign policy throughout the 1930s follows this train of thought: Abyssinia, Spain and Czechoslovakia were links in the chain of government reasoning which linked British behaviour to a policy of surrender.

After Munich Collingwood's feelings about the government's appeasement policy had reached such a level of animosity that, according to his close friend, T. M. Knox, 'he visited the headquarters of the Labour Party and begged its leaders to oppose that policy with all their strength' (Knox 1969: 166). When we realize that the Labour Party was in disarray over British policy towards Germany we see more clearly why in appealing to its leaders Collingwood was not pushing at a completely open door. Aversion to fighting a capitalist war remained strong among its left wing. Indeed, Stafford Cripps was close to being alone in the Labour Party when 'he begged the front bench to rearm before Hitler struck' (Manchester 1988: 383). Motivation is the key. Cripps had no interest in joining a war which, even if victorious, would preserve the economic status quo. Moreover, Cripps had opposed all proposals for sanctions and rearmament which during the 1930s might have deterred Hitler's expansionism. Support for a Cripps-advocated Popular Front against Fascism of necessity included the acceptance of a degree of rearmament, but of much more significance was the opportunity it presented of bringing Chamberlain down.

Most thought the Oxford by-election was about appeasement. For many on the Left, however, the main focus was the future of socialism in Britain and how it could be achieved. Disagreements over electoral tactics were, as ever, at the heart of the internecine warfare that developed. In this respect, the impending Oxford by-election stood as a test not merely of the level of support for appeasement in the country, although this was important enough, but of the Labour Party's authority in relation to the Popular Front.

Much is made of Collingwood's philosophical liberalism, and yet it is sectarian nuance which dominates the final chapter of his autobiography. During 1938 the Labour Party was divided between those, mostly among its leadership, who favoured the possibility of a coalition government and those, largely among its rank and file, who favoured an attempt to challenge the government, even to bring it down. The Labour leadership believed in taking the longer view while the Left argued in favour of an immediate Popular Front to fight Fascism. Collingwood saw no reason to stand alongside the Labour leadership in their decision to soft pedal on their opposition to appeasement or in their cautious approach to intervention in Spain. The Labour leadership was sceptical of claims that the National Government represented fascism within Britain that was about to destroy democracy and civil liberties: Collingwood on the other hand held both these propositions to be true. In Oxford at the time, Collingwood was thought to have shifted to the Left. The best explanation of this is the simplest. He had. From any other perspective, Collingwood's stance is unintelligible. It was because he adopted Popular Front views that he determined to beg Labour Party leaders to adopt a tougher stance. Similarly, if the Labour leaders had been already so disposed, they would not have needed begging.

However, the Labour Party leadership had no intention of supporting the Popular Front. Distrust of Communism played a large part in this, as did fear of factionalism and usurpation from within if the Front was to prove successful. Labour was timid over rearmament and unwilling to dilute its principles and risk loss of electoral support. The Labour Party hierarchy was quick to impose party discipline but struggled to make its own position plain. Collingwood's strong political language in his autobiography signals almost as great a rejection of the Labour Party's front bench as that of the government's.

It looked as if the choice facing the Oxford electorate when the by-election was called for 27 October 1938 would be a familiar one, divided as many were between a Labour Party whose foreign policy represented little more than drift and a Conservative government which, in Collingwood's words, was 'truckling to the Fascist powers' (AA 164: the anonymous review of *An Autobiography* in *The Scotsman*, 24 August 1939, said that it 'ends with rising choler and a most vehement attack on the National Government for their Spanish Policy of Non-Intervention and, in this critic's view, Pro-Fascism'). After the prime minister's return from Munich on 1 October when peace was greeted with relief, but also with the widespread and dispiriting feeling that something dishonourable had taken place, the choice was also felt unenviable. Even more so in Oxford perhaps than in the country at large, since this was the first test of public opinion after the Munich agreement: Drusilla Scott comments that, 'people felt helpless and isolated, unsure of the principles involved or what action they should demand' (Scott 1971: 242).

Into this atmosphere of crisis and division stepped A.D. Lindsay who, as Master of an Oxford college, a retiring vice chancellor of the university and a philosopher with an established reputation as a radical liberal, had been asked to stand as an Independent Progressive candidate against the Conservative, Quintin Hogg, with both the Liberal and Labour candidates withdrawing in his favour. To educated observers it must have seemed as if T. H. Green had been reborn. Green had called Tsarist Russia 'a state by courtesy only' (for Collingwood's discussion of Green's view see TLP, 212–16); few in Britain in 1938 would have extended this to Hitler's Germany.

At the time of the Oxford by-election, Popular Front policies represented 'an extraordinary mixture of political opinion' (Scott 1971: 249). Support for Lindsay came from a few Conservative rebels, but mainly from partisan believers in Liberal, Labour and Communist ideas who disagreed about much, but not about the contempt which they thought Chamberlain and his policies merited. The Marxist-inclined Stafford Cripps argued that fascism derived from capitalism and imperialism: not until these malignant forces were removed would there be a chance of peace. Neither Collingwood nor Lindsay went quite so far, Collingwood arguing that it was the same 'Spanish formula' at work in each of the crises that the government faced during the 1930s, but refraining from the complete Marxist analysis which Cripps followed. Lindsay more predictably called the government to order for its weakness in failing to back the League and the Labour Party doctrine of collective security.

An ability to speak about politics in terms of generalities was a part of the appeal of the Popular Front. Denis Healey, an undergraduate student at Oxford at the time of the by-election, remembers that 'sectarianism was discouraged in favour of the broader simplicities of the Popular Front' (Healey 1990: 36). Healey was one who in 1938 was impressed by Communism as the only unequivocal opposition to Hitler but was quick to realize that this was yet another simplification, one soon falsified by events.

In Oxford, omens in favour of popular unity were not promising. The decision to invite Lindsay to fight the by-election on an anti-appeasement platform was immediately contentious, as was his decision after much soul-searching to take the job on. Patrick Gordon Walker, the official Labour candidate, had been unwilling to stand down, but found himself deserted by a Labour Party National Executive Committee reluctant to impose its authority on a local Oxford Labour Party branch that on 15 October 1938 had voted by forty-eight votes to twelve in favour of Lindsay as candidate (Gordon Walker 1991: 86, entry dated 15 October 1938), significantly with three liberals, Lady Violet Bonham Carter, Dr. Nathaniel Micklem and Roy Harrod, with Richard Crossman from Labour, as his main backers (Howard 1990: 327, fn. 19). Lindsay was 'more a joint Liberal/Labour candidate than a "Popular Front" one' (Howard 1990: 74), which we should scarcely find surprising since Lindsay was a Labour Party member, as well as a high-minded supporter of radical causes. Some days after his removal as the by-election candidate Gordon Walker noted in his diary, 'A popular front of Lindsays would be worse than a Liberal Party' (Gordon Walker 1991: 89, entry dated 20 October 1938), reflecting both his commitment to the Labour Party's policy of taking the long view and his belief that a Popular Front with Lindsay at the helm would soon crack under the strain of welding together an anti-appeasement strategy that worked. While Lindsay, whom Collingwood knew well, was treated with the utmost respect in Oxford radical circles, not everybody regarded his ideas with the same seriousness; as Isaiah Berlin remembered in a letter to Crossman, 'His ideas seem to me like huge buses looming out of a vast London fog and then being swallowed up again in the darkness' (Berlin 2013: 146; Isaiah Berlin to Richard Crossman, letter dated 11 February 1963).

While his local Labour and Liberal Parties were quarrelling about the terms of their approach to Lindsay, together with its consequences for the official Labour candidate, Collingwood was at home in Oxford having completed the first draft of his autobiography and preparing to leave on his long recuperative voyage to the Far East. With one of the candidates the Master of Balliol and the other a

Fellow of All Souls the contest was popularly seen as very much a University affair. (Whiting 1994: 551–2) Despite, or even possibly because of, his experience in academic politics Lindsay was the more professional of the two candidates but still could not quite conceal his dislike of the brasher aspects of democratic politics. Frank Pakenham, later Lord Longford, tells this story, 'I remembered my unhappy drive with Sandy Lindsay, Independent Progressive candidate, on Polling Day 1938. Lindsay, most upright and sensitive of moralists, was sorely exercised about a poster issued without his authority and proclaiming that a vote for Hogg is a vote for Hitler' (Pakenham 1953: 147). Folklore has it that the originator of the poster was the linguistic philosopher J. L. Austin, a convinced anti-appeaser and possibly overenthusiastic Lindsay supporter. Oxford philosophers were as much in disagreement over who to support as the rest of the Oxford electorate, with Gilbert Ryle backing Lindsay and the formidable H. W. B. Joseph his opponent. Budding politicians were similarly split, with Harold Macmillan and Edward Heath siding with Denis Healey in giving their backing to the Lindsay side (Harrison 1994: 407–8). Support for appeasement as a policy does not necessarily signify an appeaser's mentality. Other loyalties can come into play, as they did for the philosopher H. W. B. Joseph, a Hogg supporter, when he remained true to those members of his Oxford College who fought and died for Germany during the First World War by persuading the College to erect a permanent memorial to them (Glover 1999: 175).

What is remarkable is the presence of so many competing political beliefs, including communists, sheltering under the Progressive umbrella. Lindsay was aware of this, but in placing his faith in a unity capable of rising above his supporters' deep differences he was contributing an obscurantism of his own. The Popular Front meant different things to different people, with the Liberals alone in believing in a set of overarching political ideals to which all, whatever their particular allegiances, might subscribe. Underestimation of the limits of political manoeuvrings was one result of this.

The divide in Oxford over appeasement was generational as well as political. Opposition to appeasement came mainly from the young. Those who had experienced the Great War were prepared to extend trust in order to avoid another world conflict. There were exceptions, including J. A. Smith, who was Collingwood's predecessor in the Waynflete Chair of Metaphysics at Oxford and a seminal influence on his life and thought. Smith knew Lindsay well and was a considerable help to him in his early days at Balliol. Indeed, among others, especially T. H. Green, Lindsay looked to Smith as the source of his devotion to college teaching and to his belief that philosophy had a social purpose (Scott

1971: 41–4, 113). Of the many letters to Lindsay praising his courage in standing as a candidate, two are from Smith. In the first, Smith writes, 'May I assure you of my support in your protest against the past, present and future foreign policy of Chamberlain's government? In view of the desirability of this protest I suspend for the time all possible differences arising from my lifelong attachment to the Liberal party.' (J. A. Smith to A. D. Lindsay, letter dated 17 October 1938, Lindsay Papers, Keele University Library). When Smith refers to the suspension of past differences he does not mean their abolition. The differences remain but are held in abeyance in favour of a principle which overrides them. None of this made disagreement over appeasement, or 'the past, present and future foreign policy of Chamberlain's government', as Smith delicately refers to it, less intransigent.

Collingwood's preferred political language is principle, and principle can be assessed in terms of its application as well as its foundations. A significant number of those who supported the Popular Front did so because, like Stafford Cripps, they were committed to 'a heady invocation of class as the guarantor of ultimate victory', as his biographer puts it (Clarke 2002: 79). To Cripps and those who thought like him class analysis provided bedrock. In the autumn of 1938 Collingwood sympathized with much of this and in his letter of support to Lindsay, written just three days after Smith's, comes close to despair over the public apathy he thought existed at the time. He praises Lindsay for his determination to stand as a candidate which 'shows that the spirit of English democracy is not extinct' (R. G. Collingwood to A. D. Lindsay, letter dated 20 October 1938, Research Companion, (hereafter RC): 150), blaming the Chamberlain government for permitting this crisis to develop.

The issues Collingwood raises in his letter were at the heart of the campaign as it was fought. Brian Harrison accurately describes Lindsay's broad political stance when he says that his 'unsectarian socialism enabled him to combine membership of the Labour Party with the claim to have been a lifelong Liberal' (Harrison 1994: 395). Collingwood certainly aimed to be unsectarian, and he was a lifelong liberal, although one with predictable worries about liberalism being insufficiently robust in its own defence. As Richard Crossman points out, 'he could have collaborated with Cole in the study of social history, with Lindsay in his attempt to maintain the tradition that ethics and politics are not parlour games but the training of men and women for social and political work' (Crossman 1958: 107–8).

Smith's letter focuses on appeasement as policy rather than Chamberlain as its main defender. Collingwood's position is the reverse, although there is no doubt that he was also opposed to the policy. Even so, Collingwood's bitter attack on Chamberlain does mark a divide between those who were opposed to the policy but not the policymaker and those who were solidly against both. For many in the Popular Front Chamberlain was not to be trusted whatever his policy. There is surely no doubt that this was Collingwood's view, but his letter expresses his distrust of the electorate, too. Once again this was a common view. The argument, mainly although not entirely from the Left, was that people had become so beguiled by the peace terms agreed at Munich that they were blind to the political reality. There is, however, a difference between 'the spirit of English democracy' and the manifestation of it in the result of any particular election. It is this difference which Collingwood elides when he writes of this spirit at the close of his letter, 'I hope that it still survives among those who have to vote next week.' (R. G. Collingwood to A. D. Lindsay, letter dated 20 October 1938).

The Oxford by-election campaign became a tempestuous affair. For supporters of Patrick Gordon Walker, the official Labour candidate, 'the spirit of English democracy' died with the lack of assistance given to him by the Labour Party National Executive Committee and his (democratic) removal by his local branch. Lindsay was not without a degree of political cunning, but, as Christopher Hill remarks, 'he could not believe that it was possible for a man to have convictions on which he did not act' (Hill 1960: 643), a proposition of which Collingwood may be considered a doubtful embodiment since, as he says of himself, there were times when 'I lived as if I disbelieved my own philosophy' (*AA* 151).

By 1938 Collingwood had arrived at a set of political convictions which, if they did not match his philosophy in every detail, appeared at one with his times even if not all voters agreed with him. Persuading supporters of the pro-appeasement candidate Quintin Hogg that they might be wrong was not at all plain sailing, as Lindsay came to realize when, on the stump during the campaign, he encountered a man who asked, not unreasonably, 'now that our prayers have succeeded in bringing peace from the Munich agreement, is it not ungrateful to doubt and to question that peace?' Lindsay's answer resonates with the sounds of the manse and the study. He said,

> 'suppose you had a child desperately ill. All night long you pray without ceasing, and in the morning she seems better. You thank God that your prayers have been answered. Then, later on it is discovered that owing to some error in the doctor's treatment, she is going to be disabled for the rest of her life. Would your gratitude to God for saving your daughter's life prevent you from calling in a better doctor who might restore your daughter to health? That is how I feel about our present precarious peace. I am sure that Mr. Chamberlain did his best, but I know that it was also he who brought us very near to war. I am sure that it

is owing to his policy that we are now in such a very dangerous situation. That is why I oppose him.'

(as quoted in Hopkinson 1984: 30)

In common with the Labour Party, Lindsay defended collective security as the way to deter German expansionism and attacked Chamberlain's government for not having given more support to the League in the crises which had afflicted international relations during the 1930s. Like the Labour Party, cautious on the subject of rearmament and hedging his support with concerns about industrial democracy, Lindsay saw rearmament as necessary for a defensive war, though he had little to say about any interventionist role in the affairs of other states. So he opposed the activities of the German and Italian governments in Spain but failed to identify how opposition might be realized beyond a refusal to ratify diplomatic agreements. In fact, on Spain Collingwood went further, arguing that what was needed was 'only a fair field. If the government could once extemporize and equip an army, the rebels' fate was sealed.' (*AA* 160–1).

The foreign policy of a government depends in part on the reactions and responses of other states and so is not entirely within its gift, but the biggest influence on the formation of voters' views seemed to be the prime minister himself. When the result of the election was declared on 27 October 1938 it became clear that Collingwood's fears of voter apathy were baseless. In an exceptionally high poll Hogg defeated Lindsay by 3,434 votes, a substantial swing against the government but also representing the highest Conservative turnout since 1922 (McLean 1973: 140–64).

Patrick Gordon Walker was quick to produce reasons for the defeat. One of these he thought was the focus on foreign policy which was the central element of Lindsay's campaign. Gordon Walker wrote to the *Oxford Mail* the day after polling arguing that it 'was initiated in middle class and University circles. There has been no shortage of money in a most lavish campaign. The programme of this Democratic Front to a large extent reflected the views of people who are rich enough to afford the luxury of ignoring everything except foreign policy.' (Gordon Walker 1991: 92, fn. 39). The Lindsay Front, as Gordon Walker was prone to call Lindsay's campaign, was a distraction within the Popular Front, itself another distraction from socialism as represented by the Labour Party, in Gordon Walker's view 'the strongest force in England against fascism' (Gordon Walker 1991: 90).

Gordon Walker was accused of sour grapes, but he did compliment Lindsay, and his reasons for the failure of Lindsay's campaign are perceptive. Gordon

Walker came out firmly against the Popular Front or any amalgam of progressives which might weaken the Labour Party as the main opposition to the government. On this view the Lindsay Front was simply a useful device through which a variety of far left groups, including Communists, could exert their influence. A few days after being removed as the Labour Party's official candidate, Gordon Walker wrote a long account of the background to the Lindsay candidature in his diary, saying amongst much else that

> the prime cause was the international crisis. An hysterical frame of mind was created largely in the middle class and University circles (it was therefore stronger in Oxford than it will be in some other places). It concentrated itself on the worst, most obvious fault – namely hostility to Chamberlain himself. People persuaded themselves that this was important. Quite ludicrous ideas about the importance of Lindsay's victory were evolved. That it would check Chamberlain, lead him to alter his policy, frighten Hitler, etc.
>
> (Gordon Walker 1991: 86)

To readers of the final chapter of Collingwood's autobiography this should be familiar. The onslaughts on Chamberlain, the fears for democracy, the accusations of perfidy and weakness were standard ways of speaking for those like Collingwood who had no interest in a link with the dissidents on the Conservative right and, yet, had come to distrust the Labour Party. As Gordon Walker writes, again in his diary, 'If you are for the Lindsay front you must reconcile yourself to breaking LP's and destroying the strongest force in England against fascism, namely the tough loyalty and defensiveness of the Labour Party.' (Gordon Walker 1991: 90).

Against this background Collingwood's political opinions at the time of Munich become intelligible. Moreover, Gordon Walker's scorn for the Lindsay Front was less the expression of a sore loser than a reflection of political reality since, despite some initial electoral success, the Popular Front gradually withered away, with the Labour Party being the main cause of its decline and the major beneficiary of it. During this process Collingwood's allegiance to Popular Front ideology remained unchanged. Indeed, during the first summer of the war Collingwood stationed himself once again to the left of the Labour Party, now in the coalition government, when he wrote to *The Times*, with Lindsay as one of his co-signatories, warning about the dangers to democracy arising from the policy of internment (R. G. Collingwood to *The Times*, letter dated 11 July 1940, RC: 183). The fear of fascism within, a stock belief of the Popular Front, had re-surfaced.

In Oxford, once the implications of Lindsay's defeat had sunk in, his supporters rallied round. On 28 October Smith wrote again to congratulate him on his efforts, saying that 'time alone was wanting to make an even more complete success. I cannot thank you too heartily for enabling me to take part in a movement which is, I believe, bound to grow' (J. A. Smith to A. D. Lindsay, letter dated 28 October 1938, Lindsay Papers). Collingwood, too, after a delay because of the distance letters had to travel between Oxford and Bali where he was staying, replied on 8 December 1938 to a letter from his wife, Ethel, which had been posted on 27 October 1938, the very day that the results had been declared. In his reply he says that he was 'especially interested to see how many people you have found who take the correct view of the present-day political situation in England', and that 'I begin to form the impression (based also on what my Dutch friends tell me about internal affairs in Germany) that the dictator states are only being kept on their legs by the execrable Chamberlain and the bloody-awful Halifax' (R. G. Collingwood to Ethel W. Collingwood, letter dated 8 December 1938, Teresa Smith Archive, (TS/PLTR 190) part cited in Wendy James, 'A Philosopher's Journey: Collingwood in the East Indies', in *AWOW* 546). One in Oxford who had no confidence in the 'spirit of democracy' at all was A. L. Rowse who 'declined to campaign for Lindsay against Hogg. As he put it, "Thank God that I at any rate didn't waste any time trying to persuade an idiot vote."' (Green 2011: 239).

Given that the voters in Oxford had kept 'the spirit of democracy' alive, Collingwood's talk of the 'correct view' on appeasement and his low opinion of the efforts of Chamberlain and Halifax to avoid war can seem, if not hysterical as Gordon Walker thought the Lindsay front's mindset to be, then wide of the mark: there was no 'correct' view on appeasement at the time nor, it might be added, has there been one since. Not everyone in Oxford had been optimistic about Lindsay's success. Brian Harrison records that 'of the 26 fellows of All Souls who speculated on the outcome only 7 predicted that Lindsay would win, and then only by a small majority', (Harrison 1994: 407) (although it is important to note S. J. D. Green's view that while some in All Souls were animated by it the Oxford by-election was an event in which 'other fellows of the College took surprisingly little interest') (Green 2011: 253), although this may be more a case of the fellows backing their own horse. Even some of Lindsay's supporters had doubts. As Robert Pearce comments, 'The Master of Balliol had high prestige in academic circles, but not among the general public, over half of whom, according to Tom Harrison of Mass Observation, "didn't know Lindsay from Adam"' (Pearce, 'Introduction', Gordon Walker 1991: 10); but then by the same argument not many among the general public would have known Hogg from Adam either.

Collingwood's autobiography was written from the perspective of a present in which two concerns dominated his thinking – the rapprochement between philosophy and history and between theory and practice. This sounds like an echo of the unity of thought and action found in the early work, *Speculum Mentis*. Yet it is less of an echo than a modifying of some of the ambition which marked that book. Collingwood asserted in 1939 that 'the chief business of twentieth century philosophy is to reckon with twentieth century history' (*AA* 79), a statement which points to links between philosophy and politics but does not quite tell us what they are. In terms of attitudes towards past cataclysms and anxieties for the immediate future, history in 1938 was not bound by the Oxford by-election. Even so, a philosophy which aspires to bear upon life must do so in particular circumstances. General principles can shift the gaze, but the gaze must come to rest somewhere.

The 1938 Oxford by-election was not the event of world historical significance that more than a few, especially on the University side of the town, hoped it would be. For Lindsay's supporters it promised a reaffirmation of the link between theory and practice which T. H. Green took as the benchmark of social responsibility. In fact, appeasement as policy sailed on, but into increasingly choppy waters, until it was irretrievably damaged by the behaviour of a dictator abroad. A Balliol-inspired connection between liberal theory and political practice failed to produce unanimity of view. Some of those who supported the Progressive Independent candidate would certainly have thought of themselves as progressive but not because they were liberal. As Collingwood had written to his friend, the Italian philosopher, Guido de Ruggiero, some ten years or so earlier, about the change in political attitudes, 'your conception of an idealistic liberalism will find, I think, very few favourable readers. It will remind people of Green, and Green is out of fashion – today the fashionable colour is red!' (R. G. Collingwood to Guido de Ruggiero, letter dated 4 October 1927, RC: 122).

By 'red' it is likely that Collingwood meant 'Bolshevik', but by the end of the 1930s Bolshevism had metamorphosed into Communism which, with liberalism increasingly seen as politically irrelevant, if not the ideals of freedom and justice which it claimed to represent, was regarded in Oxford and elsewhere as the only meaningful challenge to Fascism. Action was the key to the final chapter of Collingwood's autobiography, just as it was to those castigated by Gordon Walker in his diary for their hysteria in crying 'We must *do* something' (*AA* 152) when faced with what was thought of as an avoidable war. It is this feeling which lies behind Collingwood's praise for Marx, that he was not a politician negotiating passively with his enemies but a 'fighting philosopher' (AA 152), one who translated his theories into action. There is so much hyperbole in Collingwood's final chapter that it is hard not to read it as an example of exactly the mood that Gordon Walker denigrates.

In mid-October 1938 action took the form of support for Lindsay and the Popular Front. As we saw, Collingwood sided against the Labour Party leadership and was with its rank and file in hoping for a realignment of the Left in order to maximize the strength of an anti-Chamberlain coalition. As an historian of this period writes 'there seems little doubt that had it not been for Munich, agreement on a single candidate would not have been possible' (Eatwell 1971: 125). Both Labour and Liberal Party leaderships had strong reservations about an electoral pact. Even after Lindsay's candidature was confirmed, support for it from the Liberal leadership was expressed in terms which must have left Collingwood dissatisfied. *The Times* quotes the Liberal leadership as 'pledged to work for unlimited appeasement without surrender to force', which communicates exactly the kind of fence-sitting required for the new party political amalgam to work (*The Times*, Friday, 21 October 1938). Labour Party leaders nationally, too, were initially unwilling to underwrite a local party which had shifted towards the radical Left. Further, compared with the Liberal Party,

> the 'university' on the other hand, held a much stronger position in the counsels of the City Labour Party, and it was within the walls of Oxford's colleges that many of the most ardent exponents of a pact were to be found. The most prominent members of this group were G D H Cole and City Councillor Frank Pakenham. They were supported by a large 'city' Labour group which contained a small Communist cell – indeed at least one of the key offices in the constituency Labour Party was held by a Communist at this time.
>
> (Eatwell 1971: 125)

It is not difficult to see why the Oxford by-election has been described as 'a political quagmire' (Todman 2016: 147). As the campaign was fought out it increasingly took on the character of a referendum. A debate on a single issue became muddled with questions about which candidate would best represent the constituency. Uncertainty existed on the matter of policy, too. On the surface the question to be decided was the appeasement of Germany, but what was appeasement? Was it a policy or an ideal which might be pursued in different ways? Both sides stressed that what united their supporters overrode any individual political allegiances they might have. Neither side wanted to appear too distinctive. Thus, Lindsay, as the Progressive Independent candidate, tried hard, but, in the eyes of some, failed to illuminate the fog by stating that 'International appeasement was not a policy, but a purpose towards which policies must be directed.' (*The Times*, Friday, 21 October 1938). Whether appeasement was a policy or a purpose it is clear that Lindsay had the harder task in defending an alternative to it (Trubowitz and Harris 2014: 289–311). Collective security, an alliance with Russia, a ring of small states which might act as a deterrent, increasing the rate of British rearmament, out and out pacifism, all these and others had been considered and rejected as for various reasons impractical. And, yet, there was no doubting the extent of Lindsay's appeal, at one point in the campaign 'he was forced to deny that he had received a message of encouragement from Stalin.' (Eatwell 1971: 128).

Whatever encouragement Lindsay took from Collingwood's letter of support it was not in the form of policy. In fact, Collingwood goes out of his way to exclude it by writing at the close of his autobiography, 'I am not writing an account of recent political events in England', (*AA* 167) a statement which seems not a little disingenuous given his references to contemporary political events and personalities in the final chapter of his autobiography and his use of these to explain how they 'impinged upon myself and broke up my pose of a detached professional thinker' (*AA* 167).

Opposition to the British government's foreign policy together with a hatred of almost everything associated with Chamberlain was common ground between Collingwood and most of the Lib/Lab and Communist figures who made up the Oxford Popular Front, but few of these, apart from the candidate himself, might have shown much interest in the view that aid for the groundwork of Fascism came, albeit unintentionally, from a small number of Oxford philosophers who during the early years of the twentieth century understood their subject as neutral regarding the affairs of life. Many might have been flummoxed by it since the chain of reasoning which links realism as a philosophical doctrine with appeasement as a practical policy does seem obscure. Nevertheless, this was a fixed point in Collingwood's mind during the period before the Oxford by-election. Yet, we should note the support given to A. D. Lindsay's candidature by J. L. Austin and Gilbert Ryle neither of whom had much time for philosophy understood as a theory of life. H. J. Paton and H. H. Price, two Oxford philosophers who were in varying degrees intellectually close to Collingwood, but were, again in varying degrees, distant from analytical and linguistic philosophy, also gave their support (*The Times*, Friday 21 October 1938). The resolve with which Collingwood concludes his autobiography is his own. No doubt Austin showed similar determination in campaigning assiduously on Lindsay's side. Lindsay was a philosopher who was 'preoccupied with the importance of participation in political affairs' (Eatwell 1971: 126), as on this particular occasion was Austin. It was the argument that mattered first, then the election. It is hard to believe that Collingwood would have thought differently.

Explanations for Lindsay's defeat varied from the highly partisan to the social scientific. Few followed what might have been Collingwood's line in blaming Chamberlain for concealing the truth from the electorate or Lindsay's that the prime minister had never informed the electorate what his policy was. None blamed the defeat on Oxford philosophy's pusillanimity in standing up to the rise of Fascism. Post by-election criticism of the Progressive Independent candidate was strong. The Liberal who stepped down, Ivor Davies, described Lindsay as 'the worst Parliamentary candidate I have ever encountered. (Pearce, 'Introduction', Gordon Walker 1991: 10), and, yet, such is the nature of electoral politics that the best often appears as the worst. Lindsay had fought an honest campaign and where 'the issues were complex Lindsay sought complex answers' (Eatwell 1971: 130), a stance which certainly distinguished him from many of Chamberlain's critics, but did little to increase his electoral appeal. The Popular Front might have been united against Chamberlain, but it was disunited on almost everything else. More importantly, it was opposed by the Labour Party which effectively meant its end as an independent political force. Small wonder, then, that Collingwood had tried to get the Labour leadership to take the opportunity the Popular Front represented at the time rather than the long view. And, yet, it was the long view which won out. As Quintin Hogg, the victorious candidate commented in a hindsight article some forty or so years later, 'a democracy can only go to war united. In September 1938 the nation was deeply divided' (Hogg in Hopkinson 1984: 30).

In Oxford, philosophical and political allegiances produced some unexpected divisions, not only between those who supported Hogg and the majority who supported Lindsay but also between Lindsay supporters, such as A. J. Ayer, whose philosophical account of moral and political beliefs seemed to leave them shorn of practical significance and those like Collingwood who wished to explain moral and political beliefs in terms of an idealist account of mind and action. Ayer was one of the radical left in politics who saw a parallel between the British government's indifference towards unemployment at home and its impassivity in the face of Fascism abroad, a view which the Collingwood of 1938 might well have supported (Rogers 1999: 144). Collingwood's problem here is transparent. Philosophy in Collingwood's view was not a purely technical exercise wholly detached from life. An account of moral beliefs, such as Ayer's, which turned them into what they are not falsified their meaning and so could not without inconsistency be isolated from life. And, yet, in his life Ayer treated his moral and political beliefs with complete seriousness. Moreover, he acted on them, so epitomizing the committed professional thinker which in 1938 Collingwood desperately wanted to be. The solution to this puzzle is obvious, but it is not one that helps Collingwood since it requires exactly the separation of theory and practice that he was determined to avoid.

The roots of Collingwood's belief in the unity of theory and practice are to be found in T. H. Green and the philosophical idealism which forms the basis of his liberalism. As Brian Harrison remarks, 'For late Victorian Oxford intellect was not enough: it must result in action' (Harrison 1991: 229). In the context of 1938, however, the Popular Front intermingling of liberal progressives and Communist Party supporters left only confusion. So much so, in fact, that E. R. Dodds felt it necessary to be absolutely clear about where Lindsay stood politically, writing, 'I have stated the facts of this matter carefully, since Lindsay was later described, quite incorrectly, as a Communist stooge. The Communists gave him their uninvited and noisy support, but it was the Pink Lunch and not the Communists who originally put his name forward in lieu of Gordon Walker's.' (Dodds 1977: 131 fn. 1).

The Pink Lunch Club was an informal group of left-inclined Labour and Liberal intellectuals, mainly from Oxford Colleges, who met in Oxford from the early 1930s onwards to discuss contemporary social and political issues in the light of socialist theory (Dubnov 2012: 120–1, 240 fn. 83). One who knew both G. D. H. Cole and Collingwood at this time, also attending meetings of Cole's group as a student in Oxford, was Ralph Glasser whose memoir of his time at Oxford is rightly regarded as a classic. After recording his feelings of estrangement at meeting Crossman and Cole, and his dissatisfaction with the procedures of linguistic philosophy, he says that,

> An exception, far from generously recognized, was R G Collingwood in his luminous exposition of the proper business of philosophical enquiry, in lectures and in the Olympian sweep of his book *Speculum Mentis*. Its opening sentences I would remember in all the years to come: 'All thought exists for the sake of action. We try to understand ourselves and our world only in order that we may learn how to live.'
>
> (Glasser 1988: 124)

G. D. H. Cole was a leading member, and although he had initial reservations about Lindsay's chances as a compromise candidate, he did give him his support.

Given Collingwood's political inertia at the time it would have been not a little surprising if he had been a member or attended meetings. Moreover, the realist philosophical assumptions which most of the group shared would scarcely have encouraged him. However, affinities between the Pink Lunch and Collingwood's political mood in 1938 are strong, reflecting the growing recognition that political commitment was unavoidable and that an academic life which was out of touch with social and political affairs was failing its ideals. Opposition to appeasement was a great deal more demanding, however. It required more discipline than most of the parties involved could manage. The result was that after Munich feelings of shame mixed with anti-Chamberlain generalities came to dominate popular debate.

Outside Oxford the economist, John Maynard Keynes, saw the Popular Front as a vehicle for revealing Chamberlain's Munich agreement for what many believed it actually was, 'a put up job between him and Hitler' (Skidelsky 2000: 38), before going on to say that he believed Chamberlain would soon call a General Election on the back of it and that a bringing together of opposition to Chamberlain overrode every other consideration. The contempt which Keynes felt towards Chamberlain mirrors that of Collingwood. However, as Keynes's biographer rightly points out, 'the rational difference between Keynes and Chamberlain was wafer thin' (Skidelsky 2000: 37). Few of Chamberlain's critics were prepared to admit it, but the 'two parallel roads of conciliation and re-armament' (Feiling 1946: 365) which the prime minister was determined to follow were in terms of practical politics the only ones available. The idea hinted at in Collingwood's final chapter that an alternative way of restraining Hitler was simply awaiting discovery was and remains a fallacy. As is the view that Chamberlain's policies might have worked, if only they had been executed by a very different kind of politician.

The argument that Collingwood's autobiography is a great work despite its final ten pages is one that is easily made. It has to be said, however, that without them a good deal of the immediacy of Collingwood's feelings, including his shame and fury at what he along with many people at the time saw as political cowardice, would have been lost. So when *The Times* came to review the work some ten months after it was written it was the 'fearless sincerity' (*The Times*, 15 August 1939) of the final chapter which caught the reviewer's eye. As much as it was intended as a signpost for the future Collingwood's rousing conclusion was bound up with the situation in which it was written, one in which cheers for and invective against a British prime minister went side by side. On its publication, events which were fresh in Collingwood's mind in 1938 had become stale. Moral attitudes, however, are different. And, so the reviewer's praise for Collingwood's sincerity and fearlessness retains its point because it refers to the directness and honesty which characterize his writing, as well as his determination to speak in the present voice.

Sincerity, then, certainly, but what did Collingwood have to fear? His was not the responsibility of office, or, indeed, of power, which burdens office holders with deciding what can be publicly said and when. Nor did Collingwood play an active role in the public arguments over appeasement. It can be argued that the disdain that marks his treatment of Chamberlain over the Czechoslovakian crisis achieved little, except perhaps concealing the issues which made it so difficult to resolve. As Collingwood says himself of the agreement reached at Munich, 'I was less interested in the fact itself than the methods by which it was accomplished' (*AA* 165). Keynes thought of Chamberlain as a swindler; Collingwood thought of him as a trickster; both were common views though neither had much reality, especially when we notice Collingwood's unwillingness to consider alternative policies. Most serious-minded discussion of British foreign policy at the time, as S. J. D. Green puts it, 'took cognizance of the possible necessity for resistance, the need for rearmament, and the fine line to be drawn between settlement and disagreement' (Green 2011: 243). And, yet, apart from a few vaguely expressed remarks about Britain having discarded her political liberties, empire and influence in Europe Collingwood says nothing. Hardly anyone advocated unilateral British military action in relation to Czechoslovakia. Lindsay certainly knew the price that had to be paid as a result of the agreement and was deeply disturbed by it, but he reserved his faith in collective political pressure on Germany and kept silent on all other questions concerning immediate action (Scott 1971: 248), and Collingwood, given his sceptical approach to British rearmament, was in no position to advocate it.

Confirmation of Collingwood's fulminations against British foreign policy and those responsible for it comes from the reaction of his publishers, Oxford University Press, when they met to consider his autobiography for publication in November. By this time the Oxford by-election was over, although other by-elections were set to take place and the brittle, anxious mood in the country remained. The confidence inspired by Munich was beginning to evaporate, but Collingwood had always scorned Chamberlain's very real popularity immediately after Munich and had used hard words to explain it.

The Delegates of Oxford University Press were worried. An historian of the Press writes of their uneasiness after having read what he describes as 'an alarmingly controversial if not defamatory little book in which the crisis through which European civilization was passing appears first in the shape of an intellectual disease affecting academic life in Oxford' (Sutcliffe 1978: 247). Collingwood's touchy, excitable prose reflects the time in which the book was written, but for a number of the Delegates considering the manuscript it was the wholly overwritten, exaggerated tone of the final chapter which caused most concern and so he was asked to modify it (Sisam to R. G. Collingwood, letter dated 18 January 1939, Clarendon Press Archives, Autobiography File LB8083, for Collingwood's reply, see RC: 88. For discussion of this and other matters relating to the consideration and publication of *An Autobiography* by the Press, see David Boucher and Teresa Smith, 'The Biography of an Autobiography', in *AWOW* xxiii–xxvi).

When Collingwood's autobiography was published in July 1939 the situation facing the British government in Europe was dramatically different from that which existed when the book was written. During its writing, and even when the Press were considering it for publication, war seemed avoidable, but by the summer of 1939 it was little short of inevitable. We cannot examine the manuscript as the Delegates, who included Lindsay, did because the original manuscript is no longer extant, but their reactions do tell us something of what it contained. Concern was expressed about the use of the word 'traitors', specifically in connection with the then chancellor of Oxford University, Lord Halifax, who was foreign secretary in the Chamberlain government. Halifax was a leading, although not untroubled, supporter of appeasement and the Munich settlement, and a political bête noire of Collingwood's (Boucher and Smith, 'The Biography of an Autobiography', *AWOW* xlvii). That Collingwood felt able in his original draft to accuse a member of Chamberlain's government of treason may not be surprising given his hatred of appeasement, but by mid-March 1939 when he revised the proofs of the final chapter he removed it. His reasons for this can only be a matter of conjecture: that it was described as a piece of 'vulgar abuse' by one of the Delegates may have been contributory (Clarendon Press Archives, Autobiography file, 12 November 1938). In making this charge against Halifax Collingwood's was not a lone voice. Both Chamberlain and Halifax were regularly accused of treachery at this time (for one politician's view see Ball 1999: 135, where we find 'but clearly we must preserve the peace if we can – and this obviously is what Neville is out for – even if it means his being called a "traitor", etc.'; entry dated 25 September 1938).

The Delegates also asked Collingwood to review his remarks on Spain. The absence of Collingwood's first draft is important here since we do require his exact words for us to make sense of the complaint that he had attacked the behaviour of the Nationalist forces from weak evidence. For intellectuals in Britain, observing Spanish political life from the outside, Spain was a complexity within a complexity. Incidence of extensive atrocities by both sides made commitment suspect. Collingwood reserved his greatest anger for the attitude of the British government, but he withdrew any statements which were unsupported by evidence. In any case, when the autobiography was being written the endgame in Spain was being played out, and when Collingwood came to revise his final chapter Spain had become no more than a stepping stone to the immeasurably greater conflict which followed. Even among those who were sympathetic to Collingwood's stance regarding the general political rights and wrongs of the Spanish conflict it was felt that the remarks on Spain were 'out of keeping' with the book's autobiographical purpose because they expressed the sense of 'an immediate political crisis' rather than the recollection of past temper and attitude (Sisam to R. G. Collingwood, letter dated 18 January 1939); even in their toned down form Collingwood's remarks on Spain reveal a consistently left-wing political position. From this perspective British newspapers were simply propaganda sheets telling lies about the republican government and its supporters (*AA* 159–60). Unsurprisingly, George Orwell took a similar view, one which led him to question the whole idea of objective historical truth (Thomas 1965: 47–8). Collingwood in the autobiography as it was published took a rose-tinted view of the role of the communists in the Spanish struggle, one not shared by his close friend and former student, Tom Hopkinson, who wrote of 'the ruthlessness and treachery of the Communists which ended by destroying the Government side's resistance and paving the way to a Franco victory' (Hopkinson 1953: 25).

In 1995 I wrote that 'at the time *An Autobiography* was published it was read as a political act' (Johnson 1995: 13). And yet the approach to war in 1939 was such a helter-skelter of events that, in the short time between composition and publication, pronouncements in the book which had a point during the crisis over Czechoslovakia and in the run up to Munich were by August 1939 relevant only as the confirmation of long-held views or as hindsight. By the time of its publication Collingwood's autobiography had become not the decisive political intervention he was perhaps hoping for, but simply a part of the story of his life as he wanted to tell it.

It is not Collingwood's low and vituperatively expressed opinion of Chamberlain which sets the final pages of the book apart. Keynes, too, as we have seen, was another who expressed a violent dislike of the prime minister, regarding him as 'the lowest, flattest-footed creature that creeps', and finding it impossible to avoid the feeling 'of having been *swindled* as never before in our history' (Self 2006: 329). What sets Collingwood's conclusion apart is its direct concern with his political present. Not only does Collingwood restate his autobiography's main theme that the philosophers of his youth, 'for all their profession of a purely scientific detachment from practical affairs, were the propagandists of a coming Fascism' (*AA* 167), he also makes an explicit commitment to action, as his praise of Marx, the hero of the book's final political reflections, comes close to requiring him to do.

Political debate imposes responsibilities on those who engage in it, but Collingwood wrote as an autobiographer for whom personalities and events were important insofar as they affected the picture he had of himself. This varied over time, sometimes rewarding him with approval, but on other occasions giving rise to resentment, frustration and dislike. Not only was the story of his life as he told it unique to him, but his diagnosis of the crisis Europe faced at the time of Munich came from his own experience and was bound by Oxford and the philosophical views he first encountered there. Collingwood aspires to say what is true, and his success in that is a tribute to the book as he wrote it, but his frame of reference is himself. He is the essential subject and the world is important if and when it impinges on his thoughts and feelings. So when *The Times* review says that the personal political opinions expressed in Collingwood's final chapter 'cannot be called extrinsic to the argument' (*The Times*, 15 August 1939) of the book as a whole, this is what is meant. It is the autobiographical genre itself that is being emphasized. In the story he tells of his life Collingwood describes how the philosophical doctrine of realism and its practical effects provoked his particular anger, but in the world outside entirely different considerations rule. Here the policy of appeasement which he so much decried was articulated and defended by a government, and by others, including *The Times* for a lengthy period, quite independently of any philosophical position at all. Collingwood's autobiography is not an exercise in self-justification, as it would have been if he had seen it as an opportunity to answer his critics, or if he had tried to show that he had nothing in the shape of an opinion or an action to apologize for or to regret. Neither is it a private diary or memoir nor, very differently, an assessment of the foreign policy options open to the British government in 1938, as it might have been if Collingwood had been invited to address the discussion group prompted by Sir Arthur Salter, Gladstone Professor of Political Theory and Institutions at Oxford, which met at All Souls in order to provide a forum for academics and politicians to exchange ideas about the appeasement of Germany, an enterprise in the linking of theory and practice which might otherwise have appealed (Green 2011: 240–2). By making the history of his political views known and by charging the 'minute' philosophers of his youth with a political responsibility which would not have occurred to many, Collingwood was inviting public debate and criticism. In all this the key voice, as it must be in any autobiography, is Collingwood's own. After the German occupation of Prague on 15 March 1939, when 'even *The Times* abandoned appeasement' (Doerr 1998: 243) Collingwood's abrasive opposition to the prime minister continued. In 1938 Collingwood was drawn to Marx's stress on the unity of theory and practice. He felt the power of radical political ideas. But to be systematic a left-wing programme requires a base in theoretical Marxism. Was Collingwood the Marxist that many in Oxford thought he had become?

2

One cheer for Marx

When in July 1939 Oxford University Press published Collingwood's *An Autobiography* those who knew its author well were about to receive a shock for there in the final chapter Collingwood announced himself an admirer of Karl Marx (AA 152–3). To be sure, Collingwood rejects both Marx's metaphysics and his economics. But the object of Collingwood's admiration, Marx's belief that it is the business of philosophy to make the world better, is not a minor matter. It is an essential part of the ideological structure of revolutionary socialism as Marxists understand it. A significant few in Oxford believed that Collingwood, if not a fully paid up Marxist, had become a fellow traveller of the Left.

For the liberal political philosopher that Collingwood was, and for the Asquithian liberal that in politics he was originally and for much of his life remained, any suggestion of affinity with Marxism requires justification. Radical Tories, Liberal Imperialists and even Ruskin-loving environmentalists of Collingwood's generation might have inclined to philosophy to support their views, but Collingwood's approval of Marx is different. Drawing practical conclusions from liberal premises depends on those premises being true. Collingwood thought that the metaphysical and economic foundations of Marx's doctrines were false, and yet he went out of his way to praise Marx's view that philosophy bears the closest possible relationship to life. What made an academic working behind his college gates hold up a nineteenth-century philosopher of revolution as his ideal of philosophy in action? When Collingwood wrote *An Autobiography* the weight of liberal principle was in the past. It was his disillusionment with the failure of liberalism, together with his opposition to the Chamberlain government and his reluctance to commit himself to the rearmament policies of the anti-Chamberlain Right, that made him prey to the Left. In 1933 E. H. Carr said, 'There is a point up to which we are all Marxists now' (as quoted in Haslam 1999: 54). Quite what that point was varied with the individual case, but when Collingwood wrote the story of his life he had reached the stage where he believed that Marxism was the 'gloves-off' (AA 152–3) philosophy that was needed.

The true account of Collingwood's praise for Marx starts in Oxford. Marxism was a theory of revolutionary action as well as an analysis of oppression. And in Oxford during the 1930s, though much of it was nascent (Susskind 2011: 26), the academic study of Marx and Marxism went side by side with involvement in left-wing politics. Between 1936 and 1938 (Collingwood began *An Autobiography* in July 1938), it must have seemed as if the whole University was moving to the Left. While being sympathetic to Marx's identification of exploitation within capitalist societies Collingwood had remained too much the liberal democrat to accept Marxist politics. In 'Man Goes Mad' written in late summer of 1936 he described 'socialism, in the Marxian form in which it alone is a vital force in the world today', as carrying 'along with it too much dead weight in the shape of relics from the age in which it was born' (MGM in PE 324–5). Of these relics Collingwood included enlightened dictatorship, universal history, political and economic utopianism, and the glorification of war in the shape of class struggle. In 1936 Collingwood looked to a rejuvenation of liberalism, but two years later he says of his relation to Marxism that 'all that stood in the way of closer agreement was the second R. G. C., the academic or professional thinker' (AA 153).

It was a standard assumption shared by Left-wing thinkers during the 1930s that any effective facing up to the European dictatorships lay exclusively in their hands. But of those who drew attention to Collingwood's leftward shift only R. H. S. Crossman made the connection between his opposition to appeasement and his support for Marx, the fighting philosopher. Of Collingwood he writes that 'the events of 1936–38 made him suddenly aware that the ruling class of this country was conniving at the destruction of Europe's liberty and of his own' (Crossman 1958: 108). Crossman's choice of words is instructive. Only a Marxist analysis of power in British society could explain the British government's willingness to bow to the European dictators. Fellow travellers of the Left needed to be polarized so that the conflict within British democracy could be sharpened: liberal opponents of appeasement should be made to see that their liberalism, far from reinforcing opposition, actually constituted an obstacle to it.

For many during the 1930s Marxism offered commitment and hope. Its method of analysis told liberals why liberal democracy was not working. To progressive liberals the only credible destination was communism. As Goronwy Rees explains in his memoir of the Thirties, the communist always managed to impose on liberals a picture of himself 'as a man of superior moral integrity, as the fighter who is always in the front line, unhampered by the bourgeois inhibitions and reservations by which the liberal was afflicted' (Rees 1971: 117). During the 1930s Collingwood was never a communist convert, but he was disillusioned with liberalism, and so for a short period he was prepared to countenance Marx, even if it was a Marx shorn of his basic doctrines and separated from his role in Soviet ideology.

In the months preceding the Second World War when Collingwood's political soul-searching began, he was faced with a situation in which principle and the needs of the time were at odds. Policies which promised the avoidance of war were accompanied by high moral and political costs, and those which seemed to make war more likely offered no guarantee of victory. The uncertainty which marks this period is reflected in Collingwood's own political opinions. History had become an unreliable guide.

Such dilemmas came to a head after the Munich agreement in the autumn of 1938. There was scope for genuine conflict of view. Moreover, as we have seen, arguments over the pros and cons of appeasement did not follow Party lines. Not only did Collingwood support a Popular Front against the appeasement policies of the Chamberlain government, he supported it against a government perceived by the Left to be proto-Fascist, and indeed the language he uses to describe the foreign policy of the Chamberlain government – 'the Spanish formula' – does sound very much like the Stafford Cripps-inspired doctrine of the indivisibility of peace. Collingwood was no pacifist but, like many on the Left at this time who were, he was in favour of British government intervention in Spain while saying little about the rearmament that was necessary to make it effective. Again like many on the Left, Collingwood condemned the British government's negotiating stance with Hitler, while saying little about how collective security would preserve peace.

There is another sense, too, in which Collingwood became open to radical influence. Again, the issue is responsibility for war but, unlike appeasement which involved Collingwood in looking forward to a likely chain of events, the causes of the First World War involved him in looking back to reappraise Britain's role in it. At the time, Collingwood blamed aggressive Prussianism but, in 1938, with another war with Germany seemingly close at hand, he apportions blame differently. So, in *An Autobiography* Collingwood describes the Great War as 'an unprecedented triumph for natural science', and 'an unprecedented disgrace to the human intellect' (AA 90). Some ten years earlier in Oxford, another historian, A. L. Rowse, already heavily committed to the Left, had 'contended for an equal distribution of blame between the powers' (Ollard 1999: 43). In 1938 Collingwood agreed. Whether the War of 1914–18 was a Prussian war or an Imperialist one it was a war that no one wanted and so, the hidden logic of Collingwood's position implied, it was a war which need not have been fought. Collingwood was opposed to the British government's conciliation of Hitler but, from the point of view of the Left just prior to the Second World War, opposition to appeasement did not mean support for rearmament. Collingwood undoubtedly wanted the British government to stand up to aggression. With equal force, however, and like almost everyone on the Left in Britain, he did not want to be tricked into another war.

Collingwood's swing to the Left was noticed mainly by those who wanted it to be true, and it was only in obituaries published after his death that what was in Oxford hearsay became a definite claim. Few of the first reviews of *An Autobiography* made much of its references to Marx (for these reviews see Johnson 2017: 141–2). One reviewer, A. H. Hannay, did notice the oddity involved in Collingwood associating himself with Marx the fighting philosopher while at the same time rejecting Marx the thinker (Hannay 1941: 369–70). In the main, however, Collingwood's swing to the Left was described in general terms and then judged a matter for regret. R. B. McCallum, who knew Collingwood well, said that *An Autobiography* 'was regretted by most of his Oxford friends. It revealed amongst other things a sharp change in his political outlook which swung suddenly from conservatism to radicalism, a change legitimate enough in itself but requiring a much better rationalization than he gave himself in the last chapter of the book' (McCallum 1943: 467). T. M. Knox, over many years a close friend of Collingwood, took a similar line, writing 'In politics, and in college business, he was on the conservative side for most of his life, but his views turned sharply to the Left when the attitude of the British Government to the European dictatorships seemed to him to be too supine' (Knox 1951: 170).

Between July/September 1938 and late March 1939 when *An Autobiography* was written and then revised Collingwood found himself under the Marxist spell. *An Autobiography* was a child of its time and so at the mercy of events. Between late summer and early November 1938, when Collingwood sent his first draft to the Clarendon Press for their consideration, war and the avoidance of war were the defining topics of political discussion. In summary then, Collingwood thought that the Munich agreement was a betrayal, the sacrifice of Czechoslovakia was shabby, Spain represented the same supine foreign policy that guided British behaviour in Abyssinia and a fighting anti-appeasement candidate like Lindsay in Oxford was a cause for hope. Such was the ambiguity of political allegiance at the time that wanting the British government to stand up to the dictators in Europe as well as avoid war also motivated those who would not have counted themselves as belonging to the Left except by coincidence, but there was nothing illusory about Collingwood's radical views even though his residual liberalism and the shifting nature of political boundaries in the 1930s do have a blurring effect.

If Collingwood was not entirely of the Left in politics in *An Autobiography* he certainly spoke its language. So his identification of Chamberlain with the dictators in Europe, his view that Chamberlain had betrayed democracy, his support for the victims of British weakness in Abyssinia, Spain and Czechoslovakia and his hitching his opposition to the Chamberlain government to the cause of free speech in the Duncan Sandys case, together with a conspicuous unwillingness to advocate rearmament, all suggest the kind of anti-Chamberlain propaganda which in 1938 was very much the Left's preserve. Collingwood's opposition to appeasement was longstanding, unlike the Labour Party which tended to use appeasement as a weapon to attack the Chamberlain government when opportunities presented themselves and whose own policy for peace – collective security – was in 1938 an irrelevance.

Of course *An Autobiography* was overtaken by events, most immediately by Chamberlain's speech in the House of Commons on 31 March 1939 in which he gave security guarantees to Poland. Prior to this, and for much of the time Collingwood was writing the story of his life, the decision to go to war was in British hands. So the final chapter of *An Autobiography* reflects the post-Munich atmosphere in the country at large. Should peace with dishonour be celebrated or should every attempt be made to oppose a government which had lost the confidence of its people? Collingwood's angry, anxious mood expresses that disillusionment with politics which, by a strange twist of logic, often forces those with little or no political experience to get involved. If one response to the country's perilous state was desperation, another, as C. L. Mowat points out, 'was an almost frantic energy, particularly by the amateurs in politics' (Mowat 1955: 633) who, like Collingwood, were trying to get the toothpaste back into the tube.

Collingwood came to Marxism a generation late. He was imbued with T. H. Green's belief in the unity of liberal philosophy and radical social practice, but liberalism had failed to solve the deep economic and social crises of the 1920s and 1930s, and so to many at the time Marxism was a creed worthy of support. Yet Collingwood was unconvinced by historical determinism and he remained too much of a liberal to accept that the dictatorship of the proletariat would be different from any other kind of dictatorship. In his view, history was not on communism's side because it makes no sense to think of history as on anyone's side. Collingwood did not digest Marxism whole but, like many who did, he admired its capacity to link theory and practice. If he resisted Marxist historicism he valued its powers of analysis; like Collingwood, the economist, Joan Robinson, was impressed by Marx's fighting talk – she writes, 'Voltaire remarked that it is possible to kill a flock of sheep by witchcraft if you give them plenty of arsenic at the same time. The sheep in this figure may well stand for complacent apologists of capitalism, Marx's penetrating bitter hatred of oppression supplies the arsenic while the labour theory of value provides the incantations' (as quoted in Annan 1990: 181).

The struggle to advance Marxism during the 1930s was as much a matter of articulation as persuasion. Marxist economic and political beliefs came from historical and philosophical foundations, and it was felt important that the creed in which many put their faith was also convincing to historians and philosophers. In this process of argument and counter argument the connection between positions in philosophy – realist, empiricist, materialist or idealist – and their holders' political beliefs came under sharp scrutiny. Did philosophical arguments run on separate tracks such that they had no relationship at all with political views and opinions? Or was it that behind each political judgement there was a philosophical argument which had to bear the brunt of criticism when it failed? Collingwood did not believe, as did the analytical philosophers of the 1930s, that philosophy was neutral with regard to life. He thought that a 'fundamentally muddleheaded' (AA 158) philosophy led necessarily to confused politics, but he also thought that throughout the 1930s politics had turned sour (Mowat 1955: 633). For him these propositions were intertwined. It was the predominance of realism as a philosophical explanation of our knowledge of the world and of our moral and political actions which undermined both our knowledge and our behaviour. So deeply established was realism that any claim, including Marx's, that philosophy might make the world better was literally unintelligible. Collingwood believed the realists guilty of a double mistake. They did not simply find Marx's view of philosophy false. They found it false because they misunderstood the problem it was intended to solve. If Marx's philosophy was unconvincing to a realist, it was because philosophy as practical problem-solving was totally outside the realist way of thinking. And so Collingwood writes, 'In order to criticize a gloves-off philosophy like that of Marx, you must be at least enough of a gloves-off philosopher to think gloves-off philosophy legitimate' (AA 153). Some of the strangeness of Collingwood's description of Marx as 'a fighting philosopher' evaporates when we see that in 1939 this was how Collingwood wanted to describe himself. Collingwood warns that to approach Marx as if his doctrine was a purely intellectual one, or as if his mistakes were solely to do with misuse of language, is to ignore the sense in which, for Marx, ideas come alive only in practice, where practice is not a static body of theory but historical in character.

It was in the 1930s that the appeal of Marx was generated by his life as well as his writings. Indeed, Collingwood's concerns at the time of writing his *An Autobiography* are reminiscent of E. F. Carritt's worry that Marxism will not work as a guide to action when the dialectical materialism on which it rests is false, (see Carritt 1934: 123–46). Carritt's lectures on Marxism given in Oxford were heavily attended (see Ree 1984: 115); the title of one early biography, *Karl Marx Man and Fighter* (Nicolaievsky and Maenchen-Helfen 1936), captures the spirit that Collingwood was trying to communicate. That spirit, in Collingwood's interpretation, is a belief that against the background of a world going downhill fast something had to be done. Just as Marx fought against exploitation and oppression, so Collingwood wanted to fight against the forces which he thought were bringing western civilization down. A Marx before Marxism, and also before Soviet Communism, could be taken as a symbol of resistance, possibly even of hope. Marx, then, seemed to Collingwood to be everything that liberals were not. Whereas liberals like John Stuart Mill (at least in Collingwood's view) thought that it did not matter what you chose as long as you were free to choose it, Marx situated human freedom in history and showed through his life and influence how a philosophical position is at one and the same time a link to political action.

In 1936, however, the year in which a shadow-line was passed in the approach to the Second World War, Collingwood had taken the view that the intellectual basis of Marxism was 'obsolete' (MGM 325). What was needed was not more Marxism, but less, a Marxism shorn of its antiquated inheritance but retaining its philosophical pugnacity. Collingwood's admiration for Marx, the fighting philosopher, was more than rhetoric. It was specifically designed in 1939 to show that any radicalism espoused by analytical philosophers was weakened if it was not grounded in philosophical argument. And so what is most striking about Collingwood's praise for Marx in *An Autobiography* is that it has a theoretical dimension. His single cheer for Marx is connected with his own ambitions for philosophy. Marx claimed (most famously in the *Theses on Feuerbach*) that a philosophy conducted independently of life would remain arid and self-enclosed. Towards Marx's criticism of realism and of analytical philosophy more generally Collingwood was sympathetic. 'All thought', Collingwood wrote in 1924, 'exists for the sake of action' (SM 15).

Reasons for Collingwood's late enthusiasm for Marx now become clear. In the late 1930s Marx's broad strategy of developing a rapprochement between philosophy, history and practice must have been music to his ears. Revolutionary Marxists are not the only ideologues who wish to change the world in the image of theory. Collingwood's liberalism pushes him in the same direction and he stressed, as Marx had done, that human beings make their history, even if they do so in conditions that are not wholly their own (see Haddock 1995: 134–5; also Oldfield 1995: 199). Collingwood had been angered by the complacent response he thought was displayed in Britain to the Munich crisis. Up against a British government considered by Collingwood to have been both weak and deceitful, and a body politic more than willing to accept an easy peace, the 'fighting philosopher' in Collingwood was never going to concede that appeasement was either right or inevitable. It is, therefore, the historical indeterminist in Marx that interested Collingwood, necessarily so if a persuasive link between theory and practice was to be achieved.

The relationship between theory and practice is central. Neither Marx nor Collingwood defends the view that what ought to be done in any given historical situation can be simply read off from the theory that applies to it. In Collingwood's words, philosophy does not 'descend like a *deus ex machina* upon the stage of practical life and, out of its superior insight into the nature of things, dictate the correct solution for this or that problem in morals, economic organization, or international politics' (EPP 166). It is action and what provides the incentive for it which is central to practical conduct. And so action must be at the heart of any philosophy which aspires to be close to life. Collingwood wrote the final chapter of *An Autobiography* when the British government's policy of appeasement was thought to offer the hope that war could be avoided. And so, in describing Marx as 'no mere fighter, but a fighting philosopher' Collingwood was telling his readers why he thought appeasement was a catastrophic blunder and why, as a philosopher, he was determined to fight against it.

At this point praise for the 'fighting philosopher' shifts from practice to theory. According to Collingwood's understanding of the relation between thought and action no problem is merely practical and no theory devoid of practical implication. As a practical argument Marxism relies on theoretical premises as it also does on making inferences that are valid. Collingwood rejects Marx's premises but, like Marx, he wants a 'gloves-off philosophy', and so, unlike the realists, he can appreciate the force of Marx's aspirations. It was not, however, only Marx's premises that caused Collingwood to doubt Marx's approach. In *The*

Idea of Nature, published in 1945 but written from late summer 1933 to autumn 1934 and delivered as lectures in Oxford in the Michaelmas Term of that year, he set aside, as he had Hegel's, Marx's account of the relation between philosophy and practice, accusing both of confusing temporal relations with logical ones and of ignoring the sense in which

> detailed work seldom goes on for any length of time without reflection intervening. And this reflection reacts upon the detailed work; for when people become conscious of the principles on which they have been thinking or acting they become conscious of something which in these thoughts and actions they have been trying, though unconsciously, to do: namely, to work out in detail the logical implications of those principles.
>
> (IN 2)

As Collingwood was becoming aware of the terrible political transformations occurring in Germany and in Italy he was also reformulating Marx's account of the relation between theory and practice and applying it explicitly to all areas of thought and action, not just that of science (Inglis 2009: 207). Collingwood's opposition to realism holds the key, but when he says that realists find little sense in a 'gloves-off philosophy' we should not conclude that for the anti-realist Collingwood, any 'gloves-off philosophy' will do. An insistence that in order to criticize Marx it is necessary to understand the questions he raises does not mean that other questions cannot be asked or that to the same questions different answers cannot be given.

So, under the impact of events Collingwood's political views moved to the Left. Doctrines central to Collingwood's theory of history and of its relation to philosophy and practice play a significant role here. Of these the logic of question and answer and the idea of re-enactment are most important. Collingwood is saying that in order to understand Marx's thought it is necessary to re-enact it, and re-enactment positively invites a critical attitude and the personal involvement of the historian in the system of thought under investigation. Collingwood writes of the historian, 'This criticism of the thought whose history he traces is not something secondary to tracing the history of it. It is an indispensable condition of historical knowledge itself' (IH 215; for discussion relevant to Marx, see Dray 1995: 58). Additionally, if the historian attempts to grasp the history of an idea, as Collingwood writes, 'into which he cannot personally enter, instead of writing its history he will merely repeat the statements that record the external facts of its development: names and dates, and ready-made descriptive phrases' (IH 305). Here Collingwood's attack on realism is hard at work. Collingwood approached Marx in the spirit of action, one in which, as he says, 'the difference between thinker and man of action disappeared' (AA 151).

In praising Marx for wanting a philosophy 'that should be a weapon' (AA 153) Collingwood was deliberately following the example of T. H. Green who had a similar ambition for himself, although it needs stating that Collingwood does not stand to Marx as he does to Green. Both Collingwood and Green were writing in the broad idealist tradition of philosophy. And so when Collingwood looks for a philosophy to inform practice, Green provides a model. By contrast, Marx's philosophy is, to Collingwood, no model at all. Marx's dialectical materialism, economic and historical determinism and its realism leave Collingwood unimpressed. Collingwood values Marx as an historian who was acutely alert to the cracks and strains in history, but in terms of Collingwood's core philosophy Marx's ideas strike no chords. Collingwood's thought was always permanently closed to materialism. He has no truck with attempts to interpret history by analogy with natural science. He totally rejects the idea that history can tell us anything about future states of affairs, and he considers class warfare to be 'the explicit negation of the state' (SM 228). Moreover, Collingwood warns us that the practical consequences of Marx's doctrines, immense though he thought these to have been, are no guarantee of their truth (Van der Dussen 1981: 398–9, fn. 127, where Collingwood is quoted as writing of Marx, 'The practical consequences of his teaching have been, perhaps, the most important feature in general politics in the last hundred years. But it does not follow that his philosophy of history is likely to satisfy a critical historian. That, indeed, it has never done.').

So what sense is there in Collingwood admiring Marx for being a 'gloves-off' philosopher when he thought that Marx's own philosophy was going nowhere? Collingwood believed that Marx, while sharing his practical ambition for philosophy, lacked the theoretical resources to deliver it. As one writer explains Collingwood's point of view, 'Analytical philosophy has no method to integrate meaning with historical activity and cultural development. … On the other hand, Marxism confuses the understanding of the meaning of an action, which is an historical inquiry, with the means to achieve a specific end' (Eisenstein 1999: 92). Thus Marxism 'treats the meaning of human action as an object of consciousness rather than an integral part of consciousness' (Eisenstein 1999: 92). L. O. Mink takes a similar view. He writes that for Collingwood, 'The error of Spengler, Toynbee or Marx is that they do not and cannot regard as belonging to the process of historical change the ideas in terms of which they characteristically explain the process of historical change' (Mink 1969: 177).

From Collingwood's perspective then Marx was only half-right. As opposed to those who thought that philosophy was a wholly neutral activity Collingwood was with Marx. But Marx, in Collingwood's judgement, was unable to free himself from the grip of natural science. This not only severely inhibits Marx's grasp of the autonomy of history but also blocks any genuine rapprochement between philosophy, history and practice. To Marx's mind, as Collingwood writes, 'the principle that historical events have natural causes' (IH 125) is basic. But to such a mind historians must remain spectators to the events they seek to explain. By not seeing the past as experience into which historians must necessarily enter in order to make it their own Marx not only 'misconceives the relationship between the historical process and the historian who knows it' (IH 164), but he must also fail in his own purpose of linking history with life. The theoretical import of Collingwood's discussion is clear. As a 'fighting philosopher' Marx was right about one element in the rapprochement between philosophy, history and practice. But when the other elements are so retrograde, as Collingwood thought Marx's reliance on pigeon-holing historical schemes obviously was, then this insight forces the philosopher's hand. Collingwood interprets Marx in terms of his dialectical materialism, and so it is scarcely surprising that he relegates Marx's historical assumptions and methods to what he calls 'the embryology of historical thought' (IH 126). The autonomy of history, as Collingwood conceives it, that is, as a body of knowledge which is systematic but wholly different from nature, is history in its mature form. As *An Autobiography* makes compellingly clear, without this development in the understanding of history any link between history and philosophy must remain stillborn. Moreover, as the Collingwood who 'used to cheer, in a sleepy voice, whenever [he] began reading Marx' (AA 152) deems it important to add, without the will to convert ideas into action, any genuine rapprochement between theory and practice will also fail.

From *Speculum Mentis* onwards it was a 'gloves-off philosopher' that Collingwood wished to be. In that book he argued that if thinking was simply a matter of factual discoveries then 'the philosopher would do better to follow the plough or clout shoes, to become a slum doctor or a police-court missionary, or hand himself over to a bacteriologist to be inoculated with tropical diseases' (SM 15). Collingwood was neither a Marxist nor a realist. And yet his opposition to the latter surely clouds his estimate of the former. In criticizing Marx Collingwood says that we need to understand the problems Marx intended to solve and since the foremost of these was a practical problem – how to make the world better – it is as a solution to a practical problem that Marxism should be assessed. But this argument does not work. Marxism is both a solution to a practical problem and an account of human action and how it is determined or influenced by the economic conditions surrounding it. No doubt Marxists argue that these two claims are connected and that it is impossible to assess the one without reference to the other. But it must have been obvious to Collingwood that Marxism is not a solution to a practical problem in the same sense as mining is a solution to the problem of extracting minerals from the ground. Marx's philosophy is heavily engaged in what constitutes the problem as well as in providing the solution to it.

When Collingwood lectured on historiography in 1936 he had been clear why Marx's understanding of history had gone wrong. 'Dialectical materialism', Collingwood wrote, 'was still materialism' (IH 125). In 1939, however, both Marx and Marxism are viewed by Collingwood from a different perspective. *An Autobiography* was written in the summer of 1938, and its preface is dated 2 October 1938. Collingwood received the proofs of the book while visiting the Dutch East Indies, read and revised them during late February and March, returning them to Oxford University Press on 22 March 1939. *An Essay on Metaphysics* followed closely on from this; its preface is dated 2 April 1939, and Collingwood started writing it at the end of October 1938 and finished towards the end of March 1939. Both works then are contemporaneous, but they also reveal important connections with other writings of the same period, specifically *The Principles of Art*, which was written in 1937, the preface, dated 22 September 1937, and parts of *The Idea of History* which were written in 1939 and which were intended to be included in *The Principles of History*, also written at the same time.

To get to grips with Collingwood's admiration for the gloves-off philosopher of *An Autobiography* we need to turn to *The Idea of History*, and to get to grips with what he says there about magic and politics we need to turn to *The Principles of Art*. Collingwood claims that in order to understand the work of any philosopher it is necessary to grasp the question which it was intended to answer (Van der Dussen 2013: 319). Marx's question was: how can philosophy make the world better? Collingwood was sympathetic. Two sections of *The Idea of History* written in 1939 tell us why. In the first Collingwood writes of Marxism as one of many schemes of universal history which rely on pigeon-holing for their methodology, 'If any of them has ever been accepted by any considerable body of persons beside the one who invented it, that is not because it has struck them as scientifically cogent, but because it has become the orthodoxy of what is in fact, though not necessarily in name, a religious community' (IH 265). By 1939 then the body of doctrine in whose name Marx wanted to change the world had become, for Collingwood as it had for many others, a religion. Not in

Collingwood's case a religion which inspired his faith or intellectual conviction, but a religion, nevertheless. To this picture of Marxism, one which was gaining currency in the 1930s, Collingwood, in the second section under consideration, makes a remarkable addition, arguing that 'In these cases, or at any rate in the case of Marxism, historical schemes of the kind in question proved to have an important magical value, as providing a focus for emotions and in consequence an incentive to action' (IH 265–6).

The nature of human action is once again Collingwood's main concern, but what is new in this passage is Collingwood's reference to Marxism as a form of magic. This is important because magic, a term applied by Collingwood to emotion discharged in a particular way and for a particular purpose, is a mode of expression which Collingwood believes no society can do without. In saying that Marxism provides an emotional focus and a stimulus to action Collingwood is surely right, but what gives these attributes their magical value? In what sense is Marxism a kind of magic? Not, we can be certain, in the sense in which Collingwood speaks about magic involved in activities and practices. As Collingwood says, we think of practices such as wedding ceremonies and coronations as accompanied by magic because they involve appeals to emotions designed to have a practical effect (PA 74). Marxism is certainly designed to have practical effect, and it may be considered a practice, but it is also a body of doctrine which is distinct from any emotions it might stimulate or attract. The labour theory of value is hardly merely a series of incantations aimed at producing the appropriate emotional discharges.

According to Collingwood magic is neither a pseudo-science nor a neurosis. To call an activity magical is not to think of it as a half-formed approximation of something else. Equally, magic is not just hocus pocus. In Collingwood's view, magic is a means to an end and the end is the arousing of emotion. So, Collingwood writes, 'Magical activity is a kind of dynamo supplying the mechanism of practical life with the emotional current that drives it' (PA 68–9). When magic is removed, a society loses that which enables it to publicly identify and reproduce its emotions. Or, to put it another way perhaps, no society will survive on the basis of intellect alone. Collingwood's general argument has been thought compelling, but its application to Marxism is surely not. We can think of Marxism as wanting to model the world after its own image. In this it can be seen as providing, Collingwood says, an emotional focus and a stimulus to action. But there is nothing here which gives Collingwood the licence to call these magic. And the reasons for this are clear enough. The image of a classless society is not simply a means to the remodelling of actual societies, as if a Marxist could turn to other images should it fail. It is an essential element of Marx's doctrine. The arousing of emotions of solidarity should accompany the Marxist aim of a complete transformation of economic, social and political life, but only after the transformation has taken place. The magic of Marxism, whatever that may have been, is not then magic in Collingwood's sense. Certainly Marxism shares with magic the need to have a practical effect, but the practical effect of magic is about the evocation and re-evocation of the emotions: this is not true of Marxism. Magic, in Collingwood's understanding, is a necessary accompaniment to sets of beliefs, activities and practices, but it is not a substitute for them. So whatever magic does for Marxism it cannot establish its truth. And Collingwood was in no doubt that Marxism was 'a philosophical blunder' (NAPH 40) and that, as he writes of Marx, 'the practical consequences of his teaching have been, perhaps, the most important feature in general politics in the last hundred years' (R. G. Collingwood, 'Lectures on the Philosophy of History 1929', as cited in van der Dussen 1981: 398, fn. 127).

Neither thought was especially original but the caveat which Collingwood added in 1929 brings home his point. The practical effects of a philosophical doctrine are no guarantee of its truth. And so Collingwood decided that the defects in Marxism were so serious that the key to its influence must lie elsewhere. We should notice just how important this conclusion is. The driving force of Collingwood's attempt to link theory and practice is his philosophical idealism. Collingwood never denied that Marx's economic interpretation of history contained elements of truth. None, however, were able to disguise its basic falsity. And so Collingwood concludes that Marxism is neither philosophy nor history but a religion, one that, unlike Christianity, contains no transcendental truth, but which meets the requirements of religion, as Collingwood listed them in 1937: it is 'a creed, or system of beliefs about the world, which is also a scale of values or system of conduct' (PA 73). As a religion, Marxism, no less than Christianity, needs a magical dimension in order to express and focus the emotions which accompany it but, as with Christianity, the magic cannot be a substitute for the beliefs.

An Autobiography is monopolized by history – its philosophy, method and relation to life. The high water mark of Collingwood's enthusiasm for Marx was March 1939 when he was revising the proofs of the final chapter of *An Autobiography* during his voyage to Java. On that voyage too he wrote and revised much of *An Essay on Metaphysics*. In that work Collingwood finds in Marx a reflection of his own interest in how deep lying social and political changes occur. Again, it is the historical indeterminist in Marx that excites.

Collingwood writes, 'Where there is no strain there is no history. A civilization does not work out its own details by a kind of static logic in which every detail exemplifies in its own way one and the same formula' (EM 75). Here the historical indeterminist in Collingwood is sharply critical of the historical determinist in Marx. Collingwood makes the connection between knowledge of such strains and any resultant freedom of action quite explicit. Unlike the historian in his study whose ignorance of the creakings and crackings of history affects no one except himself (a reference which brings to mind Collingwood's way of talking about the gap between theory and practice in *An Autobiography*), 'the man of action cannot afford to neglect them. His life may depend on his ability to see where they are and to judge their strength. It was not by gunpowder alone that Cortez destroyed Montezuma; it was by using gunpowder to reinforce the strains which already tended to break up Montezuma's power' (EM 76).

The contemporary resonance in Collingwood's example is hard to miss: Britain, when Collingwood was away writing *An Essay on Metaphysics*, was facing external threats as well as tensions at home. Might Germany as a potential aggressor be weakened through strains within its way of life? Or would Britain need to re-arm to confront it? At issue was the capacity of individuals to find genuine answers to questions like these, and there was a strong sense that the possibility of authentic choice had been diminished by the situation in which the country found itself. Collingwood believed that human beings are responsible for what they do. It is an idea which is basic both to Collingwood's ethics and his philosophy of history. Moral conduct makes sense only on the assumption that the choices made by individuals are their own. History is not pre-determined, but made. Even so, Collingwood also thought that 'For a man about to act, the situation is his master, his oracle, his god. Whether his action is to prove successful or not depends on whether he grasps the situation rightly or not' (IH 316). If there were any runes for the kind of situation Britain was in during 1938 and 1939 they were hard to read and, in any case, few readings were the same. Authenticity of choice remained the prime consideration for liberal intellectuals such as Collingwood, but in the situation facing the country authenticity alone could not say what the choice should be. Solutions to the problem of avoiding war were as various as accounts of the problem itself.

Collingwood's broad solution to the problem of political judgement, at least as he expresses it in *An Autobiography*, is to turn to history, but we should notice, as Alan Donagan points out, 'that historical insight is not a substitute for a principle of action, whether self-interest or morality' (Donagan 1962: 242). But neither is a principle of action able to specify what each situation calls for. And so

Collingwood comes to think of duty as itself historical. Each individual must look within themselves to decide what their duty is in any given situation (NL 17.8). In summary, in philosophical terms Collingwood's allegiance to Marxism was skin deep. He had no truck with social utility as a morality in which present suffering had to be accepted as the means to an end (FML 145–53). No revolutionary can guarantee the future. In Collingwood's view, 'the revolutionary can only regard his revolution as progress in so far as he is also an historian, genuinely re-enacting in his own historical thought the life he nevertheless rejects' (IH 326). The important word here is 'genuinely' since progress in economic life (which Collingwood does acknowledge) (IH 331) is not a matter of destroying capitalism but of searching out what is true and false in it. Indeed, the 'inhibitions and reservations' which Marx takes as characteristic of bourgeois life flow from a theoretical picture which Collingwood rejects. He writes of Marx 'his attack on the "bourgeoisie" nowhere contains any attempt to state a case against the "bourgeoisie". There is demonstration that the "bourgeoisie" have done pretty badly as owners of property; there is no attempt to show that any alternative owners had done, or would have done, or would do, any better' (NL 33.78). Typically, Collingwood takes Marx's assault on the bourgeoisie as an assault on freedom itself. The failure of Marxism is theoretical. Marx's condemnation of the bourgeoisie is, Collingwood believes, the rationalization of an emotional attitude.

Politically, Collingwood's allegiance to Marxism was also shallow: after abandoning his attempt to explain the rise of Fascism and Nazism in the language of class and class consciousness he continued to oppose Chamberlain's policies. Indeed, Collingwood's Marxism peaked in the spring of 1939 and from being a slogan to jolt people into opposition to appeasement Marxism returned to being the body of ideas which failed as philosophy and history. No history could be a source of practical wisdom if it mis-identified the characteristics of its age. In the inter-war period these were the aggressive dictatorships which dominated international diplomacy and intimidated democratic governments into bending to their will. Inability to predict and explain the key political phenomena of the 1920s and 1930s was for Collingwood, as it was also for Hugh Trevor-Roper, one of the younger generation of Oxford historians who would go on to play a role Intelligence during the War (Sisman 2010: 70), Marxism's most culpable error.

Collingwood believed that the ways we speak about the world shape our behaviour in it. Marx scorned the idealist neglect of the material conditions of life, advocating instead a revolutionary creed in which class struggle would overcome injustice and end exploitation. During the 1930s many Marxists believed that history was on their side. Many liberals, by contrast, followed the Enlightenment in believing that liberalism was true quite independently of time and circumstance. Collingwood disagreed with both. And so, when a future war hung in the balance, Collingwood called on Marx to advocate action against passivity, fighting qualities against the willingness to give in to the bully. When the future war turned into a present one Collingwood came to see that the Marx he had praised in *An Autobiography* had served his purpose.

In England in the first few months of 1940 the Chamberlain government was running out of ideas and support. A new leader, Winston Churchill, both resolute and impatient to take the fight to the enemy, was waiting in the wings. In a letter to Chadbourne Gilpatric, the American Rhodes Scholar with whom he sailed the Aegean Sea in the summer of 1939, Collingwood said, 'When I wrote the Autobiography I was being a good deal impressed by Marxist ideas, but since then I have studied Marx and Marxism a bit more closely and now I can see just where they get off. A statement of the case against Marxism will, of course, have to go into the New Leviathan' (R. G. Collingwood to Chadbourne Gilpatric, letter dated 17 February 1940 (private possession), (RC: 134–5)).

Collingwood was with the Left on many of the issues surrounding appeasement, but after the attempt to explain the emergence of European dictatorship as a class phenomenon he saw the error of his ways, as he wrote to Gilpatric in the same letter, 'I gave a diagnosis (of Fascism and Nazism) in the Autobiography, but it was wrong. I tried there to give an account of them in Marxist terms, as class-war phenomena; but that was wrong – I now see them as religious phenomena: outcrops of pre-Christian religion in revolt against Christianity and therefore against civilization, which (as we understand it) is a corollary of Christianity.'

Collingwood wrote his letter to Gilpatric disavowing Marxism at the beginning of the war in Norway in the third week of February 1940. After the errors and disappointments brought on by the conduct of this campaign, the Narvik debate in the House of Commons on the 7 and 8 of May 1940 brought Chamberlain down and Churchill to the Premiership. 'Action this day' would be the new mantra for the conduct of the War. Collingwood had got the leadership he wanted, even if it was not quite in the form that he had imagined it in 1939. Whatever value Collingwood placed on Marx the fighter in *An Autobiography*, by the first winter of the Second World War he had renounced Marxism completely. Fascism and Nazism had to be defeated, but the means of victory were to be found in Christianity, together with a liberalism reformulated philosophically so as to satisfy the conditions of a post-Hobbesian age.

3

A philosopher at Delphi

When Collingwood returned to Oxford in late August 1939 war was imminent. He had spent that summer on board the *Fleur de Lys*, a schooner yacht, sailing the Aegean Sea with a carefree bunch of undergraduates from his own university. Collingwood's generation had experienced world war and knew the human costs it entailed, but his fellow sailors, though full of plans for the future, knew little of what to expect.

No one could miss the uncertainty that was in the air. Collingwood's journal of the voyage, *The First Mate's Log*, records encounters with representatives of states whose Nazi and Fascist ideologies had done most to bring about what he perceived as a crisis of civilization. The young students, perhaps more prone to action, were less reflective. Even so, as Collingwood records, among the topics they discussed after visits to places like Delphi, where the oracle appeared to offer a solution to human ignorance in the face of the future, was the nature of human knowledge and different ways of acquiring it. Was everything about human life in the lap of the Gods or is there for human beings some measure of control?

The *Fleur de Lys* was bound for modern Greece, but it was ancient Greece which gave Collingwood his model for public intellectual engagement. Possibly to pre-empt charges of historicism Collingwood judged Socrates the ideal philosophical critic. It is likely that during this voyage Collingwood set his one cheer for Marx aside and began planning *The New Leviathan*. Socratic question and answer is both a method for scrutinizing a society's basic assumptions and values and a standing apart, with the philosopher (in this case Collingwood) acting as the self-appointed assessor.

If they had been taught by realists the crew of *Fleur de Lys* would have seen knowledge as the generation of facts. They would have learned that information is diverse and ever-increasing, hence the threefold problem of packaging, access and use. Early solutions include the guide, the handbook, the dictionary and the encyclopedia. In our world, although not in theirs, it is the computer that rules because it stores, processes and discriminates between information at a speed and in quantities that no encyclopaedia, however large, could ever do and provides almost instant access to everything that is available. Knowledge as information is universal, transferable and immediate. Collingwood is not convinced. He argues that having information about something is not equivalent to knowing it. Where knowledge is concerned there is much more to be said.

In Collingwood's view knowledge is reflective. Information provides us with fact apprehended as true or false. By contrast, knowledge comes from apprehension only in the most straightforward cases. Whether theoretical or practical, knowledge comes from thinking about a given topic in a particular way. Information may be useful, but the cutting edge of knowledge is not empirical fact but questioning. Thinking worthy of the name approaches a problem – say, the refusal of a car engine to start, the authenticity of a medieval manuscript, the behaviour of an electron or that of a recalcitrant state in time of war – in the light of the relevance of the questions, the procedure for raising new questions once answers to the original questions have been found, and a method of assessing each answer so that it can be determined correct or not. The questioner, as Collingwood says,

> is no longer satisfied by what swims into one's mouth. One wants what is not there and will not come of itself. One swims about hunting for it. This ranging of the mind in search of its prey is called asking questions. To ask questions, knowing that you are asking them, is the first stage in high-grade thinking: the first thing that distinguishes the human mind from the sea-anemone mind of the 'realist' theory of knowledge.
>
> (EM 37–8)

Information is a side issue because the quality of the reflection does not depend on the quantity of information and because reflection will not work unless it is self-reflection. Both types of knowledge model face the problem of use. Knowledge as information, no matter how much is stored or how quickly the processing or the access, does not tell us which information to use or when to use it when these are relevant questions. Having information that something is the case, no matter how certain we are that it is the case, is different from knowing what to do about it or knowing how to go about doing it. Knowledge as self-reflection depends on information only in the barest sense: the aim is rather to understand ourselves better. Moreover, self-knowledge is linked to action in ways that knowledge as information is not.

For those who see knowledge purely as information progress comes from knowing more, storing it better and being able to move more quickly from one source of information to another, but in Collingwood's view insight and experience count for more. Whether oral or written, contemporary judgements depend on history. Collingwood thought of historical understanding as a model for human understanding in general. Consider a past event like the Battle of Waterloo. Information about it, such as the numbers of troops killed, the numbers taken prisoner and the numbers who survived, tells us something important. But information about a past event is not the same as knowledge of it. Lists of names and numbers may be factually correct, but their factual correctness provides knowledge only in the most minimal sense. For Collingwood knowledge is not propositional but interrogatory. In the case of a past event like Waterloo knowledge comes from the historian re-enacting the thoughts in the minds of those who ordered the battle and of those who participated in it. Without such re-enactment evidence would merely be information and so, Collingwood argues, historical knowledge would be impossible.

The idea that knowledge is self-knowledge came to Collingwood early. And yet in the history of philosophy the Delphic injunction 'Know Thyself' puzzles philosophers almost as much as it did those who first encountered it. On the one hand, self-knowledge is seen as subjective, too beset by inwardness to deliver an objective standpoint. On the other hand, in Hegel and in the tradition which followed, the Delphic command aims not at individuals, each of whom is looking to establish their own kind of self-awareness, but at individuals seeking to uncover a common humanity. In this latter picture, ways of understanding such as art, science, history and philosophy are the best way of meeting the Delphic command because they express the comprehensiveness of human knowledge without losing sight of its diversity. Unlike dialects which are regional expressions of a common language, art, science, history and philosophy are distinct ways of understanding, each with its own criteria of intelligibility and appropriateness. For philosophers the command 'Know Thyself' is impossible to obey if it lacks any account of the kind of knowledge needed to obey it. If so, the command will speak to no one. But to Nietzsche that is precisely the point: self-knowledge is nullified when it is thought that enlightenment can be found in advance. Collingwood, too, is sceptical. A command that spoke to everyone in the same way, and in the expectation of the same response, would be one that construed knowledge as based on the model of natural science. By contrast, genuine obedience to the command requires a readiness to follow it and awareness that all advice needs interpretation if it is to be acted on. Collingwood thought that historical knowledge passes the Delphic test. In historical knowledge the past is not apprehended as fact, but re-enacted as thought. Historical knowledge offers the reflexivity that science lacks. Unlike those who argue that knowledge means one thing, justified true belief, say, or verified fact, Collingwood pictures knowledge as a complex activity in which stating, propounding, supposing and questioning each has a different role to play. However, the oracle's injunction, as Collingwood understands it, has a more general application. It runs counter to, and is even a warning against, the assumption that human beings are omniscient or, as Protagoras claims, that 'man is the measure of all things'. Collingwood's own response to the oracle comes from the impression it made on him when he visited its site during his voyage. Collingwood writes, 'Sunrise at Delphi is Apollo's theophany: the apparition of the god whose terrible command "know thyself" men have been trying to obey since it was first given' (FML 61). Philosophers were especially vulnerable to the oracle's demands. So Collingwood calls the oracle's instruction a 'riddling command' (FML 62) because it seems to lack focus. Socrates considered it obvious that his knowledge of his own ignorance was not true of others, and so he took on the job of identifying claims about knowledge or moral goodness that were self-contradictory or confused but, as Collingwood came to see, the self-knowledge to which Socrates commits himself is 'no mere process of self-examination' (FML 63). Collingwood's discussion of the 'riddling' nature of the oracle's command is provocative. As Socrates did the Athenians he teased and irritated his fellow sailors. When the oracle warns against the idea that there is nothing which human beings cannot or should not know it seems to be suggesting that knowledge is necessarily finite or, in Collingwood's language, that there must be a match between question and answer: 'A highly detailed and particularized proposition must be the answer, not to a vague and generalized question, but to a question as detailed and particularized as itself' (AA 32).

So, irrelevance, over-ambition or even pride is the oracle's target here. Knowledge seekers overreach themselves when they aim at what is essentially unknowable, or when they aim at what it is possible to know but employ means of finding out that are over-optimistic or anachronistic. Here there is a sense of the limits of human knowledge conveyed in ancient Greece through a contrast with that of the gods. One of the most frequent questions asked of the oracle was which god should I worship? Whether one's life would be happy or unhappy, long or short, relatively healthy or plagued with disease, these were matters believed to be under the control of the gods and so worship of the right god would determine how one's life went, but these were the wrong questions and the oracle's injunction must surely be understood as pointing this out.

Collingwood's description of the Delphic command as 'riddling' also has force because the oracle seems quite deliberately to leave those set on following it bereft of the means of doing so. The oracle's supplicants are like those who want their fortunes told. They want to know the future before it happens. Human beings no more want to remain ignorant of themselves and the world they inhabit than they want to miss a racing certainty. But the oracle leaves them with questions but no answers. They hear the command, but they do not know what it means and so they cannot follow it. The oracle's 'terrible command', as Collingwood describes it, brings this home. Human beings must find the knowledge source themselves. In their search for this they see that the source cannot be self-authenticating and so they will want to know its grounds, how it was derived, where it came from and so on. But the oracle's instruction provides no external information, so to speak. There is nothing independent of the ways we think that can help us. This is surely Collingwood's conclusion, and his philosophical idealism is hard at work in helping him to reach it, for in his most Hegelian work he makes precisely this point: 'the mind is not one among a number of objects of knowledge, which possess the peculiarity of being alone fully knowable; it is that which is really known in the ostensible knowing of any object whatever' (SM 315). Knowledge then in Collingwood's view is better thought of as knowing, and all knowing is self-knowing. It is not a passive reception of facts but an activity, one which, at least potentially, is transformational. Collingwood writes that 'a boy leaving school with a memory full of facts is thereby no more educated than one who leaves table with his hands full of food is thereby fed' (SM 316). Unlike information, which is 'something stored and laid on like so much gas and water' (SM 316), knowledge is shaped by the questions that are asked. As many of the pilgrims to Delphi were to discover, some questions are unanswerable, not because they are misdirected or the information is unavailable, but because it makes no sense to ask them. Collingwood sometimes speaks misleadingly of philosophy as the sovereign form of knowledge; misleading because this loses the distinction between knowledge and information that he most wants to stress. By contrast, philosophy aims to clarify ways of knowing by showing what each on its own is unable to reveal. In other words, philosophy is the best resource we have for fully obeying the oracle's command. Distinguishing questions that are intelligible from those that are not is philosophy's concern.

Nothing in Collingwood's distinction between knowledge and information commits him to downgrading the object of knowledge. Coming to think about the object (whatever it might be) in the right way is basic to knowledge as Collingwood understands it, but this does not mean that the nature of the object plays no part. Historical questions, for example, arise in the context of historical knowledge, and the object of that knowledge is the past. The past, however, is dead. It can be remembered, but memory is not history. Rather, in history the past is not remembered but re-enacted on the basis of the evidence. Historical questions lose their intelligibility when the historian treats the past solely as the remembered past. Similarly, historical questions lose their intelligibility when the importance of the past is assessed by reference to what follows it. To say that one event in history can be judged important only because of events which come after it is not an historical assertion because it is question begging. And what makes it question begging is that the future is not a possible object of knowledge. What has not yet happened cannot be known and what cannot be known is no basis for judging what is known. We do, of course, look back on events and judge them as important or not in the light of what followed, but at the time we do not know what will follow. Past, present and future display different logics, and Collingwood may be understood as pointing this out.

For the oracle at Delphi self-questioning is the signature mark of the human species. Collingwood tells us that we come to know ourselves by understanding how we have come to be what we are. It is through philosophical investigation into knowledge that the claims made by science and history are clarified. Metaphysics, as that branch of philosophy which tells us how to uncover the presuppositions of a given way of life, is also an historical exercise, but this does not alter Collingwood's point. Without philosophy supplicants to the oracle leave dissatisfied.

As Collingwood surely intended, this gives philosophy a role in human affairs which exceeds most actual estimations of it. In other words, obedience to the Delphic instruction has an importance which goes beyond the individual attempting to carry it out. The public importance of the Delphic instruction is bound up with public reflection. A society which heedlessly leaves its way of life to succeed or fail just as it stands will not pass the Delphic test. Collingwood's conclusion is blunt. The artist who just happens to get the marks on the canvas right is no artist. The historian who is blind to the way his prejudices drive his conclusions is no historian. An empire building society like Athens in the fifth century will come to grief if it leaves its economic and political aims unexamined. How can a democracy possess an empire? The question with which Thucydides needled the Athenians could not be left unanswered. Indeed, Collingwood's use of the oracle's command is relevant to his own autobiography: this he argued would be merely an exercise in self-justification if self-knowledge in the form of historical inquiry into one's own past was not brought to bear.

Delphic injunctions are seldom unambiguous. We have talked about perhaps the most famous, 'Know Thyself'; another, found on an inscription on the walls of the temple to Apollo and surely uttered in the same spirit, is 'Observe the Limit' (Guthrie 1950: 184). This also seems readily open to interpretation in the light of Collingwood's new logic. Collingwood thinks that questions are the cutting edge of knowledge. They work only if they are linked with the right degree of precision to the subject matter in hand. Limitless interrogation is as much lacking in purpose as limitless information. Unanswerable questions also indicate that the mind of the questioner is idling. Questions which are in principle unanswerable have contexts, and it is this that establishes whether, or why, a given question is meaningful or not. The limit here is one of meaning. To interrogate the past in the expectation that it is recoverable exactly as it was lived is to ask a question that is impossible to answer. Similarly, the political philosopher who asks questions about the nature of sovereignty in the belief that governing the state is like running a business is seeking answers which the subject matter cannot provide.

When Collingwood says that philosophy is the best resource we have for making sense of Delphic utterances he does not mean that philosophy's role is instructional. Philosophy has the more indirect job of clarifying the questions that are asked. It remains the questioner's business to ask them and to respond to the answers received. Even so, the gap between the two activities, the search for clarity in what we question and then how we question is not without potential ambiguity. Questioners will feel that the questions they ask are intelligible as they stand. Socrates argues that the unexamined life is not worth living, but on whose conception of 'worth'? Questioners who approached the oracle did so with a specific purpose in mind. They wanted to know how best to live, certainly as individuals possessing their own particular fears and anxieties, but also as members of a society in which the possession of common values was itself valued.

Collingwood terms the oracle's command 'terrible' because it throws human beings back on their own resources. Human beings have to understand that if they are to find answers at all then they must do so by themselves. Socrates took the instruction 'Know Thyself' as an injunction to live a philosophical life. It was the only way of reconciling his ignorance with the knowledge required to obey the oracle's command. And yet what of the oracle itself? Its commands reflect beliefs. Are these to be examined and criticized by philosophy in the same way as the philosopher examines and criticizes beliefs from any other source? At issue here is the oracle's authority. If the oracle is open to criticism from philosophy then its commands are no different from any other. If it is closed to criticism then its commands are self-authenticating, to be taken on trust or beyond truth and falsity. One solution is to think of the oracle's commands as broad generalities, so vague as to provide any questioner with some degree of satisfaction. What is the good life for human beings? Which kind of state best allows its citizens to live a happy life? Questions such as these reflect a universal interest. But the oracle's answers seem evasive. So when questioners worry about how they should make proper return to the gods for their goodness Socrates tells them of the oracle's reply: 'According to the law of the city' (Guthrie 1950: 187).

Now Collingwood's description of the oracle's commands as 'riddling' comes into its own. It looks at first sight as if the oracle is providing substantive advice in the form 'simply obey the law'. But what of cases in which the law as it stands may be adrift of the attitude required. A better reading is that the oracle is deliberately returning responsibility to the questioner. It is saying that whether the law is adequate or not cannot be decided in advance. You have to assess it. Given that criteria of assessment vary – a rule can be assessed in terms of its civility, legality or justice – it is your responsibility to decide which questions to ask. I cannot help you there. There is work for you to do.

We might think that an oracle which apparently confessed to ignorance was being very wise – or very foolish. In Greece it was sometimes thought that intoxication was a factor, either in the gods or in those who spoke for them. There were occasional suspicions of human interference at a political level. Whatever the contemporary doubts, however, one precept can be drawn. Philosophy should be less oracular, and one way of achieving this is by being more respectful of the possibilities in language as it is used. Socrates would certainly have shared this view, and it is surely this counsel that Collingwood took from his visit to Delphi. Beliefs about how best to live invite philosophical examination, but they are closed to intervention at the level of specific advice. What Socrates learned from Delphi was that obscurity and mystification can be unmasked. By asking the right questions in the right way claims which have the appearance of soundness can be shown to be unconvincing. In this conception of philosophy method is central. Collingwood thought this too.

Collingwood's employment of his Socratic inheritance is his own, indicated by his distinctive stress on history. Human beings are temporal creatures. The questions they ask derive their intelligibility from contexts and practices which exist in time, and so historical knowledge is at the heart of self-knowledge both for individuals and societies. All societies, Collingwood argues, rest on presuppositions which make their ways of life what they are. Some presuppositions are so fundamental that they resist interrogation. In these cases questioning is empty because the question is incapable of freeing itself from the presupposition it is inquiring into. Metaphysics can show us what these presuppositions are, but beyond that it cannot go. This sense of unanswerable questions is Collingwood's own. Neither Socrates nor Collingwood see philosophy as a wholly academic exercise, one to be conducted in complete neutrality with regard to the object under investigation. And yet Thrasymachus-like interlocutors are as common in life as they are in Plato's dialogues. Philosophy, in Collingwood's view, should not be undertaken too far from the sound of battle. When on 13 July 1939 he visited the oracle's site on the island of Delphi, with the future uncertain, the oracle told him more than the commonplace truth that people often know less than they believe and that their sovereignty over nature and history is conditional. Information, Collingwood says, is 'the talent buried in the earth' (SM 78). By contrast, questioning is 'the soul of knowledge' (SM 78).

Self-knowledge in Collingwood's hands is neither as abstract nor as non-political as it may appear from these remarks. He believed that civilizations decline more often for reasons internal to themselves than from attacks from outside. When a civilized society is weakened by self-doubt, or is beguiled into following false gods, then barbarism's work is done for it: 'If a people who share a civilization are no longer on the whole convinced that the form of life which it tries to realize is worth realizing, nothing can save it' (EM 140, see Newman 1979: 478).

Whether or not appeasement was a false god Collingwood believed that the appeasers in the British government knew a great deal less than they thought. Those whose responsibility was to put the policy of appeasing Nazi Germany into practice were not short on questions. Nor had they lost faith in a civilized way of life. The problem was that in Collingwood's eyes they were asking the wrong questions. Here Collingwood's logic of question and answer works in tandem with his historical sense. When the leading appeasers looked inside themselves they found the injunction that was the mainstay of a Christian attitude to politics: seek peace and follow it. So the question which was uppermost in their minds was how to achieve a lasting European peace. For those who believed that politics should bend the knee to morality it was the right question to ask, possibly even the only one. Indeed, for many years Collingwood had held this view. But, as the logic of question and answer requires, questions derive their sense from the contexts in which they arise and so, against the background of an intractable German revanchism, the appeasers' question served only to make a bad situation worse. Those who petitioned the oracle wanted advice that would help them in the world as it is not as it might be. Not for them Plato's quest or, as Collingwood called it, the 'wild-goose chase after some object that could be called absolutely good or "good in itself"' (NL 11.56).

The First Mate's Log reveals Collingwood sure of his political ground. When towards the end of its voyage the *Fleur de Lys* docked in Messina on 13 August 1939 Collingwood was drawn by the impecunious state of the harbour master into highlighting the failures of the Italian export trade, and he reminds his readers how these were 'officially blamed on the sinister activities of Mr. Anthony Eden' (FML 170). He continued with his rebuke to those 'few people in England who believe that Fascism stands for efficiency and that democracy spells muddle' (FML 173). Behind Collingwood's words lies another reproach to the British policy of appeasement, in this case of Italy. Mussolini's policy of economic self-sufficiency was intended as preparation for war, but the reality was that it simply disguised Italy's basic economic fragility. Anthony Eden, the 'notorious anti-Italian hawk' (Maiolo 2010: 226) in the British Foreign Office had resigned in February 1938 in protest against the Chamberlain government's policy of accommodating Italian ambition. As Collingwood's reaction in his log is surely meant to imply, negotiation with the dictators does not work: stand up to them, especially those whose purpose is paper thin, and they will crumble.

In Britain throughout the summer of 1939 the mood was variable, possibly even contradictory. It was, as Daniel Todman describes it, 'a mix of patriotism, fatalism, anger and optimism' (Todman 2016: 188). Against this clamour of attitudes and opinions it is tempting to think of Collingwood as a Cassandra-like figure, one that is uniquely capable of identifying the dangers to which the tribe is blind or, if seeing, is unable or unwilling to remove. However, Collingwood's was never a Delphic voice, although that is sometimes the impression he creates. In fact, much of what Collingwood says on specific issues is little different from views expressed by others of a progressive frame of mind who were equally concerned to respond to what looked like certain war in an intellectually convincing and radical way. Common ground is the belief that Nazism would not be overcome without Britain having first freed itself of its own weaknesses. George Orwell was one who certainly thought this, so targeting not liberal ideals as such but the way in which an imperialist and capitalist society turns them into their opposites. Orwell's is Thucydides's question in a modern context. It is a style of questioning shared by Collingwood who, less seriously but with the same methodology, asks how the countryside can be enjoyed in a car-owning democracy without turning into what it is not? Neither Orwell nor Collingwood were shy of being their nation's moral and political conscience. At the start of the war both confound the enemy without with the enemy within, Orwell more comprehensively and systematically by revealing what he takes to be the fundamental elements of British political life as it existed historically in 1940 and Collingwood with more circumspection the loss of civil liberties accepted by the British state at war. As Robert Colls comments of Orwell,

> In April 1940 he was claiming that *if* he thought 'a victory in the present war would mean nothing beyond a new lease of life for British imperialism he would be inclined to side with Russia and Germany'. He said it knowing that Nazism was a monstrous, brainless, and enslaving empire led by a maniac – but he said it all the same.
>
> (Colls 2013: 140)

And Collingwood writing on the very day war was declared 'If this country went Nazi for the sake of beating the German Nazis, victory in the field would be the worst fate' (R. G. Collingwood to T. M. Knox, letter dated 3 September 1939, RC: 148).

Liberal causes embody liberal principles. At least, that is the theory. But for the left-inclined during the 1930s and at the start of the Second World War liberal causes offered nothing more than the opportunity to exploit liberalism, even perhaps to bring it down. There is then a divide between those like Collingwood who saw liberalism as being insufficiently robust in its own defence and who attempted to strengthen it and those with a different kind of political motivation who supported liberal causes out of political convenience or as means to the end of socialist revolution.

As Collingwood's cruise on the *Fleur de Lys* was nearing its end one entrenched political belief was shattered. The non-aggression pact between Germany and the Soviet Union signed in the early hours of 24 August 1939 did not simply confirm that war was imminent. It destroyed any hope that Communism was the best defence against Nazism. The reason for this was as much a matter of logic as ethics. If Marxism was true, how could it align itself with its most vociferous and despised opponent? Reactions differed widely. When the students on board the *Fleur de Lys* heard of the Pact their response according to Collingwood was total disbelief, only to have the news confirmed at Antibes. But what exactly had been confirmed? It looked to many that the two dictators had defied logic. Implacable enemies had become allies. P and not-P were the same, or, as a number thought at the time, they had made water run uphill.

The effect of the Pact on Communist sympathizers in Britain varied. For those who took it for granted that logic had a moral face, namely the demand for consistency in ethical and political judgements, the result was bafflement. Others lost all hope. For those who thought that Moscow could do no wrong the Pact was simply reasoned away as an exercise in realpolitik, a means to an end, a temporary appeasement in order to gain time or protect the Soviet Union's achievements. Along with many on the Left Collingwood went far to equate the Fascism outside Britain with what he thought of as the Fascism within. He had come close to calling the British prime minister a dictator and he had excoriated appeasement as no more than a way of accommodating Nazi rule and ambition. With the arrival of the Pact, however, this political stance was brought rapidly to an end. Between two agreements – Munich in September 1938 and the Nazi-Soviet Pact just under a year later – British views about the possibility of war were at the mercy of events. *An Autobiography* breathed the atmosphere of Munich just as much as it vilified a British prime minister. There was a reasonable hope for peace, but only if Germany could be persuaded to change course and if Britain could find the politicians to make her do so.

Interrelationship between thought and events is evident in Collingwood's writing during his voyage to the East Indies as well as his stay there. Kristallnacht on 10 November 1938 together with the German occupation and dismemberment of Czechoslovakia in March 1939 made the British people aware that there would be no negotiated peace. Collingwood had left Liverpool on 22 October 1938 on board MV *Alcinous*. *An Autobiography* had been completed during the summer of that year. During the voyage he worked on *An Essay on Metaphysics,* and after arrival, during January and February 1939 on *The Principles of History* (for details of the composition of this work, in particular the manuscript entitled 'Notes on Historiography', see PH 235). It is scarcely surprising then that connections between these works are multiple, especially when we note that revisions to *An Autobiography* were also ongoing during March 1939.

Events in Germany while MV *Alcinous* was off the coast of Somaliland in early November 1938 gave no cause for optimism. Kristallnacht, the state-sponsored pogrom against the Jews, was a brutal harassment which received world-wide condemnation. While travelling between the East Indian islands in mid January 1939 Collingwood reflected on this in the light of the errors which he argued made history impossible and falsified doctrine in religion and politics. Historical facts are not like biological facts. Collingwood writes 'the unity of a common way of life and the unity of a common pedigree are different things between which there is no necessary connection' (PH 237). In Germany, however, it was Rassentheorie, the racial ideology at the centre of Nazism, which ruled. And, in Collingwood's view,

> Modern Germany thus stands officially committed to the same error which infected ancient Jewish thought, and which Paul exploded – the error of regarding a given community's historical function as bound up with its biological character, i.e. with the common pedigree of its members – and thus persecutes the Jews *because it agrees with them*. Intellectually the Jew is the victor in the present-day conflict (if you can call it that) in Germany. He has succeeded in imposing his idea of a chosen people (in the biological sense of the word people) on modern Germany: and this may explain why the victims of this persecution take it so calmly
>
> (PH 237; italics in original)

One writer finds this commentary 'chilling' (Bates 1996: 49), but we should remember the historical irony which is hard at work in it. George Bernard Shaw, who thought that 'Judophobia is as pathological as hydrophobia' (as quoted in Holroyd 1991: 421), also 'defined Hitlerism as a government founded on the idolatry of one person laying claim to the world on behalf of Germans as the Chosen Race' (Holroyd 1991: 431). Or to put the point differently – Rassentheorie is a biological theory and nothing else. As Collingwood makes clear that is emphatically not the case with Judaism (see PH 236).

Few people take persecution calmly, especially when it takes the form of public defamation, discrimination and ostracism, all under the terrible guise of normality: when, however, aligned with the belief that Hitler would not last and that the many Jews who thought of themselves as no less German than their Christian fellow citizens believed that the worst was over, then a noble stoicism in the face of adversity might well stand for calm, especially when, as was the case in Germany when Collingwood wrote these remarks, there was little by way of an alternative available to them. In 1935 the Nuremburg Laws defined Jewishness in racial terms. The incorporation of Rassentheorie in law had an impact on Collingwood since in lectures given in 1936 he links it to an earlier German thinker, stating that 'Once Herder's theory of race is accepted, there is no escaping the Nazi marriage laws' (IH 92). He writes of Rassentheorie not only that it was 'scientifically baseless and politically disastrous' (IH 92) but also that 'we are not inclined to be grateful to Herder for having started so pernicious a doctrine' (IH 92). Collingwood stresses the Jewish faith as symbolic of a common way of life animated by a common set of beliefs.

In 1938 Collingwood described biological history as a monster, one whose malign presence infected systems of thought otherwise as remote from each other as icebergs are from heat waves. Rassentheorie, Jungian psychology and ancient Judaism were the examples he gave (AA 140, PH 236). Judaism is a religion as well as a sign of common ancestry, a distinction which was of little importance to its Nazi persecutors, but when Collingwood speaks of Judaism it is its character as a community united by a common faith that is his key focus. In this context Collingwood's reference to calm as a reaction to persecution gains explanatory force from the fact that it is precisely faith not biology which gives rise to the possibility of genuine security and consolation. Calmness, in other words, does not necessarily mean passivity, as it would do if the reaction to persecution was racially defined, but neither does it imply a claim of inviolability.

If Collingwood in 1938 had seen himself as 'the temporarily suppressed conscience of the Labour Party' (Crick 1980: 246), as the Independent Labour Party (ILP) almost certainly, and Orwell more than likely, did then by the time of the Pact he must have realized that such political grandstanding was over. Germany would have to be fought and defeated. It was now time for serious politics, since the Pact showed not only that Communism was no bulwark against Nazism and that the reverse was true, but more significantly that a double totalitarian bloc, one in which Stalin would give substantial material aid to the Nazi regime, was about to impose itself across Europe. In these new circumstances support for the ILP vanished, as it also did for the idea of a Popular Front. Collingwood's options were narrowing. In this new context Collingwood's fear was first of the Soviet Union being brought into the war in alliance with Germany and second that a German victory over Britain and France would lead to a massive increase in Soviet strength. In this oracular mood Collingwood thought that without these developments Britain would win through (R. G. Collingwood to T. M. Knox, letter dated 3 September 1939, RC: 148) but with them the danger to Britain multiplied a hundred-fold, and so he came to the realization that, although he considered the Chamberlain government abhorrent, it was by a large margin the lesser of the evils that Britain was being called on to face. After the Nazi-Soviet Pact he saw too that if ideologies so devoid of moral purpose were to be defeated then often severe compromises would have to be made. The book which he was to call *The New Leviathan* would not adequately encompass its time if it did not address this as a certain requirement of victory. It is tempting to explain the changes in Collingwood's political mood and utterance by reference to what the historian Peter Clarke calls 'the iron grip of circumstances' (Clarke 2002: 194). After all Collingwood was participating in a shift in opinion which was both a rational response to events and common to many in Britain at the time. *The Manchester Guardian*, for example, adopted a stance close to Collingwood's that the Pact was not solely one of non-aggression but of friendship, with all the deep strategic threats that this implied (Gannon 1971: 281–3). Such similarities are scarcely surprising. Collingwood thought that real thinking always began from practice and returns to it, a view which reinforces the idea that it was during the late summer and autumn of 1939 that the plan for *The New Leviathan* was beginning to form in his mind.

Two concerns central to the design of *The New Leviathan* derive from this time. One was the recognition that the war would pass beyond safeguarding the autonomy of states to raise matters basic to any human life worth the name. The Director of the Institute for Advanced Study at Princeton wrote to Thomas Jones in the early spring of 1939 'Humanity and the right to live one's life in an orderly way is a right that transcends the occupation of Albania or the theft of Czechoslovakia' (Jones 1954: 433). Intimations of the war to come were placing in jeopardy precisely those relationships, activities and values without which a civilized way of life would be impossible either to conceive or live. By the time of the British declaration of war on 3 September 1939 this insight had become a general one, with the major part of the British press in full agreement. The issue was no longer Czechoslovakia, Danzig and even the fate of Poland, but as the *Sunday Times* of that day resolutely describes it – 'the peace and liberties of the world' (Gannon 1971: 287).

The implications for Collingwood's slowly germinating purpose throughout the period of the Phony War to write the work of political philosophy which matches such resolve are clear. Collingwood's visit to the island of Delphi reinforced a long-held view. All knowledge is self-knowledge. The European mind is no exception. A philosophy of politics which was adequate to the crisis of his time would require a philosophy of mind. Without inquiring into the capacities of human beings to live a civilized life at all too many questions would be begged, with the result that Collingwood's aim would not be met. Reference to 'the iron grip of circumstances' is therefore only half right. It conveys the sense in which hopes are dashed or new ones raised as circumstances change – an all too common experience, especially in wartime – but it misses the search for a higher synthesis which characterizes the argument of *The New Leviathan*. Nor should this argument be considered an exercise in futurology. Collingwood had his own reasons for doubting the oracle's prognostications, but like Hobbes who argued that 'things to come have no being at all, the future being but a fiction of the mind' (Hobbes 1651: part I, chapter 3), he was wary of soothsayers.

As the hard-headed Hobbes says himself, the priests at Delphi made their answers 'ambiguous by design, to own the event both ways' (Hobbes 1651: part I, chapter 12). Collingwood's writing on the political convulsions of the early years of the war reflects circumstances but also reaches beyond them with the elucidation of a civilized way of life as its primary aim.

4

Talking with Yahoos

In 1938 Collingwood's picture of Europe is something like a wilderness populated by Yahoos. The liberalism he defends is shaped by his philosophy of mind and his account of practical reason, but his true focus is a lot more specific. The Yahoos of Jonathan Swift's *Gulliver's Travels* give him a starting point. What interests him in his account in *The New Leviathan* is why it is hard to think of creatures lacking civility as human beings at all. He distinguishes talk of the swarming of bees from talk about the seasonal migrations of pastoral villagers. Rightly, Collingwood says, we express our sense of this difference in the language we use. For the villagers seasonal migrations are part of their manners and customs but, in Collingwood's words, 'we do not say that it is the custom among bees to swarm on occasions of a certain kind. We say that they do swarm on such occasions but not that their doing so constitutes a custom' ('Goodness, Rightness, Utility', NL 398). What fascinates Collingwood (as it does Hobbes) is the nature of the connection between our customs, manners and laws and our humanity. In the context of a nation fighting for survival, basic questions like these are primary. Questions to do with the kind of country Britain might be if victory is achieved presuppose exactly those norms of civility which are under threat. Liberalism faces the problem of establishing a just political order while remaining neutral between different conceptions of the good. For his part Collingwood rejects utilitarianism and contractualism as complete solutions and calls instead for reconciliation between politics and civility. The logic of civility – as an ideal and as a standard of conduct appropriate to a civilisation at a particular stage of its history – is Collingwood's main concern.

What human activities would look like in the absence of civility is the central issue. To investigate this Collingwood does not imagine civility obsolete, as if civility is a fashion that can become outmoded. Rather he asks us to think of the loss of the concept of civility as being more like losing an essential condition of human life than a particular custom or practice. Could we call such a life human, if civility is lacking? By contrast, if civility is a general condition of human life then by what process is it achieved?

Civility is exactly what the Yahoos in Swift's *Gulliver's Travels* lack. They represent the state of natural unsociability that Collingwood's thinking needs (see NL 30.7 for Collingwood's account of his sources). Indeed, in the novel, Gulliver describes Yahoo behaviour as, in various degrees, odious, repulsive and base, descriptions of a kind that we cannot easily imagine him making of his fellow human beings. The Yahoos are different, and it is with the character of this difference that Collingwood is concerned and which we need to specify. Collingwood stresses that the Yahoos are always with us (NL 30.8), but they are not always with us in the sense that Collingwood says the poor are (NL 38.71). For a liberal this difference is important because whether the poor are always with us depends in large part on the principles of justice we are prepared to adopt. By contrast, in what sense the Yahoos are always with us depends on the philosopher's purpose in taking them outside the boundaries of Swift's novel.

Understanding a primitive society involves showing how its rules and practices make sense, but getting to grips with the Yahoos is different in kind. This is not merely because they are creatures of Swift's imagination. When readers understand the Yahoos, it is because they possess the ability to reflect on their feelings, possibly to reject them as the primary motivation for their actions. Coming to terms with the Yahoos, therefore, is akin to coming to terms with ourselves, as Swift makes Gulliver believe that returning to his own kind is a poor best compared with the honesty and transparency of life among the Houyhnhnms.

Swift portrays human life in terms of the contrast between the brutish Yahoos and the pre-eminently rational Houyhnhnms. Whereas there is nothing in Yahoo life that controls the passions or shapes them into human warmth that is affectionate and discriminating, the Houyhnhnms live at the opposite extreme. They see the passions as significant only in their being the unlucky consequence of the human possession of bodies. By distinguishing themselves from both these types, human beings find what comfort they can. Swift reinforces this view by making Gulliver attempt – and fail – to model his life on the pure reason of the Houyhnhnms. And yet, as Swift wants his readers to realize, Gulliver's apparent choice between the Yahoos and the Houyhnhnms is a false one. He cannot escape his self-disgust at being thought a Yahoo by turning to the Houyhnhnms: for him as a human being their life too would be equally unliveable.

What Gulliver comes to see within the novel Collingwood elucidates outside it. Swift wants to show Gulliver falling into the trap of wishing himself more like the Houyhnhnms than he can possibly be, so they will be persuaded to believe that all that separates him from the Yahoos is the 'Tincture of Reason' that they lack. Collingwood sees this too. He writes 'the idea that man, apart from his self-conscious historical life, is different from the rest of creation in being a rational animal is a mere superstition' (IH 227). Collingwood's remark gives little support to the idea that human feelings can be made the subject of historical knowledge: 'so long as man's conduct is determined by what may be called his animal nature, it is non-historical; the process of those activities is a natural process' (IH 216). And Collingwood sees with equal force that the ability of human beings to give reasons for what they do is one that the Yahoos conspicuously lack. But these impressively true statements, in Collingwood's view, do not take us to the heart of the matter. It is the inability of the Yahoos to identify the feelings they have that is the fundamental deprivation. When Collingwood speaks of the Yahoos as physically resembling human beings but lacking their intelligence, he speaks as Swift does. And he is at one with Swift, too, when he refers to the Yahoo poverty of culture and industry. Like Swift, again, Collingwood stresses the Yahoos' permanent quarrelsomeness, their lack of agreement and their incapacity to settle an issue between them except by force. Collingwood, however, has philosophical concerns that shape what he wants to say. Swift describes the Yahoos as 'the most unteachable of all Brutes' (Swift 2003: 217 hereafter cited as GT). Since this is the essential characteristic of the Yahoos, Swift is telling us forcibly that theirs is a state that cannot be rectified. Collingwood, in describing the Yahoos' mental development as arrested 'just short of free will' (NL 30.52), helps us to see why.

Yahoos, in being stuck with their feelings and nothing more, are what human beings would be like if deprived of a social existence. In Collingwood's view, to lack a social existence is to lack a language. The inability of the Yahoos to attend to their feelings by naming them explains why their restlessness can never be calmed. Swift hints at this. He points to the Yahoos needing to be 'continually watched' (GT 249) if their passions are not to run riot. But the need to closely observe the Yahoos arises only because they are incapable of watching themselves. Yahoo feelings are like the feelings that human beings experience when they are unable to understand them. The difference is that for the Yahoos all feelings are like that.

What Collingwood does in *The New Leviathan* is to recreate the Yahoos on his terms by treating them not as a flight of literary fancy but as a hypothesis.

In this new philosophical guise Yahoo behaviour is open to redescription. So Collingwood reformulates the Yahoos not as the solitary individuals of a Hobbesian state of nature but as gregarious creatures who take a ferocious and obsessive interest in their own kind. Yahoo life is 'poor, nasty, and brutish' (NL 30.6). Likewise Collingwood redescribes the Yahoos as more imitative than the individuals postulated by Hobbes. So Collingwood writes, 'There is a kind of imitation quite independent of the action imitated; and the Yahoo herd would be as imitative as a herd of monkeys' (NL 30.65).

Neither gregariousness nor imitativeness is sufficient to give the Yahoos a language as Collingwood understands it. Yahoo imitation comes with a complete inability to understand what they are imitating. Collingwood criticizes the view that language acquisition comes from an instinct to imitate, that language is acquired by copying what others say. This, he writes, is 'an idle fiction' (PA 241). And it is not hard to see why because no amount of copying can provide the self-consciousness and self-expression that language requires. Instinct, in other words, does not capture the fact that it is our wanting to express something that is significant in the acquisition of language.

Like prelinguistic children Yahoos are awash with feelings, but no amount of repetition, vigorous pointing, signalling or gesturing will help the Yahoos discover what their feelings are. Their lives may be lustful but the meaning of their desires – why they desire this rather than that, and to what degree – is permanently mysterious to them. This is why Swift describes them as howling, whining, roaring and groaning. Their cries are as 'noisome', as Swift puts it (GT 249), as their lives. They do not speak, nor indeed do they whisper, mutter or mumble.

Yahoos are not savages, in Collingwood's understanding of the term. Savagery, for Collingwood, is a relative condition. It is a state of being relatively uncivilized so absolute savagery is an empty class (NL 41.11). The Yahoos, however, lack the rudiments of civilisation. They possess no language. They are the captives of their feelings. They cannot share a social existence and since they are incapable of choice the route to rational freedom, as Collingwood understands it, must be permanently blocked off to them. We cannot describe the Yahoos as barbarians, either. Barbarism, in Collingwood's view, is distinct from savagery because it seeks the destruction of civilisation (NL 41.12). Barbarians must have an understanding of the civilisation they want to overthrow, and this is something that the Yahoos cannot attain.

For Collingwood, clarifying a feeling is to give that feeling a meaning. It is what happens when we become conscious of our feelings. By contrast, not being truthful about the feelings we have is a sign of a 'corrupt consciousness' (PA 282–5), perhaps taking the form of sentimentalizing our feelings or trying to disown them. A 'corrupt consciousness' is close to the state of being self-deceived: individuals who deceive themselves about their feelings must at least know something about those feelings to present them as other than they are. Yahoos' feelings, however, have them in such a tight grip that they cannot present them as other than they are because they do not know what they are. Collingwood's insistence that the Yahoos will not go away means he must transform the Yahoos so that they feel at home and know why they do. This he does by formulating civility as an ideal. By means of a process of social and political education in which civility is the pre-eminent aim Yahoo feelings are controlled, and so Yahoos become adjusted to living peaceably with others.

While Swift's Yahoos are nothing but their bodily feelings there is a sense in which Collingwood is right to say that our feelings are always with us. The feeling of sadness is never merely the report of a neutral observer on an independent bodily state, say, tears in the eyes. A Yahoo is similar to a young child who feels the cold before being able to name the feeling, or an adult who experiences a feeling not previously encountered, say, jealousy, and struggles to understand it. For the untransformed Yahoos, as Collingwood might express it, the move from non-agreement to agreement is permanently closed. They lack an inherited and public set of rules that establish meaningful usage, 'hat-doffing experiences', as Waismann terms them (Waismann 1968: 32). Yahoos cannot learn because they have nothing that they can regard as an achievement. Human beings learn, say, not merely that ropes exist but that they can use them for a variety of purposes – tying knots, mooring boats, hanging people and so on. Learning how to moor a boat goes together with learning how to sail one, or, in a more complex case, learning how to speak may go with learning how to speak in an assembly. Such learning depends on the activity having been achieved, and since societies are temporal entities, it follows for Collingwood that this is an historic achievement of civilization itself. We see here a resemblance with Wittgenstein who argues in *On Certainty* that 'if experience is the ground of our certainty, then naturally it is past experience. And it isn't for example just *my* experience, but other people's, that I get knowledge from' (Wittgenstein 1969: 35e–36e, 275).

It is clear that our knowledge of the Yahoos does not come from history. We might imagine Gulliver thinking of his voyage to the land of the Houyhnhnms as an historical account of the Yahoo life he finds there. But this would not be history as Collingwood understands it. History involves the reconstruction of thought. Insofar as Yahoos occupy a realm of pure feeling historical knowledge of them is closed. A history of human feelings might be possible on Collingwood's terms, but only if feelings are in some way essentially related to thoughts or if they express concepts, judgements or beliefs. Interestingly, a history of Houyhnhnms would also be hard to visualize, but for different reasons. We might think of it as akin to a history of logic.

Yahoos are fated to live only in the present. In Collingwood's view, the conditions for the transmission of knowledge 'are that there should be a community in which inventions are not hoarded, but taught' (NL 36.59). So the communication of knowledge can only take place in a society where teaching and learning are understood as simultaneous activities imbued with the spirit of agreement. In the absence of civility (for this is what such agreement implies) there could be no historical continuity. So, in Collingwood's account, the rules of civility are transmitted as rules of grammar or as rules of a conversation within which individual inventiveness takes place. Since the Yahoos lack this they can copy and mimic but they cannot know why.

Collingwood understands civility as an ideal to which any actual state of affairs is a more or less adequate approximation. This implies that civility needs historical expression if it is to be more than an abstract set of rules. Civility takes its reference point from 'the ideal condition into which whoever is trying to civilise a community is trying to bring it' (NL 34.7, Connelly 2003: 270–84). It is an ideal to which actual civilisations can only approximate. As Collingwood writes, 'the process of civilisation would thus be one of asymptotic approximation to the ideal condition of civility' (NL 34.56). Thus no actual political society can ever embody civility completely. Collingwood tells us that, 'the community's condition never becomes one of pure civility and the barbarous elements never vanish' (NL 34.55).

In an imaginary conversation between Collingwood and Gulliver, talk of how civilized an existing society is in relation to an ideal might make sense. Unlike the Yahoos and the Houyhnhnms whose natures exclude complexity, Gulliver is contrived by Swift to be receptive to a world that displays different degrees of imperfection. So when Collingwood argues that conditional rules of civility – being civil to particular individuals in particular social circumstances – rest on 'the ideal of civility as such', it is not difficult to think of Gulliver asking what form such an ideal might take. Collingwood's reply would leave his philosophical readers in no doubt about what he means. There is, he writes, 'an ideal of universal civility; civility on every kind of occasion, civility under any kind of provocation, civility to every kind of person' (WCM, NL 494). This order of ideal Collingwood explicitly associates with the Sermon on the Mount. Civility, for

Collingwood, can never mean simply 'the way we behave', so he presents us with universal civility, civility unqualified by any social or historical variation.

Collingwood thinks of civilisation as a process of becoming. Civilisation means refraining from diminishing another's self-respect and refraining from the unconditional use of force over them. No civilisation, Collingwood insists, can ever totally remove elements of savagery which remain within it as 'primitive survivals' (NL 9.5), and any civilization can find itself threatened by barbarism. As we have seen, Yahoos in Collingwood's account are neither savages nor barbarians. And yet the Yahoo, Collingwood stresses, is always with us.

Civility is a requirement for those who realize that on occasion they may have to employ force or fraud to achieve a political good. On this subject Swift has Gulliver speak directly: in explaining to the Houyhnhnms that in his country young horses are castrated to help make them tame (and therefore useful). Gulliver is, in effect, showing us how human beings, as distinct from Yahoos and Houyhnhnms, and, indeed, young horses, sometimes need to use force to counter force, so encouraging the civilizing process on its way.

Collingwood understands a political society to be a conditional undertaking in which civil communication is necessarily incomplete. One indicator of this is the need for each successive generation to receive a political education. Another is regression to a non-social state in the form of criminality. Another, again, is the unavoidable use of force, as Collingwood puts it, 'not arbitrary or unneeded force, but force absolutely necessitated by the impossibility of ruling without it' (NL 29.45). This arises in defence of civility itself and in relation to the incompleteness of the process by which non-agreement is transformed into agreement. Disagreement belongs to the character of politics, and so Collingwood writes, 'it should be observed that war in the general sense of political strife is the evil that is inseparable from the political good' (EPP 103).

Liberals are right to be troubled by cases where liberal governments act uncivilly to defend civility, but does Collingwood's Yahoo starting point adequately capture the issues at stake? For Collingwood, all political societies are subject to loss of reason in the form of emotions uncontrolled or feelings unchecked. But this way of thinking is a weak explanation of the dilemmas that liberal governments are sometimes called upon to face. The choice on these occasions is not between one policy based on reason and another on the unfettered release of the feelings. The intransigence of political morality derives from circumstances in which rulers encounter, as Edmund Burke puts it, 'the dreadful exigence in which morality submits to the suspension of its own rules in favour of its own principles' (Burke 1982: 240). Collingwood overestimates the work which civility is able to do in such circumstances. Civility places a value on the avoidance of arbitrariness. The result is a presumption in favour of equality. However, the distinguishing feature of the Yahoos is not arbitrariness as opposed to non-arbitrariness, but randomness. Since they are unable to name their feelings they have no way – partial or impartial – of attaching them to objects in the world with any degree of reliability or consistency. Liberal societies do not automatically become Yahoo when they face the situation that Burke describes. The notion of liberal political societies regressing irresistibly from reason to feeling lacks the moral fine shading needed to capture the dilemmas at stake.

For liberals, lying is open to conditional justification, but cruelty is quite another matter; in Judith Shklar's famous phrase, the liberal humanist regards 'cruelty as the worst thing we do' (Shklar 1984: 44). What the liberal fears is not only incivility manifested as servility, humiliation or exploitation but barbarity which is outside the frame of rational discourse on which liberalism relies. Unlike savagery, which is always relative, civilized to a degree and no more, barbarity is an active 'hostility towards civilisation' (NL 41.12). And yet Collingwood thinks this liberal fear is unfounded because barbarism is ultimately at odds with itself – 'all it does is assert itself as will and then deny itself as will' (NL 36.94). It is outside the conceptual circle that enables conversation between the civil and the uncivil. Rudeness and discourtesy can be pointed out, but, if cruelty is a psychological state, then the sadistically cruel cannot be argued out of their cruelty.

Civility impinges on moral concepts such as cruelty, servility and humiliation that do not fit easily into morality understood as a formal system of restraints. Collingwood does attempt a detailed description of their content when he writes, 'there seems to be a difference in kind between even the grossest and beastliest incivility, the sort that would not trouble to warn a man before firing a shot where his head happens to be, and the cruelty of killing or hurting him for the sake of killing or hurting him' (NL 35.78). The ideal of civility excludes cruelty in all its forms, including the cruelty that can arise from over-civility such as Montaigne's report that he had seen 'people rude by being over-civil and troublesome in their courtesy' (Montaigne 1905: 50): behaviour which should, perhaps, concern liberals as much as obvious forms of disrespect. Collingwood aims to protect civility from the Yahoo feelings that are always with us, but it is difficult to see how this can be achieved without diminishing civility's formal claims. Uncivil behaviour that is disrespectful but falls short of the use of force, such as scorn, indifference or contempt, is described by revealing the specific logic of the moral concepts concerned. Additionally, as Collingwood himself notes, there will be circumstances in which civility may have to be suspended or involve exceptions and exclusion clauses. Arguments over these, such as disputes over the treatment of strangers, are morally substantial and so pull civility closer to moral and political debate.

Civility promotes mutual trust and so is the appropriate response to the conditional nature of politics as Collingwood understands it. He tells us further that living up to the ideal of civility means gradually reducing the incidence of servility and humiliation. In Collingwood's liberal politics the problem of civility lies in seeing how it can be extended both to its declared enemies and to those who simply do not share its assumptions. Collingwood's solution is shared by Brian Barry, who asks how liberal practices can be justified to those who are not liberals. Barry considers the principle of neutrality according to which a liberal state is required to remain neutral between differing conceptions of the good. Non-liberals are not required to change or abandon their substantive beliefs. However, neutrality can succeed only if non-liberals are already predisposed towards it because it requires them to understand their substantive beliefs as preferences or opinions. Further, as Barry suggests, liberals are best advised not to apply the neutrality principle to their own beliefs because that would assume that 'liberal beliefs are on all fours with dogmatic beliefs' (Barry 1990: 1–14). If liberalism cannot persuade non-liberals by means of the neutrality argument it should 'go on the offensive' (Barry 1990: 14), as Barry puts it, in terms of its own values. Thus, Barry writes, 'given the choice between trying to persuade non-liberals to accept the principle of neutrality and trying to discredit their beliefs, I think that the second is clearly the better strategy' (Barry 1990: 14). In *An Autobiography* Collingwood agrees that liberalism is weakened by its search for neutrality. J. S. Mill's view, as Collingwood understands it, that 'people ought to be allowed to think whatever they liked because it didn't really matter what they thought' (AA 152–3) he thinks is false to the relation between thought and practice and, as Barry comments, it is 'radically unstable' (Barry 1990: 14) from the standpoint of moral psychology. So the failure of liberalism for Collingwood springs 'not from weakness or falsity in the principles of liberalism itself, but from the failure to put those principles consistently into practice' (MGM 327).

The standard liberal response to the dilemma which Edmund Burke describes is to build into political institutions and practices virtues in which citizens can put their trust. If civility is valued instrumentally, individual citizens will treat each other civilly so that they can more readily satisfy their different and possibly conflicting wants. If, on the other hand, civility is more like a formal condition of political life, then behaving civilly may sometimes have a price. When expectations are stable civility can be both sensible strategy and a condition of social transaction but, in more discordant times, the qualities of a good citizen can collide. Here, as Adam Smith reflects, the signs of civility, the dispositions 'to respect the laws and to obey the civil magistrate, to promote the welfare of the whole society of his fellow citizens' (Smith 1976: 231) conflict and lead to very different imperatives in conduct. Collingwood, like Smith, is aware that in non-ideal circumstances 'a departure from the rules of civility must be provided for in the rules of civilisation' (NL 35.48), but how and when this departure takes place, and what suspensions of civility it allows, constitute the tests which politics imposes.

In Collingwood's liberalism too, individuals place their faith in rationally based structures rather than personal character or temperament, following a standard pattern in singling out the rule of law as a necessary feature of a civilized polity that operates as a foundation for trust. By respecting the law, individuals are Collingwood writes, 'daily more and more able to control their own desires and to crush all opposition to the carrying out of their intentions' (NL 39.92). Spinoza's notion of reason domesticating the feelings is here hard at work. The rule of law acts as a buttress to civility. Subscribing to law is evidence that Yahoo type urges are being restrained, even though in its day-to-day practice law is as vulnerable to incivility as any other human activity. Law will destroy itself as law if, for example, lawyers clothe their profession in privilege or mystique. As Hegel illustrates, 'to hang the laws so high that no citizen could read them is injustice of one and the same kind as to bury them in row upon row of learned tomes, collections of dissenting judgements and opinions, records of customs, etc.' (Hegel 1967: 138). Swift too contrives that Gulliver should trust the law but not always the lawyer. In his happy life among the Houyhnhnms Gulliver lists the human vices and false representations he is content not to miss; here there is no 'Physician to destroy my Body, nor Lawyer to ruin my Fortune' (GT 254, and for further remarks on lawyers, see GT 229–31).

Collingwood's vision is of a civilization that arises out of, and thinly overlies, a condition of uncontrolled feeling. What dominates this picture is fear of the Yahoos and what they represent. As we saw, the state is licensed to use force to counter force, to encourage the civilizing process on its way. The problem is, however, that civility is not a model for justice. Moreover, given that many new and possibly radical social and political demands depend on justice, or at least appeal to a concept very much like it, then Collingwood faces a serious difficulty.

A state based on civility is simply too minimalist to respond to the aspirations of his age.

The reasons for this are clear enough. Civility depends on the presence or absence of something, namely, force. Ideally, we live up to civility by abstaining from the use of force. This tells us all we need to know about what civility requires. But we would not be told all we need to know about justice if we said that we live up to it by abstaining from injustice. Defenders of Collingwood will argue that what civility distributes is respect. Since respect should be distributed equally it must be the concern of justice. So Collingwood writes that 'to recognise the freedom of others is to respect them' (NL 37.14). But there is little point in arguing that civility distributes respect if respect is a good that cannot be distributed. Clearly respect, although undeniably a liberal good, is not a good like an opportunity or a resource like an income. More importantly, Collingwood's association of respect with freedom neglects the connection respect has with worth. It is not simply the freedom of oneself and others that instigate respect but whether or not the ends advanced by freedom have worth. To these difficulties we might add the sceptical thought that treating others with civility has particular value because it permits peaceful and possibly cooperative relations when respect is minimal or awaiting confirmation or even absent. Thus, to subsume justice under respect confuses the distribution of benefits and burdens in a community with the ways that individuals attach worth to their own projects and to those of others. Defenders of Collingwood may nevertheless insist that the equality of respect that civility enjoins is all that justice should be concerned with. In other words, Collingwood, by placing justice under the rubric of civility, is keeping its subject within limits. But this does not square with what Collingwood actually says. For Collingwood, even a 'slight contrast' between rich and poor undermines civility. The problem is that it is only through the application of a principle that is distributive in kind that the extent of slightness in the contrast can be identified and addressed. And this is something that civility is logically precluded from doing.

Gulliver's Travels is scarcely a religious tract. Collingwood, however, sees in religion a set of beliefs that civility needs. His ideal of civic virtue is not simply a particular conception of the good that he assumes is shared by others. Collingwood insists that an individual 'cannot criticise the civilisation of his society from a detached, external point of view' (WCM, NL 499). His discussion of civility as an ideal bears on his understanding of progress (IH 321–34); the difficulties in Collingwood's determination not to allow civility to be construed independently of history are well illustrated in some remarks of Wittgenstein's. During a discussion with Benjamin Farrington in 1943, Wittgenstein commented,

> When there is a change in the conditions in which people live, we may call it progress because it opens up new opportunities. But in the course of this change, opportunities which were there before may be lost. In one way it was progress, in another it was decline. A historical change may be progress and also be ruin. There is no method of weighing one against the other to justify speaking of 'progress on the whole'. Farrington said that even 'with all the ugly sides of our civilization, I am sure I would rather live as we do now than have to live as the caveman did.' Wittgenstein replied: 'Yes of course you would. But would the caveman?'
>
> (Wittgenstein 2003: 363)

Collingwood's view raises the question of how philosophy can establish civility as an ideal, and here he turns to religion for support. The difficulty is how Collingwood's understanding of faith as expressing an 'inward flame' can fit with his view of civility as a shared practice. More specifically, civility as an ideal does little to clarify its connection with justice since the economic injunctions of the Sermon on the Mount might be satisfied in a variety of ways: for example, by requiring the rich to give away all they have, or by allowing them to keep what they have only if this makes the poor better off. Given the equivocal nature of such interpretations it is hard to think of them as absolute presuppositions of civility. Thus there remains a tension between civility as a feature of an historical practice and civility as a universal ideal that is never completely eliminated. It is worth noticing that this is not a difficulty that troubles Swift. Swift characterizes Yahoos and Houyhnhnms reductively: reason is understood in terms of the absence of passion and vice versa.

In a famous essay Orwell describes *Gulliver's Travels* as great art even though he thinks that the view it represents 'only just passes the test of sanity' (Orwell 1998: 417–31). Orwell admires *Gulliver's Travels* while disagreeing with the moral and political ideas it contains. For his part, Collingwood does not share Swift's pessimism or feel himself bound by Swift's description of the Yahoos. In Collingwood's reconstruction, the Yahoos are an abstraction representing one aspect of human behaviour. Yahoos cannot understand their feelings because they lack the capacity to selectively attend to them (Swift refers to their 'undistinguishing appetite') (GT 240). Selective attention in us, however, is not a matter of introspection, as if all we gain over the Yahoos is a shrewder capacity for self-exploration. Slightly misleadingly Collingwood speaks of feelings as standing to thinking as foundation does to superstructure (PA 157–64), misleading because understanding our feelings is a matter of grasping the rules that govern the expressions we employ to convey them. So, Collingwood writes, 'one does not first acquire a language and then use it. To possess it and to use it is the same. We only come to possess it by repeatedly and progressively attempting to use it' (PA 250). Thus from Collingwood's standpoint what the Yahoos lack is a public world. Yet this does not lead Collingwood to envy the Houyhnhnm way of life, as Gulliver is contrived by Swift to do. Indeed the opposite is the case because, from Collingwood's philosophical point of view, the Houyhnhnms are almost as irrelevant to a human conception of civility as the Yahoos are. They have little idea of agriculture, industry and science. In their politics (surely barely worth the name) tellingly they possess no word for 'opinion', hence no understanding of disagreement and, as Swift makes abundantly clear, no concept of war. So the human difficulties that Collingwood means to address in his understanding of civility would be beyond their grasp.

Importantly, Collingwood does not regard the Yahoo elements in us as beyond teaching. His philosophy of language makes the central claim that it is the expression of their feelings in language that enables human beings to make sense of them. Liberalism, in Collingwood's writings, is 'on the offensive', to use Barry's phrase, because Collingwood circumscribes what can be justified in civility's name. Collingwood writes that 'we can pity the sadist, but we cannot allow him to be observing the rules of his own civilization. He has no civilisation. He is nearer akin to a Yahoo than to the *animal rationale* that obeys the rules of a civilization whether high or low' (NL 35.92).

So for Collingwood the Yahoo in us is not the Yahoo as described by Swift. Where we ordinarily distinguish between our appetites and our desires, and our desires and our passions, Swift gives the Yahoos no such ability. Since the Yahoos live permanently in the here and now their emotions appear to them as little more than physical reactions, as outside their control as an itch or a blink. Yahoo behaviour is, therefore, like that of a human being in the grip of a sneeze or a shiver, except that for the Yahoos that is all there is. Being in the grip of a sneeze is what it is like for a Yahoo to experience hunger or fear or anger. Small wonder then that, as Swift describes it, life for the Yahoos is a constant frustration.

By contrast, Collingwood thinks of the Yahoo in us differently. There is an intellectual component in our emotional life linking it to our beliefs, thoughts and judgements. It seems clear, therefore, that Collingwood can only understand the Yahoo in us by parting company with Swift. Orwell writes, 'Swift falsifies his picture of the world by refusing to see anything in human life except dirt, folly and wickedness' (Orwell 1998: 429). Swift does not just inform us about our Yahoo feelings. He says that we are nothing but those feelings. Satirist and philosopher now perceptibly slip apart. Irony and deliberate exaggeration are no use to Collingwood. Equally, an historical study of barbarism and savagery is of little use to Swift. No matter how thorough our attempt to locate them, there are no Yahoos in history. That is not the sense that Swift gives them.

The use of the Yahoos as an abstraction which is common to Swift and Collingwood deserves a little more attention. An abstraction involves taking away from a complex idea everything believed essential to it. As an abstraction the Yahoos are neither an historical nor an anthropological fact. Their existence is conceptual. In conducting this thought experiment Collingwood aims to 'strip off in thought' (NL 30.73) the features basic to the idea of society – language, rationality and free will – such that 'the remainder is the Yahoo herd' (NL 30.73). Swift's Yahoos are the embodiment of nastiness. Collingwood's Yahoos tell us what human beings **can** be like and why their feelings need educating and restraining, if not coaching out. Yahoo behaviour – imitativeness, brutishness, total incapacity for intelligent appreciation and choice – is what human beings shun, and so it should come as no surprise that Collingwood considers it not only a failure of sociality but the most virulent source of war.

Collingwood's methodology here is an established procedure in social contract theory, a way of thinking about human society and politics to which he is indebted. Nevertheless, it raises difficult questions, the most serious of which Collingwood is certainly aware of. We might phrase the question like this – if the Yahoo in us is a tendency and not the Yahoo as described by Swift then why introduce the idea at all? And so Collingwood asks 'If the thing is an abstraction, if it never exists and never can exist as a fact, why trouble to paint a picture of it?' (NL 30.74).

Collingwood's answer stresses the existence of the Yahoos as an idea. Why, then, is it an idea which is necessary to what he wants to say? The Yahoos represent human life arrested, as Collingwood says, 'just short of free will' (NL 30.52). Since as Collingwood argues free will is the defining characteristic of human action and since change is an essential feature of human life in its temporal aspect, there must always be the possibility that free will can be modified or even reversed. In order to understand how this can happen Collingwood says that 'we have to know what the changing thing is changing into and what it is changing out of' (NL 30.75). The job of the Yahoos as an abstraction is to provide criteria reference to which enables us to make sense of what is happening at least at one end of the process of change when this occurs. For the Yahoos as an abstraction free will is permanently out of reach. For the Yahoos in us it can be suspended, sometimes seriously or damagingly. Without the picture of the Yahoos as an abstraction, changes of this kind would remain brute facts and as such would be hard or even impossible to assess. Where this is the case there is the need for a measure. Collingwood argues that there is nothing independently of our own understandings that can guarantee change is for the better. There is nothing in the historical process. There is nothing resembling a law of progress which ensures that change will always be an improvement. It is, therefore, important to human beings that they 'know which end of the process is the right end and which the wrong; so that granted we need not hope ever to reach the one or fear ever to reach the other' (NL 30.79), we can at least tell which is which and which is made more or less likely by any specific change.

When Collingwood talks about human beings becoming Yahoo by allowing their appetites to rule he appears to postulate a single relationship between two states, one in which appetites are held in control and the other in which they rage about in primitive disorder. In this conventional picture, human beings in a Yahoo state are completely enslaved by their appetites and desires. In this condition human beings would scarcely recognize themselves as human. War would be like two mastodons fighting over a piece of meat.

The problem with this picture is obvious. By operating with an either/or list of possibilities it makes the Yahoo tendency in us too much like the Yahoos in Swift and is, in any case, not what Collingwood actually says. For Collingwood the anti-realist facts gain their significance from the ways we think about them. What enables us to recognize any slippage into Yahoodom is not the fact of change itself or the phases through which it passes but the abstraction from our own behaviour which the Yahoos represent. When changes of this kind take place, their initial and terminal poles – the state prior to change and the state after it – are not facts but abstractions from facts. Without them it would be impossible to estimate what sort of change has happened and to what degree.

When Collingwood was writing *The New Leviathan* trust in the foundations of civilized life was at a premium. Western civilization was commonly thought to express the humane Christianity which, in spite of often culpable failures to live up to this ideal, would see it through the trauma to come. Collingwood hoped to clarify ideals such as this and in so doing make the gap between ideal and actuality more apprehensible.

In Collingwood's political philosophy, as it is in that of Hobbes, insecurity counts as one of the highest human fears. The Leviathan exists to authorize, guard and protect, but Collingwood argues that these functions will not be convincing unless the state is anchored in a philosophy of mind which delineates human capacities, interests and desires. It is therefore unsurprising that Collingwood gives prominence to threats and insecurities which come from within us. Whether from self-deception, or a false estimation of its power, the greatest danger to a civilization arises from the failure of self-knowledge. Hobbes would have agreed. Vainglory, or pride in our terms, is one example. Vainglory is clearly not the full-scale regression into primitivism represented by the Yahoos at their worst. Pride as a cognitive state presupposes too much by way of mental capacities to act as the rock bottom pursuit of appetite which is the defining feature of the Yahoos. And yet a misplaced estimation of power is what vainglory is all about. All are prone to the belief that the Yahoo is never in them but always in others. As we saw, Collingwood says that the Yahoo in us is never completely overcome. His meaning is surely clear. Believing oneself or a society to be invulnerable, or better than it is, or convincing oneself that the situation is other than it is, all endanger the civility which alone makes life tolerable for human beings, who are just as capable of falsely estimating their powers as estimating them truly.

Part Two

Engagement

5

Why are we at war?

The conflict between fascism and communism in the period between the two world wars left liberalism with little air in which to breathe. Liberalism gave Collingwood his earliest political beliefs, so there is little doubt that its decline touched a nerve. Denis Healey, a student at Oxford at the time and a near companion of Collingwood's on his voyage in the Aegean in the summer of 1939, remembered that 'the drumbeat of approaching war was deafening' (Healey 1989: 41).

An Autobiography contained some of the sharpest passages of political invective ever penned against a sitting British prime minister, one whose moral beliefs shaped a strong determination to avoid war. When it was written the national mood was overwhelmingly in favour of peace, but by its publication date, so close to the British declaration of war, the book's derisive treatment of Neville Chamberlain might have seemed over-played. Even so, the times appeared to be with Collingwood because the public mood in Britain during 1939 changed as events made Germany's purpose unmistakable.

We might think that political opinion in times of uncertainty is an unsafe guide, whether to policy or commitment. Oxford student politics was, as Denis Healey remembers, 'overwhelmingly of the Left in the summer of 1939', and 'in turmoil' (Healey 1989: 44), with many who had joined the Communist Party exiting in disillusionment after the Nazi-Soviet Pact and later the Russian invasion of Finland. The views of those who, like Collingwood, were suspicious of the Communist Party as a weapon in the fight against fascism appeared, as far as the political future was concerned, no better based. At the start of the Second World War Collingwood thought the German economy was brittle and, like the American President, Franklin D. Roosevelt, leader of a country not yet at war and ill-disposed to join it, he then believed that Nazi rule would be short-lived. As hopes for a negotiated peace or for a revolution within Germany itself to end the war gradually diminished and, as the nature of German tyranny was revealed, the distinction between Nazis and Germans, one which many liberals including the American President considered morally essential, threatened to become redundant.

In Britain, at the start of the conflict, the distinction between Nazis and Germans provoked extensive argument, not least in government circles. Collingwood was closer to these debates than has been imagined. And so Collingwood's reference in the final part of *The New Leviathan* to his having read political works by German refugees, his claim that some of these had failed to grasp the nature of the tyranny which had overtaken their country and his opinion that the writing of one refugee appears as little more than defeatism tells us something important.

German refugees from Nazism in Britain in the early years of the war were doing their utmost to shape British public opinion by publishing books which purported to tell the truth about life in Nazi Germany and about what Hitlerism really meant. A significant number were intended to gain British recognition for their political parties, essentially hostile to Hitler, after the war. In *The New Leviathan* Collingwood tells us of his familiarity with this literature, much of which had been available in English translation since 1939. Books like Heinrich Hauser's *Hitler versus Germany*, Heinrich Fraenkel's *The German People versus Hitler* and Sebastian Haffner's *Germany-Jekyll and Hyde*, all published in England in 1940, covered all aspects of National Socialism and German life (Baynes 1943). What characterizes these books is their concern with the opposition to Nazi rule within Germany and estimates of its strength. At the time Collingwood was writing *The New Leviathan* this 'other Germany' was a matter of dispute. Among German refugees in Britain who were politically active Heinrich Fraenkel was among the most determined, arguing that the 'other Germany' existed and should be supported. Collingwood sharply disagreed, writing of the anti-Nazi opposition within Germany, 'There are not enough of them' (NL 45.69).

The books Collingwood read on this topic linked him with a different and more disturbing world. At the start of the war Collingwood had understood Nazism as a function of pagan survivals in Germany. Among Christians it was a common enough view. He had spoken then of the fate of the Christian opposition to Nazism in Germany and had viewed the struggle to defeat Nazism as much in terms of the emotions as the intellect (EPP 187–96). Ideas which had once seemed immutable changed during the course of the war and in some cases even lost their significance. As early as 1919, Collingwood warned that the Prussianism which had only recently been overcome would 'reappear in another and more dangerous shape' (EPP 205). By the summer of 1941 Collingwood was certain that a policy based on the 'other Germany' or the 'true Germany', as it was termed by its adherents, would not gain the ascendancy. The war would have to be fought to a finish.

When the war began Collingwood thought that the British Government had been irresponsibly reticent about the reasons for fighting it. It was a complaint which many in the press and on radio sought to rectify by supplying reasons of their own. In the summer of 1940 under a new prime minister, Winston Churchill, this questioning mood continued. Some believed that, if the war had to be fought at all (and there was a significant number who entertained the possibility of a negotiated peace) then it should not be solely for reasons of national defence but in order to bring about a world in which peace, security and social justice were available to all. The Labour leader Clement Attlee, then in effect deputy prime minster in Churchill's War Cabinet, made this point with unambiguous force, saying in July 1940, 'The Germans are fighting a revolutionary war for very definite objectives. We are fighting a conservative war and our objects are purely negative. We must put forward a positive and revolutionary aim admitting that the old order has collapsed and asking people to fight for the new order' (as quoted in Smyth 1985: 134; see the discussion in Addison 1994: 126 where, speaking about Churchill's attitude to reconstruction in December 1940, he says that 'gradually it flowed around and past him, like a tide cutting off an island from the shore').

Survival may have been the overriding imperative in Britain in 1940, but calls for a better world caught the national mood because Britain had within the lifetime of a generation fought one war at great human cost only to find itself embroiled in another. *The New Leviathan* was not a party political manifesto, and yet Collingwood was sensitive to the demands for change on which, no matter how broadly expressed, Attlee and others were insistent. There can surely be no doubt that Collingwood's liberal inheritance pushes him in this direction. The influence of Ruskin, too, can be seen in the willingness of *The New Leviathan* to discuss educational and environmental issues as well as more traditional liberal concerns about disparities of wealth and opportunity and how they might be diminished. War aims other than that of defeating the enemy were very much in the air. Some six months or so into the book's writing *The New Statesman* in its issue of late August 1940 published a letter asking for the war's objects to be delineated, if not in detail then in principles which included more than national survival (Burridge 1976: 53). Someone else who wanted to talk about the aims Britain was fighting for was Tom Hopkinson, who had been a student of Collingwood's and was a close friend. He was editor of the popular magazine

Picture Post, and the issue of January 1941 contains a 'Plan for Britain', in which the future Britain was fighting for was spelled out very much along welfare state lines (Hopkinson 1982: 184–5). Collingwood clearly does try to tackle concerns which go well beyond the single purpose of defeating Germany.

Churchillian rhetoric stiffened British resolve but could not in itself provide the positive proposals for social and political reform that Attlee was asking for. Nor indeed as the war progressed was Churchill willing to conflate winning the war with discussions about the kind of Britain that might be thought desirable should victory ensue. Moreover, in May 1940, with victory and the nature of the post-war peace both strictly academic questions, and with Germany supreme in Europe and thought ready to mount a cross Channel invasion, the urgent decision to take was whether or not it made sense to continue fighting at all. *The New Leviathan* should be read in this light. In one sense Collingwood was with Churchill, and his belief that the European dictators had to be fought to a finish. Nazism had to be destroyed. But in another sense Collingwood was firmly with Attlee. For corroboration of this we need only remember the unity of purpose which connects *An Autobiography* with *The New Leviathan*. Collingwood had been a supporter of the republican cause in the Spanish Civil War. He had defended the government of the loyalist leader, Juan Negrin, against charges of communist infiltration. For the progressive left the republic's cause was the cause of all humanity. It was an ideal, one that remained vital, even after its defeat. As one writer on Negrin comments, 'Spain, in the person of Negrin, had become the touchstone of Britain's claim to be espousing human liberation in opposition to Nazi enslavement' (Smyth 1985: 137). On this view, Britain was now fighting a people's war. National security was a necessary but not sufficient reason for doing so.

Early readers of *The New Leviathan* expected it to answer the two questions which dominated the period in which it was written. Why should Britain fight on when there were so few arguments to support it? Why should people in Britain agree to fight if victory left what Attlee called 'the old order' unchanged? However, action in the face of uncertainty was what Collingwood thought much in history was about. In *The Idea of History* he complained that moral thinking in the ancient world 'attributed far too much to the deliberate plan or policy of the agent, far too little to the force of a blind activity embarking on a course of action without foreseeing its end and being led to that end only through the necessary development of that course itself' (IH 42). Ideas do not take their place in history like blocks in a school syllabus. They may be intimated or suggested, as a demand for social justice was in Britain during the 1930s, but not fully articulated; or, if articulated, as social justice was in the Beveridge Report, then not yet realized and open to substantial dispute. When we add to this picture Collingwood's view that philosophy was not a super science standing above the battle of ideas then we can see why his liberalism, principled though it was, is frequently an insufficient guide to his thinking. His self-confessed political disengagement which characterized much of his life complicates matters further.

In the summer of 1940 there were some arguments for fighting on. Collingwood shared Chamberlain's view that the German economy could be worn down. Churchill's strategy of gradually winning American involvement was thought by some to be persuasive, although during the composition of *The New Leviathan* it seemed unreal and Collingwood makes no mention of it. Nor does the much-anticipated historical presence of the Soviet Union enter his thinking. Far more important to Collingwood's mind was the sheer impossibility of any alternative. Here the distinction which *The New Leviathan* develops between civilization and barbarism is the key to his point of view. Collingwood writes, 'The defeat of barbarism, I say, is always certain in the long run' (NL 41.73), a statement which may sound like Churchillian rhetoric but actually means something quite different.

We know now that during the dark days of 1940 Churchill did contemplate the possibility of a negotiated peace with Hitler (Reynolds 1985: 147–67), even though it was in the mood of a man who might be forced to go to a disreputable tailor to pay through the nose for what he is certain will be an ill-fitting suit. Going cap in hand, however, is a poor basis for a settlement with an enemy who is both strong and untrustworthy: Churchill's decision to fight on was made as much on grounds of pragmatism as principle. When the Battle of Britain was at its height Collingwood feared the return of appeasement in high circles in government. Churchill's decision set British worries aside. Victory was far from certain, but the course had been set. Barbarism might be ultimately doomed, as Collingwood thought, but it still had to be defeated.

Both philosopher and politician saw the nihilism at the centre of Nazism, and both believed the ideals of civilization, if not their actual manifestations, to be imperishable. Collingwood's philosophy told him something more. It told him that barbarism was self-contradictory. It could not survive because nothing that is self-contradictory can survive. There is some reflection here of a doctrine that Collingwood committed himself to in 1916. Then he wrote, 'Every really good thing in the world harmonizes with every other; but evil is at variance not only with good but with other evils' (D 462–3). Common purpose among barbarians is like honour among thieves or trust among liars. It was by means of a philosophical argument that Collingwood came to see barbarism for what it was (NL 36.94), but he saw also that fighting barbarism had to be a military and political matter. Moral perspectives were certainly present but, as the war took its course and Britain found that it was no longer conducting the struggle almost alone, to the Allies the overwhelming priority was victory no matter what morally unpalatable choices this involved.

Collingwood's firm belief that human choice presumes free will reflects, if a little awkwardly, his Christianity and his liberalism. Both play a part in his rejection of the nineteenth-century doctrine of 'the evanescence of evil' (NL 496). We in the twentieth century, Collingwood tells us, have come to see that evil things do not 'begin to perish as soon as they begin to exist' (NL 5.5). Evil is historical in character. New formations come into existence as old possibilities are replaced. Collingwood's view that the defeat of barbarism is certain makes it sound as if it is predetermined, but this is far from his meaning. When barbarism is not recognized for what it is, or when it is recognized, but the recognition fails to lead to action against it, then, Collingwood says, the blindness is culpable. Given the nature of Britain's enemy, and given the dangers facing Britain after the fall of France, the British Government's decision to fight on finds in *The New Leviathan* clarification at the level of justification and general rule.

Like a number of works written during the 1930s, for example, Alfred Cobban, *The Crisis of Civilization* (1941) and Leonard Woolf's *Quack, Quack* (1935) and *Barbarians at the Gate* (1939), *The New Leviathan* saw the conflict as about the future of civilization. A few words are necessary to show how this frame of mind came about. Collingwood wrote about politics as a Christian and a liberal, and there is little doubt that he regarded the idea of the liberal state as one of the achievements of civilization. He saw just war theory in the same light. The prohibitions and permissions it lays down govern the behaviour of states at war, and they derive from, and are an approximation of, an ideal of civilization which applies to states and recognizes the kind of entities they are, but which is independent of them and provides bedrock for their institutions and conduct, their principles and their application. Collingwood speaks of the civilization of a community as a process of advancing civility. He wants us to see that what makes a state and what makes it civilized involve different concepts. He may also have thought that the more states become civilized, the more they perfect themselves as states and that the more states perfect themselves as states, the more incumbent it is for them to draw away from imperial rule or possession. However, his focus is apparent. When a civilized community faces an enemy which is barbaric, unavoidably it has to draw on arguments and emotional resources of the most fundamental kind.

Here Collingwood's philosophy of history and his political philosophy follow parallel lines. The future, unlike the past, is in principle both alterable and unknowable. Collingwood's belief in free will is as unshakeable as his view that human beings do not always use it wisely or even well. War might be thought of as a case in point. In his memoir of Wittgenstein Norman Malcolm quotes from a letter he received from him towards the end of the Second World War. Wittgenstein wrote,

> I want to say something about the war being a 'boredom'. If a boy said the school was an intense boredom one might answer him that, if only he could get himself to learn what can really be learned there, he would not find it *so* boring. Now forgive me for saying that an enormous lot can be learnt about human beings in this war – *if* you keep your eyes open. And the better you are at thinking the more you'll get out of what you see.
>
> (Malcolm 1958: 41)

Collingwood did not live to see the war through to a finish. He was seriously ill during much of the composition of later parts of *The New Leviathan*, relying on his own integrity and intellectual robustness to bring the project to completion. One of Wittgenstein's fears in giving advice to his friends was that they might think him preaching to them. Neither Collingwood nor Wittgenstein had much use for the picture of philosophy as a science, and it is surely in keeping that they should worry about the practical value of philosophy as well.

Collingwood thought that it is not the business of political philosophy to tell politicians what to do, just as it makes no sense for the philosophy of art to tell painters how to paint or sculptors how to sculpt. Collingwood is surely right. We need only ask whether the best result would be an aesthetician/artist amalgam in which artists are forever elucidating their work to themselves to understand his point. The absence of a language in which these hybrid possibilities are expressed is revealing. In Collingwood's view the distinction between forms of activity is categorical. He never abandoned it. Somewhat typically, however, this is what Collingwood appears to do. He wanted a much more uncompromising perspective, one in which 'the difference between thinker and man of action disappeared' (AA 151). But what kind of thinker? Action without thought Collingwood considered close to being unintelligible. Not any kind of thought will do either. Practical conduct requires practical thought. Policymaking, in

Collingwood's view, goes wrong if the thought behind it is derived from the wrong questions or the wrong set of assumptions. Appeasement to his mind was the defining example (although one assumption that sets politics on the wrong track is surely the idea that philosophers can tell politicians what to do).

In this way of thinking Collingwood's anti-realism and his logic of question and answer are both hard at work. Two examples illustrate the point. At the time of Munich demands for Britain to give guarantees of security to countries facing assault from Germany sounded hollow when voiced by those who, during the 1930s, were most vociferous in opposing rearmament. As was remarked, 'It was now of course illogically late to will the way if you had consistently opposed the means' (Howarth 1978: 228). Why 'illogically'? Collingwood's answer is straightforward. Questions derive their sense from the contexts in which they are raised and what makes a question apposite in one context may diminish in relevance when times change. Again, at the war's outbreak it was a common view that the biggest threat to British values would come not from a strengthened Germany itself but from the undemocratic measures that Britain might have to take in order to resist it. It was an anxiety that Collingwood shared, one which in his case was gradually and only partially dispelled by events. It is in the nature of political thinking that it proceeds not in the timeless realm of propositional logic, but in history, one in which nuance as much as principle shapes political opinions. Thus, in 1932 Collingwood followed de Ruggiero's lead in counselling against criticism of Fascist Italy from outside on the grounds that it would harm the anti-fascist cause within (Boucher 2013: 384). Liberal non-interventionism is the principle here as it was in Collingwood's cautionary remarks on aid to the covert opposition to Nazism within Germany at the start of the war. Spain was the exception as it was to almost all on the progressive Left. In mid-February 1939 Collingwood was in the Dutch East Indies writing furiously on what he hoped would be his major work on history. Back in Oxford, idealism about Spain continued to dominate political debate with, as reported in *The Times* of 17 February 1939, forty two professors signing a telegram to Halifax, then foreign secretary and chancellor of the university, urging against public recognition of the Franco government (Roberts 1991: 139). Collingwood had advocated military intervention in Spain, an opinion which might well have had more to do with pointing the finger at a British prime minister's beliefs and purposes rather than practical politics, but it was in tune with the feeling in Oxford and in one respect in advance of it.

During the first winter of the war it was pessimism which infected Collingwood's mood. Civilization had been 'thrown on the defensive' (EPP

194). It was, to adapt a phrase of Chips Channon, 'the bee which had lost its sting' (Channon 1967: 200). *The New Leviathan* was not written at the end of the war when its result was known, nor at the start when the future was unknown, but during it. For much of its composition Victory in Europe (VE) Day would have seemed a very long way away indeed. Collingwood wanted philosophy to embrace history, not be embraced by it. During the war in Britain victory was the essential aim but, as we have seen, demands for a fairer society were not far behind. In this respect *The New Leviathan* is neither ahead of its time nor behind it. It is not merely circumstantial. Whether a demand for social justice is implied or even avowed by its arguments is a philosophical question, one which depends on the account of civilization which Collingwood defends.

6

Fighting back

In July 1939 the historian R. C. K. Ensor wrote a pamphlet with the title *Herr Hitler's Self-Disclosure in Mein Kampf*. After warning his readers that traditional British sea power would not be enough to stem a German advance Ensor said,

> Such people forget that navies today are things of steel, quickly built and quickly out built. The Hitlerian Greater Germany – an impregnable Continental Block, which in man-power, steel-power, coal-power, and oil-power stood to this island as a giant to a pigmy – would not be likely to allow this island very much longer to rule the seas, or perhaps to rule anything else
>
> (Ensor 1939: 26)

By the winter of 1940 the 'impregnable Continental Block' had become a reality. Millions faced a life in which terror was the norm, which meant that resistance in the occupied countries was near to impossible. The deliverance of Dunkirk in May, however, and the Battle of Britain in the summer and early autumn of 1940 signified that Nazi domination of Europe was incomplete. Though slight and unfocussed in strategy and resources there was an opportunity to fight back. Taking the fight to the enemy became an imperative. Given the strength of the German grip on occupied Europe, the problem was how.

The composition of *The New Leviathan* spans the fall of Belgium, France and Holland together with the threat of a German invasion of Britain. Much of the book was written while Britain endured the Blitz and when the Battle of the Atlantic was fought to ensure that U-boat domination of supply routes – the development which Churchill feared most – did not become a reality. Britain was fighting, if not totally alone, then sufficiently thrown back on her own initiative to make questions of strategy hard to answer. When Collingwood finally sent his manuscript of *The New Leviathan* to the Clarendon Press in August 1941 (it was not published until a year or so later, in mid-summer 1942), the storm clouds over British security looked less threatening, but most of Europe remained firmly and apparently irreversibly under Nazi control. Pearl Harbour and the American entry into the War were still some months away, and the German invasion of the Soviet Union in late June 1941, although extensively planned and to some degree expected, was only a few weeks old. We know Collingwood's view was that barbarism – the deliberate attempt to put the civilizing process into reverse (NL 41.53) – had to be fought. And, yet, in the first months of the War while the government felt this obligation it struggled to find the means to meet it and in some quarters to justify it adequately. In 1941, when Collingwood was completing the book against the impact of events as well as his own progressively debilitating illness, the struggle against Nazism in Europe resolved itself into a debate about means when open resistance to oppression was too often self-defeating. *The New Leviathan* was the book Collingwood gave up his work on the philosophy of history to write. Unpacking Collingwood's tightly written discussion of clandestine warfare and the role of political exiles from Nazi Germany in defeating Hitler tells us a great deal.

What Collingwood says about resistance in *The New Leviathan* (NL 45.68–78) is at first sight mysterious. He refers to clandestine radio stations and anti-Nazi literature as being run and printed by 'heroes' but then almost in the next paragraph denies that there is a duty to help them. He speaks about refugees from Nazi Germany failing to understand the tyranny in their own country and being defeatist in the face of it, although we might feel that a liberal political philosopher, and a Christian would see it as precisely the duty of Englishmen and women to give assistance to those in Europe whose freedom is being forcibly removed. As Collingwood wrote to *The Times* (letter dated 11 July 1940, RC: 183) of the British Government's policy of internment, 'There are two classes of refugees whose early release is especially desirable. English internment camps hold at this moment some of Hitler's bitterest enemies – workers for German freedom who have for years risked their lives in the same battle which all England is fighting today.' The will to fight back is likely to be strongest among those who have actually experienced persecution. Collingwood is engaging with a contemporary disagreement about the nature and aims of resistance and the role of political exiles from Germany in the defeat of Nazism and the reconstruction of their country after the War.

We should begin with radio (or wireless, as Collingwood calls it), a medium of which we can be sure he is not a particular fan (PA 323). As amusement art, that is not art at all in Collingwood's terminology, radio is ideally suited to the conveyance of entertainment and propaganda. What made radio novel in peacetime during the 1930s – its range, immediacy and power to present experience as other than it is – in wartime made it a tool of persuasion and deception. Clandestine radio, in its attempt to subvert Nazi propaganda from within, was a significant feature of the war of ideas which, as Collingwood understood it, was what the Second World War was about. Collingwood wrote to T. M. Knox

> For it seems to me that we are engaged in a war of ideas, and that under the disadvantage of having lost the initiative. Nazi ideas have the explosive force of novelty; what we call "democratic" ideas are old and stale, and – *silent inter arma leges* – likely to become absolutely decrepit in war conditions, whose effect might easily be the intellectual bankruptcy of our own side, even (perhaps I should say especially) in the event of military victory. People like you and me have a clear duty to prevent this, if it can be prevented; and to diminish the evil effects if it can't
> (R. G. Collingwood to T. M. Knox, letter dated 6 January 1940, RC: 148)

So when Collingwood refers in *The New Leviathan* to 'those heroes, for example, who continue in spite of everything the Nazis can do to run their secret wireless station and keep on printing *Das Wahre Deutschland*' (NL 45.68), his readers might be forgiven for assuming that his reference was to the voicing of opposition from within Germany or one of the occupied countries of Europe. This, however, was far from being the case, and if we are to grasp Collingwood's meaning it is essential to see why. Collingwood does not actually refer to *Das Wahre Deutschland* as a radio station, but the facts are that it was both a printed publication and a radio station. Indeed, when we bear in mind Collingwood's familiarity with political works written by refugees from Germany (NL 45.75), it is likely that he knew of the existence of anti-Nazi radio stations in general and of *Das Wahre Deutschland*, the publication, in particular. Nevertheless, the two are different ways of communicating the views of the same political party, and both emanate not from the anti-Nazi underground in Europe but from Britain itself.

Here we need to step outside Collingwood's immediate frame of reference. The idea that subversive broadcasting was taking place on any kind of scale in Germany in the early years of the war is unpersuasive. Throughout the time Collingwood was writing *The New Leviathan* resistance in Germany was at its lowest ebb. Like all other forms of protest, broadcasting calls of defiance to the regime was hazardous in the extreme, as one historian of the Third Reich indicates: 'The moment war broke out, tuning in to foreign stations was made a criminal offence punishable by death' (Evans 2008: 576; for further discussion see Mazower 2008: chapter 15, especially 476–7). Indeed, so risky was opposition within Germany that even before the war *Das Wahre Deutschland* itself was forced to take to the air, first just outside Paris under the sponsorship of the French government and then, after the fall of France, in Britain where it began transmitting to Germany on 26 May 1940 when it was known initially as the 'freedom station' (Howe 1982: 72–3).

Sustaining the spirit of resistance in Europe was one of the strongest motives for clandestine radio. Indeed, *Das Wahre Deutschland* was one of the first propaganda radio stations (Balfour 1979: 465 fn. 159). It purported to be broadcasting from Europe but was in fact run and broadcast from Britain after 1940. One of the original developers was Carl Spiecker (for Spiecker, see Howe 1982: 72–82; and Bonney 2009: 14–15) who was brought back to England (under the code name of Mr. Turner) when the fall of France was imminent, in order to bring his experience of secret radio stations to the aid of the British Government whose involvement in this kind of resistance was just beginning (see Howe 1982: chapters 2, 3, 4, 8 and 9; also Pether 2011). In both guises, the radio station and the printed publication, *Das Wahre Deutschland* was the mouthpiece of the German Freedom Party, a loosely organized group of German refugees, broadly social democratic in tone, which had been formed by Spiecker in France in 1936–7. Among the Party's publications was the *Deutsche Freiheitsbriefe*, leaflets that were smuggled into Germany. Its monthly publication, *Das Wahre Deutschland*, was published in England between October 1938 and October 1940. The radio station gave its final broadcast on 15 March 1941.

The German Freedom Party was both anti-Nazi and anti-Communist. As one recent writer on the politics of German emigration comments, 'The Deutsche Freiheitspartie rejected any distinction between Communists and Nazis: A red dictatorship is as cruel as a brown one, and Stalin's crimes are no different from those of Hitler. We want nothing to do with people who defend this policy' (Palmier 2006: 109). It is a point of view which is not difficult to imagine Collingwood holding himself.

Das Wahre Deutschland was a small beginning. In the early years of the War subversive warfare was largely confined to persuasion since opposition in the occupied countries precluded active resistance. In Britain clandestine radio propaganda at the start of the War was under the control of Electra House (EH), a semi-secret department of the Foreign Office, run by Sir Campbell Stuart who was responsible to Anthony Eden, the Foreign Secretary. In July 1940, along with the sabotage departments of M.I.6 and the War Office, it became part of the Special Operations Executive (SOE), the organization established by Churchill with the instruction 'to set Europe ablaze' (for SOE see Dear 1996 and Mackenzie 2002). In September 1941, after *The New Leviathan* had been completed, and after a series of inter-departmental wrangles and personal squabbles that would not have surprised Collingwood, given his experience of bureaucratic backbiting between the various divisions of Naval Intelligence in the First World War (Johnson 2012: 78), clandestine radio propaganda came under the control of the Political Warfare Executive and its size and effectiveness increased. However, at the time Collingwood was writing *The New Leviathan*, the spark on which many rested their hopes was thought by some to be little more than a damp squib. Ellic Howe, who worked on black propaganda during the War, makes the following perceptive comments on British clandestine radio broadcasts in their literal and more innocent early days: 'The task presented to black propagandists in 1940 was to weaken German morale and to encourage the still embryonic resistance movements in Europe. My own belief is that most of the subversive outpourings during the twelve months following November 1940 were a waste of human effort and of the electricity required to transmit them' (Howe 1982: 84). And of *Das Wahre Deutschland* specifically Howe writes, 'My own impression is that Dr. Spiecker's *Das Wahre Deutschland* ('The true Germany station') cannot be regarded as a vigorous and confident answer to the Concordia Buro's NBBS, but, rather, as a wildly pathetic gesture of defiance' (Howe 1982: 74).

When *Das Wahre Deutschland* ceased broadcasting in March 1941 it was thought by many in British intelligence circles to have outlived its usefulness. A totally different approach to anti-Nazi radio propaganda was needed. In both its radio and printed publication forms *Das Wahre Deutschland* reflected the intellectual assumptions of its contributors. Their basic political standpoint was laid down in the October 1939 issue: 'we should not overestimate the political importance of emigration, and believe that a counter-government in exile could transform Germany. The revolution can only come from within' (as cited in Palmier 2006: 738 fn. 1). This was Collingwood's position, too. While Collingwood considered it 'right and proper' (NL 45.7) that support should be given to opposition groups in Germany he also thought that it was for the opposition groups **themselves** to decide where their duty lay. To support this view Collingwood draws on his philosophical understanding of duty. The concept of duty requires not only that a particular act is performed but also that it is performed by the agent whose duty it is (NL 45.7–72). In broadcasting its message Spiecker's radio station was preaching to the converted. It appealed only to those who were already convinced of Hitler's evil. Now the philosophical argument begins to shade into a political one. If, as Collingwood argues, there is a distinction between helping resistance and the duty of resistance, then the value of the help will largely depend on the extent of the resistance. The difficulty with *Das Wahre Deutschland*, both the radio station and the printed publication, was that 'neither was trying to influence the mass of Germans who enthusiastically supported Hitler and his war of aggression; they were addressing the very, very few who wanted him to lose it' (Newcourt-Nowodworski 2005: 78). Again, interestingly, this was Collingwood's own view. There ought to be in Germany 'enough to sweep the flag of the false Germany from all the lands and waters of the world' (NL 45.69), but the reality was otherwise, and so Collingwood argued that a misguided interference in Germany's affairs was worse than no interference at all (NL 45.71–2).

In 1940 the kind of interference that was likely to be effective in German affairs was very unclear, but it was soon realized in British political warfare circles that the earnest liberal outlook of *Das Wahre Deutschland* would not do. The tone of the early broadcasts was idealistic, with appeal made to the 'good German': an example of such an individual might be Collingwood's friend, Adam von Trott, whose principled opposition to Hitler led later to his torture and execution as a result of his participation in the plot to assassinate the German leader in July 1944. Since it was felt that political idealism would cut no ice in Nazi Germany the view was that the new broadcasts should make no attempt to offer a political programme, neither should they aim to create a political movement. Rather, in the words of one of those involved, 'We want to spread disturbing and disruptive news among the Germans which will induce them to distrust their government and disobey it, not so much from high-minded political motives, as from ordinary human weakness' (as cited in Garnett 2002: 43). Truth now drops out. White propaganda was to be replaced by black: it does not matter what lies are spread among the subject populations of Germany and the occupied countries as long as they produce the desired effect.

So the focus was not the means to a political end, although choice of means was important, but the end itself. The slogan 'the true Germany' was thought highly ambiguous. While the nature of the false Germany was apparent, that of 'the true Germany' was not. To the British government, whose responsibility it was to deal with the various political groupings of German exiles in Britain, each of which claimed to represent the wishes of the German people, it was often unclear just who had the authority to speak for Germany and who spoke only for themselves. Spiecker's German Freedom Party was only one of a number of groups which were competing for official British recognition and support. The difficulties facing the British government are indicated in Jean Michel Palmier's description of the Party's membership as containing 'elements that were heterogeneous and even mutually antagonistic' (Palmier 2006: 109), while Richard Bonney says that the German Freedom Party 'considered itself the foreign counterpart of a German conspiratorial opposition' (Bonney 2009: 14–15). By seeking contacts with the anti-Nazi opposition in the army and the universities within Germany, the German Freedom Party echoed Adam von Trott's belief that the spirit of 'the true Germany' was not dead but dormant. Was the idea of 'the true Germany' an intelligible belief if, as Collingwood claimed, German barbarism was endemic?

The debate over German militarism and its source in the German mind and character has a history which transcends the merely idiosyncratic (Boucher 1992: xlvii). What sparked Collingwood's remarks was not history alone. Over the eighteen months Collingwood was writing his major work on political philosophy, the German problem – not just how to defeat Hitler, but how to ensure that the political forces he represented were properly understood and defeated as well – stretched the minds of politicians, civil servants and philosophers alike. Collingwood, together with his second wife Kathleen, was active in anti-Nazi circles in Oxford before the War (Boucher 1989: 261, fn. 153). He was also a friend and supporter of a number of refugees, amongst whom we should mention Wolfgang von Leyden, Arnaldo Momigliano and Paul Jacobstall (see Crawford et al. 2017: 140, 'both Collingwood, until his early death, and Andrewes were staunch friends of refugee scholars such as Paul Jacobstall').

We can be sure that he did not take these activities lightly. During the composition of *The New Leviathan*, when the walls of Hitler's European fortress appeared unbreachable, Collingwood had asked how a civilized society should respond to barbarism, but in political terms whether the barbarism (now only a short Channel crossing away) could be defeated by political opposition from within or only by external force from outside was hard to determine. Collingwood's concern was this: that Hitler's Germany might be placated by a British government being seen to give support to exile groups who were in favour of a policy of accommodation with the Nazi regime. In 1940 the idea of a peace with Germany necessarily meant coupling peace negotiations with an acknowledgement of the existence of the Third Reich. Such a policy, as Anthony Glees notices, 'did not simply mean the appeasement of Nazis, it also implied the drawing of a distinction between Nazis and other Germans. Its proponents saw a chance of avoiding all-out war with the German people either by encouraging the anti-Nazi opposition to overthrow Hitler or else by offering attractive terms to those Germans who were thought to be politically neutral' (Glees 1982: 44). To Collingwood this must have appeared a return to the appeasement he had fought so hard against. So, even in the mid-summer of 1941 when appeasement seemed certain to have failed, he was determined to ensure that there was no going back.

In the first months of the War, a policy of manufacturing a breach between the German people and their Nazi rulers was thought in Britain to be both reasonable and persuasive. As Jeremy Lewis points out ' "Peace with the German people, certainly; peace with the Nazis, never" was a popular slogan' (Lewis 2010: 313). It was a view which did not convince Collingwood. Few early reviewers of *The New Leviathan* showed interest in its discussion of German responsibility for the War, that is, whether it belonged to a single party or was historically linked to national characteristics. An exception was D. S. Mackay who highlighted the specific argument. He writes that 'the author builds up his massive indictment, not against the Nazis and their sympathizers merely, nor against the present population of the German Reich, but against the "latent barbarism" of the German people throughout its history' (Mackay 1944: 365).

Collingwood read the books written by refugees from Germany closely. A considerable number were available, varying widely in political allegiance – conservative, socialist, communist, liberal – as well as in their hopes for a new Germany after the War. Some would certainly have struck Collingwood as defeatist, either because they believed that 'Germany existed and it was Nazi. Those who claimed to embody Germany were trying to resurrect a ghost' (Palmier 2006: 285) or because they were reluctant to support émigré opposition to Hitler if by doing so Germany was harmed (Palmier 2006: 285, where he writes of the former German Chancellor Bruning, 'His attitude infuriated a number of British political figures, and when Bruning advised the British government to maximize its concessions to Hitler, Churchill called him a 'coward'. Throughout his exile, Bruning reiterated that a future German government would not include the émigrés, whose actions had been "detrimental to Germany"').

More important than the charge of defeatism was Collingwood's claim that a number of books showed little grasp of the conditions which made Nazi tyranny possible in Germany. His view was that from as early as the fifteenth century Germans 'looked upon social experience and the freedom it implies with horror, and clung with passionate zeal to the servitude of a non-social community' (NL 33.5). For philosophical reasons as much as political ones he flatly rejected the separation of the Nazi party and the German people which in the early years of the War seemed the most convincing basis for an appeal. Anthony Glees describes the position which provoked Collingwood's objections, writing, 'Were the Nazis to be overthrown it was suggested that "the other Germany" would emerge' (Glees 1982: 57). To Collingwood's mind, however, this was historically unconvincing and represented a wish fulfilment similar to that which had deluded Chamberlain when he declared war on the Nazis rather than the German people in September 1939.

In this respect Collingwood was a political outsider. Not for him was the task of distinguishing between the émigré sheep who were predisposed to some accommodation with Hitler and the goats who knew that there was no alternative to a fight to the finish. In referring to the 'very ill service' (NL 45.74) which could be done to Britain by refugees from German oppression Collingwood declares that not all refugees were benign. It was the British government's responsibility to filter out those who could do Britain harm. Separating those whose background and motives gave rise to suspicion was one aspect of this process. Some were thought unreliable because their opposition to Nazism was superficial. So, while Collingwood was almost certainly unaware of it, one of those who cast doubt on his fellow refugees was the same Dr. Spiecker who ran *Das Wahre Deutschland*, the radio station which Collingwood admired. W. J. West quotes Spiecker's comments on the National Council of German Refugees: 'he would have nothing to do with them because he did not believe in their ideas or their methods. He added that in his view these men's real quarrel with the Nazis was that they did not hold the positions in Germany today that they thought they merited' (West 1987: 195).

Guarding against infiltration from political extremes was one of the functions of government Collingwood would surely have supported. At the time of the composition of *The New Leviathan* the threat was real. Indeed, as Ellic Howe who worked there reports, British clandestine broadcasting was itself penetrated by a German diplomat who was likely to have been at the time a Soviet agent and was later a friend of the triumvirate of those who spied against Britain: Philby, Maclean and Blunt (Howe 1982: 39, 237–8; for more on this case see Glees 1987: 84, 220–8). Collingwood was as critical of tyranny in Russia as he was of it in Germany, although in an essay written after the declaration of War in September 1939 he said that while Fascism and Nazism were absolutely opposed to liberal ideals as, he also thought, were Marxism and Leninism, 'the USSR Constitution of 1936 contains a great deal that is in harmony with them' (EPP 191). For critics of the Soviet Union at the time the 1936 Constitution was not a document in which to put much faith, especially after the Nazi-Soviet Pact that cleared the way for the Soviet expansion into the Baltic countries and elsewhere, and after the Soviet invasion of Finland.

As we have seen, in the context of radio propaganda the denial that there was any effective opposition in Germany meant that attempts at persuasion based on the contrary belief were a waste of time and broadcasts which appealed to the unity of the European working class also failed as propaganda by attacking the Nazis alone and ignoring the real enemy which was the German nation itself (the European workers' station was run by R. H. S. Crossman; for his role in clandestine radio see Howard 1990: chapter 8). For his part Collingwood never took the view that propaganda was all-powerful even if propaganda in the right hands might have a job of work to do. He writes, 'For Fascists and Nazis alike, propaganda is a useful weapon, but not an indispensable one. It is folly to identify the weapon with the hand that wields it' (EPP 192). The problem was that in the case of Germany in the early years of the Second World War few were ready to be convinced. Whether this was because the unity of Germany mattered more to them than effective opposition to the Third Reich (supposing that possible) is a secondary issue. Collingwood was of the opinion that in Italy and Germany, although 'the vast majority of the population is sympathetic to the liberal-democratic ideals and hostile to the Fascist or Nazi minority that has seized power' (EPP 191), it lacked the will to defend liberalism when its survival was at stake (EPP 191).

For the purposes of radio propaganda anti-German diatribes merely 'helped to cement the German people to Hitler when all British efforts should have been devoted to driving a wedge between Volk and Fuhrer' (Glees 1987: 121). Collingwood himself may have been vulnerable to this criticism. The power of radio to influence people and events during the Second World War was undeniable. To say that radio is powerful, however, is not to say that what it broadcasts is always true. And, as James E. Gilman rightly points out, the Nazis 'contrived to tap a reservoir of religious passion which had become largely unavailable to the devotees of liberalism' (Gilman 1986: 125). This was Collingwood's view exactly. His problem was to show how a nation he thought was predisposed to accept what he calls 'the propaganda of irrationalism' (EM 133–42) could be won back to civilized ways of living except by the use of massive and superior force.

One possible solution was suggested by Sefton Delmer, who joined British clandestine radio operations in May 1941 and became their specialist in black propaganda. He writes,

> Clandestine "Black" stations as compared with the BBC had a very difficult task in collecting an audience. They were restricted to short wave transmitters.

PID's Marxist station under the benevolent supervision of my colleague, Dick Crossman, after months of broadcasting had no audience in Germany, not anyhow so far as PID had been able to ascertain. Nor had the right wing station run by a German conservative that had preceded mine. How did I propose to attract listeners? I decided to use radio pornography to catch their attention. My "Chef" (Hitler was always called "Der Chef" by those in his inner circle, so I decided to call my veteran hero "Der Chef") became a kind of radio Streicher, except that the victims of his pornographic tirades were Nazis, not Jews.

(Delmer 1962: 63)

For more on the actual operations of British clandestine broadcasting, see Pidgeon (2003: chapter 18, 125), where we find 'The Department also operated a number of propaganda wireless stations that broadcast to occupied Europe. Two of these broadcast in German and were run by refugees, one right-wing the other a left-wing station operated by German communists. Both the leaflets and the broadcasts were of the "white" propaganda variety, that is to say that their message was simply one of encouragement to obstruct the Nazi regime.' The broadcasts were on short wave and could be picked up in Britain, as also could propaganda stations operating from within Germany; see Gardiner (2004: 115).

So both *Das Wahre Deutschland*, the freedom radio run by Dr. Spiecker (Delmer's 'German conservative'), and *Sender der Europaischen Revolution*, the Marxist station run by R. H. S Crossman, failed. Neither attracted an audience large enough to make them worthwhile. By contrast, Delmer's *Gustav Siegfried Eins* which went on the air from 25 May 1941 was a success. It was nothing but a pack of lies, but it worked. It was black propaganda, but people in Germany and in the occupied countries of Europe listened to it. It was pornographic, but it poured mockery on the Nazi leadership when they thought themselves immune from it. One Cabinet Minister who found Delmer's radio broadcasts extraordinary was Sir Stafford Cripps, whose comment after seeing one of the scripts was reportedly, 'if this is the sort of thing needed to win the war, I'd rather lose it!' (There are a number of versions of this story. Mine comes from Rankin 2008: 304; see also Crowdy 2008: 214, 'A devout Christian, Cripps described PWE as "that beastly pornographic organization" and complained this style of broadcasting would only appeal to the "thug section of the Nazi Party" and that, in his opinion, PWE should instead concentrate on broadcasts that gave hope and appealed to "good Germans".')

In spite of Delmer's successes it was obvious to many at the time that the war would not be won by propaganda alone, and Collingwood did not expect the British government to lose sight of what it was fighting for. Subversive propaganda is only one of the weapons available to a liberal state at war designed to weaken the enemy's will to fight and to strengthen the will to resist. At the close of *The New Leviathan* Collingwood's rule that barbarism never wins is spoken of specifically as an example of an inductive proposition, not a universal one. While it is likely to be true there can be and are exceptions. So, Collingwood writes,

> I do not know what the reason is why barbarists have always in the end been beaten. I do not even know whether there is a reason, that is, a single reason, the same in every case; it might very well be that one was beaten for one reason and one for another; or even that of various portions into which a single barbarist army was divided one part was beaten for one reason and one for another
>
> (NL 45.95)

Collingwood may have believed that barbarism is self-defeating, but it was still his view that the defeat of barbarism is not something that happens independently of anything people might do about it, including the creation of propaganda in defence of civilization.

Collingwood believed that the Second World War was a continuation of the First; that nationalist ambitions came about in Germany historically in the form of the misdirection of its people, and that the origins of German aggressiveness were to be found within the system of education which had made its citizens what they are. He thought too that the defeat of France in 1940 resulted not from military failure alone but from ignorance of the dialectic of political life (NL 27.62–3). Their understanding of this, he believed, gave the British people a safeguard. And so, speaking of the tyranny in Europe, Collingwood writes, 'that is why it has failed to conquer England. Whether the failure will be permanent depends not on strictly military issues but on whether the English retain the mental vigour to hold on to the lesson that political life is essentially dialectical' (NL 27.64).

The New Leviathan was written in a fighting spirit and, as one contemporary review rightly pointed out, Collingwood had 'practical issues of the gravest import at the forefront of his thought' (Anonymous 1942: 340). How do his views of what might happen and of the risks to Britain change as events progress? How does he react when strongly held certainties are directly challenged by events? We can trace his responses from the start of the War when he took the view that Germany would collapse from within and that the War was for Britain to lose. In a letter to T. M. Knox written on 3 September 1939, the day war was declared, he stated,

If Russia is not brought into the war against us, we shall win. And it will not, I believe, take very long. Both we and France are much stronger than in 1914, Germany I believe is weaker. The Germans are already hungry. Their nerve is strained by the Nazi regime into a dangerous brittleness. The same cause has sapped their initiative. Too much depends on the supreme command. They have sacrificed the friendship of their late allies, Italy and Japan and Franco's Spain, for a new ally who, if we are defeated will eat them up. Nazi Germany is doomed in any case

(R. G. Collingwood to T. M. Knox, letter dated 3 September 1939. RC: 148)

Sentiments such as these were shared by many in Britain during the first autumn of the War. Confidence in British strength and German weakness led to the view that Hitler had over-reached himself. Indeed, the policies of the prime minister, Neville Chamberlain, were based on similar assumptions. Like Collingwood, the philosopher who had subjected both him and his doctrine of appeasement to fierce criticism, Chamberlain was unimpressed by the Nazi-Soviet Pact and had little expectation of a long war since he thought that economic and political weaknesses would rapidly compel the German people to turn on the regime and end the war themselves. As Maurice Cowling comments, 'Chamberlain's governing assumption was that victory was certain' (Cowling 1975: 360). This assumption was Collingwood's too, but in the late autumn and winter of 1939, with German morale expansive, a mood of pessimism took over and he began speaking of Fascism and Nazism's ability to 'annihilate even the most widespread liberal-democratic opposition in their own countries' and to 'overwhelm' liberalism and democracy elsewhere (EPP 192).

A few months later in June 1940 the fall of France shocked Collingwood (TLP 222). Another of the planks of certainty had been removed. In July, with the Battle of Britain at its height, Collingwood's anxieties were focused on the return of the appeasement which he thought had made the war unavoidable (F. A. Cockin to T.M. Knox, letter dated 29 July 1940, cited and discussed in Johnson 2013: 168, fn. 66). During the early summer of 1940, in which a new government led by Churchill had only recently arrived on the scene, as Geoffrey Best comments, 'the British public was so battered and bewildered by shocks and disasters that if a different leader – Lord Halifax, for example – had told it that there was no point in going on with the war, it would have followed him' (Best 2005: 115). With the coming of autumn that year, however, and with victory in the air battle over England assured, Collingwood's hopes rose. While on a visit to London he observed the effects of the Blitz and how Londoners were responding to the devastation it caused. Collingwood had wished to see for himself 'what the "greatest air force in the world" could do to London. The results are conclusive. Hitler can never beat us' (R. G. Collingwood to F. G. Simpson, letter dated 8 October 1940, RC: 178).

It was perhaps Collingwood's most Churchillian utterance, but the political problem remained. How could Germany be defeated if America remained outside the conflict? As we saw, one early and widely held view was that once the German people had seen the reality concealed by Nazi propaganda – the abhorrent nature of the Nazi leadership, the economic conditions facing the mass of ordinary people and the futility of war – this would bring the 'true Germany' to light, opposition from within Germany would increase and the regime would be weakened, possibly even undermined. British leaflet campaigns in Germany and in the occupied countries were early manifestations of this idea. And yet, despite much effort in terms of time and resources, this attempt at persuasion failed. Not only was Nazi control totally unbending, but it was soon realized that the 'true Germany' was too small in numbers to have any practical effect (Cruikshank 1977: 162, NL 45.69). This was certainly Collingwood's position, although he adds a significant philosophical gloss.

Throughout *The New Leviathan* Collingwood speaks about German barbarism as a collective phenomenon. There were individuals who remained untainted by it, including some who even sacrificed their lives fighting against it, but this does not diminish the force of Collingwood's point. What makes a society civilized or barbaric involves more than the sum of its parts. And so we see Collingwood again insisting that barbarism could not be defeated from within. The impetus had to come from outside, and it could come only from civilized nations doing for German barbarism what the German people were unable to do themselves. The notion of the 'true Germany' was not a point of detail. Early British strategies for defeating Germany, such as economic blockade and, more obviously, internal opposition, were dependent on it: as we have seen, the whole policy behind British clandestine radio presupposed something like an authentic Germany, one which was temporarily (it was hoped) subdued beneath the weight of Nazi oppression.

In practical politics none of this was as abstract as it sounds. By the winter of 1940 it was sufficiently clear that hopes for an effective opposition within Germany, together with a role for exiles outside it, were unrealistic. And so within British government circles, as Anthony Glees comments, 'a slow but sure change in British policy took place, one which led to the exclusion of this exile component. Any desire to stop short of the outright destruction of Germany and of unconditional surrender smacked of appeasement policies' (Glees 1982: 6–7).

Clandestine radio broadcasting did continue (with increasing impact as Germany weakened) until the end of the War, but for the time being education, persuasion and influence were moved into the background. Collingwood saw the necessity of this. In *The New Leviathan* he says that force in politics is justified when directed at those who are incapable of political education (NL 27.38). To make Collingwood's insistently argued point transparently clear, if the German people were incapable of overthrowing Hitler themselves then Britain and her allies must do it for them.

Collingwood did not hold the view that barbarism would die as representing the will of God, the verdict of history or the result of an immutable law of politics. Collingwood's Christianity, liberalism and philosophy stand very close to one another both in his early works and late. No one could argue that its reference to *Das Wahre Deutschland* made *The New Leviathan* a politically influential work, but it shows that its author knew of the existence of the invisible war, a war fought on very different lines from open combat but with the same aim. In the light of the serial traumas which were to beset the Allies throughout their search for victory we can be sure that in his reference to strength of hand and stoutness of heart Collingwood was making a salient and even Churchillian point.

7

The New Leviathan and the impact of events

Collingwood's war was in intention and purpose a writing war. *The New Leviathan* brings Hobbes up to date by linking political philosophy to a philosophy of mind in which the development of human consciousness through connected stages plays a decisive role. Between the planning and the resulting book, however, there is a major gap. The book was to have answered five questions in five parts. Parts I to IV were intended to drive the argument forward using a broadly dialectical methodology in which the idea of contract and the logic of question and answer have significant contributions to make. The fifth question was how a civilized society should behave in the face of barbarism. In Britain in 1940 it could not have been more significant. Few whatever their part in the war effort could have set it aside. Moreover, it is a question with a universal frame of reference. No member of any society which considers itself civilized could reasonably avoid it. In the event Collingwood's five questions/five-parts structure never happened, and *The New Leviathan* was published in four parts. Part V then was abandoned, although importantly **question** five was not. So, we can be sure that at least up to 17 February 1940 Collingwood set himself five questions which he proposed to answer in the five parts comprising *The New Leviathan*. Collingwood's subsequent decision to reshape question five is philosophically informed, which makes it of more than simply textual interest. It is important to consider the historical context in which Collingwood raises it, but the question itself embraces conceptual possibilities within the idea of civilization as such. We can be certain that Collingwood changed course, and so we must ask why.

On the publication of *The New Leviathan* in 1942 and for a considerable length of time afterwards it was assumed that the plan of the work as published was what Collingwood intended. It is true that Collingwood in his preface tells his readers that his book 'is not what I should call a finished work. It has been so far finished as time and health permitted during a space of nearly two years' (NL lxi). But no one concluded from this that there was to have been a fifth part nor, indeed, should they have done since Collingwood outlines the scheme of the book on the very first page, 'Part I, an inquiry into man; Part II, an inquiry into communities; Part III, an inquiry into civilizations; and Part IV, an inquiry into revolts against civilization' (NL 1.15). Generations of readers can be forgiven for taking this statement as final. The problem is, however, that it is not. Collingwood does say why he was unable to call his book finished, but he does not tell us in what respects he thought it unfinished or how close to being finished he thought it was or whether his intentions had changed as he was writing it. Readers assumed straightforwardly that *The New Leviathan* as published was the book which Collingwood planned to write, and they did so because it repeats the four-part design of the original Leviathan, the work that Collingwood explicitly wished to renew. Pressures of time and ill-health might have had an effect, possibly on the depth of treatment of individual topics or by limiting the opportunities for re-writing, but as concerns the book's organization it might have been set in stone.

All this changed in 1989 with the publication of the *Draft Preface* to *The New Leviathan* (EPP 224–8). It is from this that we learn that Collingwood intended his book to answer five questions – 'I shall begin by asking what man is. Next, I shall ask what society is. Next, I shall ask what civilization is. Then I shall consider the revolt against civilization, and lastly I shall ask how a society which considers itself civilized should behave in the face of this revolt' (EPP 226–7). The knowledge that Collingwood set himself five questions does not necessarily mean that he intended to answer them in five parts, although the weight of probability is in this direction. It is the difference between the divisions of the book as published and those outlined in the Draft Preface which is important. The book as published stops with Part IV which concerns the revolt against civilization, whereas the *Draft Preface* reaches beyond that to consider how a civilization should respond to such a revolt. Clearly, when the Draft Preface was written this question was highly important to Collingwood. Indeed, he considered that it 'constitutes the real subject of the book' (EPP 227). It is hard to believe, then, that he did not intend a separate section to examine it.

The next development was decisive. Confirmation of Collingwood's intention not only to answer his five questions but also to answer them in five books occurs in a letter from Collingwood to his friend and fellow yachtsman in the Aegean, Chadbourne Gilpatric, which came to light in America in 2011. The letter is dated 17 February 1940, and the relevant section reads as follows,

Now I am at work on a book to be called <u>The New Leviathan or Man, Society and Civilization</u>. Dedication, of course, to Hobbes as the founder of modern political theory. Book I, Man, Book II, Society (complete theory of politics and so forth). Book III, Civilization discussion of what it is and what it involves. Book IV, the Revolt against Civilization: analysis of Fascism and Nazism. Book V hasn't found a title yet, but the question it will have to answer is what must civilized people do about the revolt against civilization.

(R.G. Collingwood to Chadbourne Gilpatric, letter dated 17 February 1940, RC: 134–5).

We can now be sure that *The New Leviathan* was planned in five parts but published in four. We can also be sure that the fifth part was never written. Nothing remotely resembling it exists in Collingwood's unpublished manuscripts. From this the question which naturally arises is why Part V was not written as planned.

A number of answers to this question can be ruled out. For example, that Collingwood abandoned the fifth part because he had become too ill to write it and was in any case writing against the clock. It is true that during the later stages of the composition of *The New Leviathan* Collingwood was facing severe physical difficulties as a result of the multiple strokes he suffered over that period. He was writing against the background of an illness which might at any moment make it impossible for him to continue. None of these answers tells the full story, however. A different answer is more ingenious, but, I believe, not persuasive. On this view it is argued that while Collingwood did give up on the fifth part he did not give up on the fifth question, and his answers to it are to be found 'scattered' throughout *The New Leviathan* (see NL xiii and EPP 228 fn. 1, where we have the view that 'the purpose of the fifth part … is partially fulfilled in the four parts that eventually comprised *The New Leviathan*').

The problem with this explanation is that it seems insufficient. Collingwood must have thought that a fifth part was needed. Why then would he abandon it and distribute his answers to the fifth question throughout the text? Was this done during re-writing and revision or as the book was being composed? Such scattering as took place was not random. Collingwood insists in his *Draft Preface* that question five could not even be raised, let alone answered, until answers had been given to the previous questions. It is this question and answer logic which makes the term 'scattered' inadequate to the task. The true story is that Collingwood abandoned his fifth part because much of the question it was intended to answer had lost its relevance.

What is certain, although merely circumstantial as a guide to Collingwood's intentions, is that after his letter to Gilpatric Part V vanishes. In two later letters to the Clarendon Press who were to publish the book, effectively a progress report which explains in detail the organization of the book into four parts, the ways his illness has affected his writing, the extent to which the manuscript has been revised and how much remains to be written, Collingwood neither makes any mention of a Part V nor gives any explanation for its non-existence (R.G. Collingwood to Kenneth Sisam, letter dated 11 June 1941, RC: 92 and R.G. Collingwood to Kenneth Sisam, letter dated 6 August 1941 RC: 92).

After Collingwood's death Kenneth Sisam, who worked at the Press and was a friend of Collingwood's, wrote to his second wife, Kathleen, saying that 'fortunately he was able to finish The New Leviathan, so that I should expect that he had planned out the amount he could finish' (Sisam to Kathleen Collingwood, letter dated 20 January 1943, Clarendon Press Archives). This must surely refer to the book as organized in the progress report, not the Draft Preface which was probably written some fifteen months or so earlier. This would be between December 1939/January 1940 and May 1940, a time when its author was relatively free from illness and when he was optimistic about completing the book as he originally planned it. It is also likely that the Draft Preface was the basis for the proposal for the book on which the Press made their initial judgement.

Our interest here is in the chronology of this arrangement as much as its logic. Part I concerning the philosophy of mind was completed by March 1940, but Part II took longer. At this stage question five seems still to have been in Collingwood's plans. Neither the letter to Gilpatric in February 1940 nor the one to Sisam at the Press in March makes any mention of a change. As Collingwood says in his letter to Gilpatric he hoped 'to have half the book written by the beginning of May', but as it turned out Part II reached chapter XXVI in January 1941, with the final section from chapters XXVII to XXXIII written and the whole part revised during April and May 1941. There is no doubt that in June 1941 Collingwood thought of Parts I and II as complete. The final section of Part II of *The New Leviathan* runs from chapter XXVII to chapter XXXIII. The dating of this section is important because it is in these chapters, particularly XXVII to XXX that much of Collingwood's answer to question five is to be found. If we are right that this final section of Part II was written during April and May 1941 (and for internal reasons this seems unquestionable) then the temptation is to assume that the views expressed there also date from that period. But this, I believe, would be a mistake. In his letter to Gilpatric written on 17 February 1940 Collingwood says that 'I have Book I and Book II taped' which implies he knew then what he wanted to say in those Books, but that Books III, IV and V were yet to be tackled. Given that Books III and IV concerning Civilization and

Barbarism, respectively, are indebted to much that he had already written on those topics in autumn 1939, then this leaves only Book V to be considered. If the views expressed in chapters XXVII to XXX do contain most of Collingwood's answers to question five, and if these reflect views he held earlier, then we should be able to conclude that the decision to give up on Book V was one that germinated in Collingwood's mind during the summer and autumn of 1940.

Circumstantial evidence points in the same direction. During the Hilary term in Oxford in 1940 Collingwood was heavily occupied, which forced him to revise his rate of progress. The effect of this was that arguments which emerged from one political context were written up in another. In other words, the views expressed in Part II of *The New Leviathan* date substantially from 1940, even though matters which bear on the missing Part V were not finally written of until later. The true story of the fate of Part V comes initially from within *The New Leviathan* itself.

At some point Collingwood decided that Part V was not going to be written. We can show why he held that view by establishing when he reached it, and the way to do that is to trace the answers he gives to the question that Part V was intended to answer. What makes it possible for us to trace these is his question and answer logic. As we saw, Collingwood says specifically in his Draft Preface that question five cannot be answered until answers have been given to the questions which precede it. Question five asks 'how a society which considers itself civilized should behave in the face of this revolt [against civilization]', a question which reveals Collingwood's preoccupation with the frailties of liberalism, as well as the feeling common at the time that when a civilized society resorts to the methods of its enemies in order to defeat them then something in its way of life has gone seriously amiss. The concern of question five is political morality. To answer it Collingwood had first to establish the capacity for deliberation which choice presupposes (*The New Leviathan* Part I), then the social consciousness which deliberation requires for its expression (Part II), then the form taken by collective choice and the political arrangements which are appropriate to it (also Part II). Towards the end of Part II Collingwood takes up the justification for war and the measures which are open to a liberal society engaged in fighting it.

We know that the basis of a well-governed polity, in Collingwood's view, is civility. It is this structure of ideas, philosophically derived and historically instantiated, which Collingwood believes provides a basis for trust in a liberal society when it is faced by barbarism and has to make hard choices in order to fight it effectively. Collingwood tells us that *The New Leviathan* was written 'in great part during the bombardment of London' (NL lxi), that is, the massive

German air assault on London and other British cities which began in September 1940, continuing through to the beginning of May 1941. It is this period which provides the context for much of Part II of *The New Leviathan*. This context fits closely with what we know of the composition of Part II, even though neither writing nor revision was smooth or uninterrupted. It offers, I believe, the best explanation of Collingwood's thinking when he reached the conclusion that Part V would not be written.

According to Collingwood's logic of question and answer, questions arise in contexts. A question which makes sense in one context may be redundant in another. Contexts do, however, vary in kind. Some questions are clearly context-dependent. Given Collingwood's linking philosophy with history we should not find this surprising, but it is an ambition with a potential price to pay. Questions which reflect their times may lose their relevance when those times change. Collingwood's fifth question, however, is philosophical, and so his answers aspire to universal relevance.

Collingwood's question five – how a civilized society should behave in the face of barbarism – is oddly phrased, almost quizzical, but when we remember the context the oddness quickly evaporates. During the first seven months of the war there was a widespread feeling in Britain that direct military confrontation with Germany might still be avoided. Hitler's offensive against the West had not taken place and Britain was only slowly re-arming. If a diplomatic solution could be found, went the thinking, then the catastrophe of war still need not occur. Barbarism might be mollified. The prime minister, Neville Chamberlain, summed up this mood when he announced early in April 1940: 'Hitler has missed the bus' (Todman 2016: 310–11). The tone and content of Collingwood's opinion of Chamberlain, which he continued to express up to and after Chamberlain's death in November 1940, matches that of the Labour Party and those further to the Left of it. Of the Labour Party in the summer of 1938 Maurice Cowling remarks 'they were saying that Chamberlain was "spineless" and "immoral", had lost touch with public feeling and was blinded by "class prejudice" to the duty to organize the "democratic powers" to resist the dictators' (Cowling 1975: 211). On almost all levels, including those of ideology, policy and the sheer emotional dislike of everything that Chamberlain represented, the affinities between Collingwood's politics in 1938–9 and the views of the Labour Party as well as those to the Left of it, as expressed by its leaders on almost all sides of the Party on many occasions, as well as its rank and file, are impossible to miss. Collingwood's denigration of Chamberlain preceded that of *Guilty Men*, first published in July 1940, but its picture of Chamberlain as 'a criminally negligent dupe' (the phrase belongs to Dutton 2001: 134) was Collingwood's opinion exactly. The sheer animosity towards Chamberlain which pours unmistakably from Collingwood's published and unpublished writing in this period is mirrored by that of the Labour Party whose hatred of the prime minister was matched only by his lack of respect for them. The issue of rearmament represents Collingwood's political position in 1938 very well. While vigorous in his condemnation of appeasement he was less than forthcoming about the need for, and the scale of, British rearmament. As we saw, he did support Lindsay's candidature in the Oxford by-election of October 1938, and Lindsay had argued in his Election Address that 'defence against air attack' should be made 'fundamental' (Scott 1971: 249), but for many on the Left, even those who supported limited rearmament, hatred of Chamberlain was a more than sufficient reason to oppose him when he attempted to bring this about. Lindsay's words are instructive. Defence against air attack was to be 'fundamental', thus, apparently ruling out what in any case few Labour Party supporters wished to hear, a large-scale investment in the army.

At this time two fears governed Collingwood's political opinions. One was the return of the policy of appeasement which he thought had made war more likely, and the other was that in order to win the war Britain would become more Nazi than the Nazis (R. G. Collingwood to T. M. Knox, letter dated 3 September 1939, RC: 148). Question five reflects both these concerns. Events, however, modified Collingwood's political focus. The disastrous Norway campaign which contributed to the fall of Neville Chamberlain, a development Collingwood must have welcomed, together with the rise of Churchill to become prime minister and the Blitzkrieg which Hitler launched against France, Belgium and Holland on the morning of 10 May 1940 all combined to make the first of his fears redundant. There would be no appeasement of Germany now, removing at least one option in the list of possible behaviour in the face of barbarism. However, Collingwood's left-inclined liberalism ensured that his second fear remained. It was surely better to risk defeat than sacrifice the liberal principles which Britain had entered the war to defend. And so on 11 July 1940 Collingwood co-signed a letter to *The Times* protesting against the government's policy of internment, or at least the manner in which it was being carried out. For a time this seemed to reduce the relevance of question five. What changed this, forcing Collingwood to completely rethink the structural role of question five in his work, was another event. This was the Blitz, which began in September 1940 and shocked the British government and people into the realization that they were fighting a total war.

It was history in the shape of the impact of events which changed the original sense and point of Collingwood's fifth question, even though neither vanished completely. Traces of the original remain in Part II of *The New Leviathan*, as in the discussion of how the choices of political policymakers are limited because

> the ruling class knows that the body politic cannot, being the kind of body politic it is, adopt that policy, (it may, for example, be a courageous policy; and the body politic may consist of irredeemable cowards) or because the circumstances are such that a given policy is judged incapable of succeeding (for example, the policy may involve a war against a power judged greatly superior).
>
> (NL 28.88)

The relevance of this to Collingwood's original question is easy to see, but such congruity did not last. After Churchill's galvanizing 'blood, toil, tears, and sweat' speech on 13 May duty pointed in only one direction, 'Victory'. In June Bertrand Russell announced in *The New Statesman* that he had abandoned pacifism so conforming to the changed public mood (Monk 2000: 241). Russell's pacifism was not shared by Collingwood, and may have been exceptional, but the overall reaction was the same. With this realization came a new atmosphere and tone. Such was the nature of Britain's enemy that the war would have to be fought to a finish. For a time in the summer of 1940 Collingwood's liberal worries about Nazism within remained but, with the bombing of London in September, when the implications of Churchill's speech were readily apparent, he saw that his second fear was as groundless as his first. The British people were united in their determination to preserve their way of life. With his fears removed Collingwood's fifth question was not shelved completely. As a total war against barbarism became unavoidable Collingwood saw that a refocused question five remained relevant.

With the involvement of America and the Soviet Union the Second World War shifted from a European conflict to a global one. Indeed, the larger meaning of Collingwood's book reaches beyond nations: civilization is not the property of one nation or one way of life but of the world. In the later sections of Part II of *The New Leviathan* Collingwood talks in this way, and his reason is not hard to grasp. Like Hobbes before him Collingwood saw little point in an account of political life which ignored human nature in its most basic and rawest form. It is true that they differ substantially over the philosophy of mind, but both write about politics on the assumption that, as Collingwood puts it, 'the Yahoo is always with us' (NL 30.8). Neither liberal internationalism nor the prospect of a perpetual peace is capable of expressing the ideas at stake here. Nor is there any role for world history, at least one in which the future is determined from outside as representing some sort of universal pattern. Collingwood states, 'Eschatology is always an intrusive element in history' (IH 54). What is much more important to Collingwood is the idea that human beings make their own history, even if in circumstances not of their own choosing, or in contexts which are both barbarous and evil. And so Collingwood wrote fatefully in the autumn of 1939: 'If he lives among wolves, as the saying is, he must howl. If he thinks howling barbarous, he must find a way of not howling. That involves teaching his neighbours not to howl; so he must find a way of teaching them' (WCM, NL 499).

It seems then that the mystery of the missing Part V in *The New Leviathan* is solved by history. It was history in the shape of the changing ideas, events and attitudes that marked the British experience of war in 1940 which made Collingwood alter his view about the need for a Part V. British stoicism, resilience and determination during the miracle of Dunkirk, the Battle of Britain and the Blitz answered Collingwood's question five beyond any reasonable doubt. In the face of new circumstances and beliefs new questions were called for, with old ones redirected to address different problems. Appeasement and the risk of defeatism were no longer on the agenda. The question now was how Nazism was to be defeated and what actions were necessary in a civilized liberal society in order to bring that end about. Collingwood tells us that his subject in the book is 'the modern European mind' (NL 9.24), in those aspects which bear on civilization and the threat against it. It is only necessary to read Collingwood on peace and war to see how much he was disturbed by the moral disintegration of Europe and why he was so strongly motivated to redraw its way of life. It is this which occupies Collingwood from the final sections of Part II to the book's conclusion.

In 1936 Collingwood described modern weapons of war as signs of madness. By the time of the writing of *An Autobiography* in 1939 it was commitment that preoccupied him. He was impressed by the close engagement in politics which the Left exemplified. As Roy Pascal remembers, 'You felt something was being done, that you weren't just sitting up in a study and thinking about the political situation' (as quoted in Werskey 1978: 217). However, unlike something that happens independently of human thoughts and interests like dawn breaking, commitment arises from system and method, possibly struggle, if not from a comprehensive bank of ideological reasoning. In 1938 Collingwood agreed with many on the progressive Left that neither the Tory Government nor the

Labour Party had done much to resist Franco in Spain. He was never a 'Red Professor' (Werskey 1978: 158), however. A unified Marxism lacked appeal to him and would continue to do so. Even though the price for this was a set of political beliefs that, for a time, played different and discordant tunes he was at least spared the convoluted justifications offered by many on the Left when faced with the prospect of fighting a capitalist war in order to defeat Nazism.

By the end of 1938, when he reacted to Munich with shame, Collingwood accepted, like the impeccably liberal-minded E. M. Forster, that the 'dilemma facing his country was that to defeat totalitarianism it would have to become totalitarian itself' (Furbank 1978: 230). By May 1941 in a mood of dark pessimism he realized that a brutal enemy would not be defeated by a liberal state wearing kid gloves and that to be effective moral and political justification must include 'what the emergency calls for' (R. G. Collingwood to G. G. Coulton, letter dated 1 May 1941, RC: 111; see Johnson 2013: 182–3, fn. 23).

As a defence of civilization *The New Leviathan* was embedded in history as well as philosophy. History because it gave voice to contemporary fears that Britain was not simply confronting a power greedy for territory and ever willing to disregard legal and moral boundaries to obtain it, but in fact facing barbarism. Philosophy because Collingwood knew that if his account of civilization was to work he would have to start his enquiry from scratch. Questions which presupposed too much about human capacities for good would not help. And yet, in spite of his apprehensions, Collingwood also understood that calls for a fairer society could not be ignored. Throughout all these changes of attitude and mood Collingwood tracks history closely. The future clearly was closed to him. It is hard to believe, however, that had he been able he would not have smiled on the BBC broadcasts his close friend, the evangelical Anglican, F. A. Cockin, made with others in 1945 which inquired into the nature of justice in the world both as it is and as it might be (see Cockin 1945). Collingwood did not discount the possibility of progress in expectations and opportunities. To this belief, however, he added a severely cautionary qualification – of the human will he writes 'The greater the opportunities it inherits, the greater the temptation to abuse them. This temptation, which no progress can abolish, is the origin of barbarism' (WCM 498).

8

The New Leviathan in 1940

When the manuscript of *The New Leviathan* was on its way to the publisher in August 1941 the nature of Britain's enemy, if not the full extent of its evil, was apparent to all except the most blinkered in Britain. As the war intensified more harrowing questions emerged. In this context Collingwood's question five gained new and harder relevance. Its focus narrowed but its subject matter – the moral limits on politics for a liberal state facing barbarism in time of war – needed to be faced.

A little textual rebuilding is needed if we are to recover Collingwood's answer. An example can help. Charles Dickens's friend and first biographer, John Forster, said of the ending of Dickens's uncompleted novel, *The Mystery of Edwin Drood*, 'It was all blank' (Forster 1874: 427). Unlike *Edwin Drood*, which was unfinished at Dickens's death, in which, as Forster says, 'the evidence of matured designs never to be accomplished, intentions planned never to be executed, roads of thought marked out never to be traversed, goals shining in the distance never to be reached, was wanting here' (Forster 1874: 426–7) *The New Leviathan* does contain the 'accomplished fact' (IH 219) which Collingwood believes is alone capable of fostering historical knowledge. True, there is an exclusion clause – 'on what I have only begun and am still doing, no judgement can as yet be passed' (IH 219). However, such is the singularity of re-thinking Collingwood's answer to his fifth question that we have no need to reason back from the solution to the problem as Collingwood states, say, the naval historian must do in understanding Nelson's tactics at Trafalgar (AA 70). Nor are we faced by the 'blank page' of unaccomplished designs which makes the task of finishing *Edwin Drood* such an artificial exercise. There is no need to reason back because we have the question which Collingwood meant to answer. Similarly, there is no need to contrive his answer since we have it, if not in a body of well-directed argument then in substantial traces of 'accomplished fact' which are in principle open to re-enactment.

To reconstruct Collingwood's answer we need to know the kind of question he is raising and what his question is about. We have much that helps us with both. We know that the fifth question is the kind of question that can only be answered intelligibly after the questions that precede it have been answered. We know also that Collingwood considered it the most important question: in terms of its formal characteristics important not in isolation but in relation to its place in the 'question-and-answer complex' (AA 38) which makes up *The New Leviathan*. Of this schema generally Collingwood writes, 'Each question and answer in a given complex had to be relevant and appropriate, had to "belong" both to the whole and to the place it occupied in the whole' (AA 37). Collingwood's fifth question then 'belongs' as the kind of question whose answer depends on answers to previous questions and 'occupies' its place in the whole as the kind of question whose answer brings the process of questioning to an end.

We know a great deal too about the subject matter of Collingwood's fifth question. By a series of steps, each of which presupposes its predecessor, *The New Leviathan* links an account of human mental and emotional development to social, political and civilized ways of living. It is a book in which the design of the whole is prior to its parts and, while it originated in lectures given over many years, is very far from being a collection of randomly arranged remarks. Collingwood's system of referencing acts as an aide memoire which in a significant way confirms the book's organization as a system of interlocking arguments.

What then is the place of the fifth question in this design? We should notice that the fifth question is not the kind of question which admits of a single specific answer. For example, it is not like the question: what is the air temperature of the room in which I am writing? What marks this difference is the complexity of its subject matter. It is more like the question that Collingwood asks in his discussion of the logic of question and answer in *An Autobiography*, 'Why won't my car go?' (AA 32). Both questions need to be subdivided into secondary questions to be answered satisfactorily. However, unlike the question 'Why won't my car go?' which is answered, as Collingwood says, by experimentation, the fifth question can only be answered conceptually and in relation to the historical present of which it is a part. Just as Collingwood's secondary question 'Is it because number one plug is not sparking that my car won't go?' produces the required answer, so Collingwood's fifth question is answered by the secondary questions appropriate to it. The fifth question retains its importance in the same way. In fact, all five of the questions Collingwood asks in the book are complex. What distinguishes Collingwood's fifth is the sense in which its terms have already been clarified by the answers given to the first four questions. Thus what Collingwood means by the terms 'society', 'civilization' and 'barbarism' as the 'revolt' against civilization shapes the kind of answers he wishes to give.

Collingwood's overall aim is to elucidate a political society which has civility as its guiding ideal. Here the philosophical method which governs Collingwood's arguments combines with his distinctive version of social contract theory to derive the principle of civility, together with the kind of political life it implies, in a systematic way. More specifically, the account of a near civil political society has to be in place before the fifth question can be answered. 'Near civil' is the term used since Collingwood says that 'political life contains an indispensable element of force' (NL 27.1), first because civility is a learned value, but not always appreciated for what it is, and second, because civility is tested by other ways of life which either have only imperfectly acquired it or reject it utterly and wish to obliterate it. This testing of civility raises hard questions which are onerous for those who aspire to conduct politics by agreement and yet remain unsentimental in their political beliefs. It is a region of political life which is undeniably troubling for liberals, but it is unavoidable and Collingwood recognizes it as such. It makes up much of the subject matter of the fifth question, and its importance is impossible to underestimate, especially in a time of war and especially when the enemy represents a barbarism as extreme as that which overwhelmed Europe during the Second World War.

If we are right in understanding the fifth question as a portmanteau question then what of the questions it contains? Such questions refer to possibilities (like, e.g., the misbehaving number one plug which was the cause of Collingwood's car failing to start). In the case of the fifth question the possibilities are not mechanical objects which may have failed but areas of conduct (or behaviour, in Collingwood's language) that occur when a liberal society is faced by the possibility of transgressing its own principles if it is to survive. When this occurs a near civil society may appear to have gone seriously wrong: by realizing the importance of this issue Collingwood is trying to discover exactly what it involves. Collingwood knows already what a civilized society looks like, and he knows already what barbarism is. But what he does not yet know concerns the kinds of incivilities (force or fraud) which a liberal society is justified in employing when it is confronted by a revolt against its fundamental values and way of life. Stoicism in the face of barbarism is a response we can be sure that Collingwood in the Britain of 1941 was familiar with, but the answer sought by the fifth question is philosophical as well as practical, and so Collingwood looks to formulate an ethical theory which encompasses what he wants to say.

Part I of *The New Leviathan* lays down the framework of ideas without which question five cannot be answered. So in his discussion of choice as the exercise of practical reason Collingwood tells us that 'Nothing can confirm the resolution with which a man regards his intention except the discovery that another intention, upon which he is fully resolved, stands to it in the relation of ground to consequent' (NL 14.33). To take Collingwood's own illustration, 'the strong resolution not to let the tent blow down acts as a ground of the weaker resolution to get out of bed at once.' Collingwood's example points to the realization that in 1940, for the war to be fought efficiently and with any reasonable hope of success, liberal methods would not be sufficient. Compulsory military service, state direction of labour and industry, government direction over large areas of the British way of life – all this was as a matter of practical logic deemed necessary if Britain was to survive and Nazism to be defeated. In the extreme circumstances in which the country found itself political morality began to appear as the only morality available. Liberal assumptions about rights and freedoms existing outside state scrutiny and control were not only put in question but radically revised and with increasing frequency set aside.

In his letter to T. M. Knox, written at the start of the conflict, Collingwood voiced the fears of many when he talked of Britain becoming Nazi in order to defeat Germany. Less than a year later, Ernest Bevin, Labour member of the War Cabinet, not entirely frivolously summed up a general mood when he said that on taking office he suddenly found himself 'a kind of Fuehrer with powers to order anyone anywhere' (as quoted in Todman 2016: 372). Then in May 1940 the Emergency Powers (Defence) Act was passed, with the threat of invasion looming the pace of internment of enemy aliens in Britain quickened, and it became obvious that Britain's war was rapidly becoming a total one. In this context the importance Collingwood attached to his fifth question is readily understood.

Collingwood wanted a 'gloves-off philosophy' (AA 153), but what did that mean? It was by clarifying the moral and political principles Britain was fighting for that *The New Leviathan* would make a contribution to the war effort. Little clarity would result if the book failed to address the possibility which concerned him most. No democracy which considered itself civilized could contemplate a completely 'gloves-off' politics morally speaking. If victory was achieved by a liberal democracy subverting its own principles, then this would be worse than defeat.

What Collingwood meant by the revolt against civilization, as he termed barbarism, was the deliberate attempt to put the civilizing process into reverse.

During the time Collingwood was writing *The New Leviathan* the exemplification of barbarism over much of Europe was Nazism. Facing up to Nazism meant fighting it, not compromising with it and not using its own methods in order to defeat it. The primary tool of Nazism was war, and the aim of war was conquest and the subjugation of the enemy. For the liberal that Collingwood assuredly was the purpose of war was peace. From this standpoint a state of total war is something of a contradiction in terms since it erases the limits on which political life depends. If the end of war is peace, then not any means can be employed to achieve it. One answer to Collingwood's fifth question looks clear. The task of facing up to barbarism could not be undertaken by adopting its methods.

And yet against the background of the conditions of modern war, as Collingwood well knew, no state, least of all one fighting to preserve a civilized way of life, could begin the struggle for survival wearing kid gloves. In the spring and early summer of 1941, as we have seen, the war was going poorly for Britain. The devastations of the Blitz, the costs being paid in human life and resources in the Battle of the Atlantic, the potential losses in the Middle East, the actual loss of Greece at the end of April and the threat to the government's strategy in the Mediterranean all combined to increase concern about the war's direction and purpose. *The New Leviathan* follows its own logic. It is not a commentary on events. Moreover, Collingwood was fighting a battle of his own to complete the book at all. It is more than probable that it was in this time of uncertainty that Collingwood wrote the section which concerns political morality. During the war, hard choices were being made, and in *The New Leviathan* Collingwood tries to make sense of them.

We can think of political morality as a conflict of goods in which no choice can be made without moral loss. Collingwood is dismissive of the idea that it is the categorical nature of moral imperatives which is the reason for the impasse. He comments, 'If a hook which is right for trout-fishing is wrong for salmon-fishing, make up your mind what fish you are after' (NL 16.74). When in July 1940 Churchill as prime minister ordered the destruction of the French fleet in the Algerian ports of Oran and Mers-el-Kebir it was, in the words of one historian, 'one of the most ruthless acts of a democracy in the annals of war' (Hastings 2009: 69). But was this ruthlessness that of a phronimos who is ruthless only when necessary or was it that of an Odysseus who was gambling on how events would turn out? Churchill had good reasons for acting as he did and was agonized by remorse, even after being applauded for his decision as one which was unavoidable if the security of Britain was to be safeguarded. Collingwood thought that 'conflict between two rules each meant to provide a partial definition for one and the same way of life' (NL 16.76) was proof that its way of life was muddled. But on this occasion it is surely Collingwood who is muddled. Churchill valued and continued to value both the imperatives whose conflict created his dilemma. His decision was, in the words of a contemporary, 'tragic but necessary and it will wake the world up to a realization that we now are fighting for our lives and have taken the gloves off' (Amery 1988: 630, entry dated 4 July 1940).

Collingwood's criticism of Kant's ethics is paralleled by his rejection of utilitarianism. Neither categorical moral principles nor a consequentialist account of human action is sufficiently fine tuned to explain a choice like Churchill's or indeed the many others which would have to be made if the revolt against civilization was to be defeated. In the face of an enemy such as Nazism it was surely right for the British people to trust democratic politicians to be ruthless when necessary. In the absence of democratic accountability in time of war, however, that 'when necessary' might too easily slip into 'when expedient' or 'when convenient' or possibly even 'when self-serving' for trust to be unconditional. Collingwood's answer to his fifth question needs firmer ground.

The New Leviathan of course was written before the events which comprehensively changed the Second World War and Britain's role in it. The German invasion of the Soviet Union converted a country which many in Britain wished to keep morally speaking at arm's length into a political ally, and the entry of the United States into the war after Pearl Harbour ensured that the war would not be completely within Britain's scrutiny or control. Collingwood's answers to the four philosophical questions which comprise the book constructed a stage for the answer to the question which he thought the most important of all, only for it to be overtaken by history. Even as *The New Leviathan* was on its way to the publisher Britain's destiny was no longer in its own hands. Nevertheless, while Collingwood was working on the closing chapters of Part II Britain remained in unique danger and pressing questions concerning political morality remained. The nature of political necessity was at the forefront of these, which makes it unsurprising that Collingwood's answers should look to Plato and Machiavelli for guidance. If Collingwood's Plato was not the philosopher of the ideal state with all its apparatus of philosophical rule, he was a defender of the noble lie, or at least a version of it. Similarly, if Collingwood's Machiavelli was not the philosopher of political realism, he was a defender of a conception of civic virtue in which rulers may have to act less than well when a political good cannot be obtained in any other way.

There is one point on which Collingwood is clear. All ruling involves deceit. Deceit is fraud, and fraud is a subspecies of force. Political morality can be conceived as fraud: concealment of intention and purpose is unavoidable in the latter and often present in the former. But there are also significant differences. Acts which would otherwise be considered immoral but which are performed to further a political good are not essentially criminal. They do not always depend on false representation, and they are not commonly performed to gain an unjust advantage for the individual performing them. Such differences are important because they reveal how Collingwood's approach to the subject of political morality narrows the number of options available to him.

The issue is the extent to which Collingwood's way of thinking about political morality prevents him from fully answering the question he set himself. Permitted behaviour in the face of barbarism is the topic here or, to put it in another way, the moral permissions liberals give themselves when they face illiberalism of an extreme kind. Collingwood argues, like many moralists before and after him, that deception is justified when it is for the good of the deceived and when the deceived are only those 'most backward in political education' (NL 27.38). Plato's influence is hard to miss, although it radically limits Collingwood's attempt to answer his fifth question since the moral crux of deception arises because it is not only those 'most backward in political education' who need to be deceived. Moreover, not all cases of political morality involve deception. In such cases, where the action and its consequences are quite explicit, the moral costs of necessary immorality are often high.

Collingwood does recognize that a rule-governed morality is tested severely by political dilemmas (NL 16.76). Even so we should be in no doubt about the degree of licence that he allows rulers, even when their ends are limited by a political good. He writes, 'deceit on the part of the rulers if it is for the good of the ruled or for the facilitation of ruling is not only justified; it is, whatever sentimentalists might say, a duty' (NL 27.29). Collingwood's opposition to appeasement (AA 161–7) should not disguise the fact that it was a lie told to those who were able to judge for themselves what he was objecting to. So Collingwood criticized the Chamberlain government for concealing the facts regarding German treatment of the Jews 'to prevent indignation from flaring up into an inopportune and hopeless war' (EPP 214). Civil relationships – mutual respect between ruler and ruled – must be undermined by fraud, but how resilient does Collingwood think civility is when faced with a politically necessary deceit?

Collingwood claims that when practising a necessary deceit the overriding imperative is not to be found out: 'if you tell the same lie to fifty thousand people, and one of them sees through it, you have backed the wrong horse: you had better not have told that lie' (NL 27.43); 'breeding new types of Yahoo' (NL 30.86) encourages political expediency because the distinction between the civil who control their feelings and the Yahoos who do not looks increasingly fragile.

It is clear that Collingwood is alert to the risks involved in deception used as a political tool. First among these is being found out or having one's bluff called (NL 27.43). And there are good and bad liars too. By way of illustration Collingwood cites Hitler as an example of the first, Mussolini as an example of the second. But again we might see this as Collingwood narrowing his field of enquiry. The fifth question concerns the moral limits of political conduct in a democratic setting. Totalitarianism completely changes the context of discussion (even if it is not difficult to think of examples of political leaders of democracies whose moral sense in politics was less than acute).

At this point the question of Collingwood's treatment of Stanley Baldwin takes centre stage. *The New Leviathan* is not altogether remote from its author's radical past. Continued vituperation of Stanley Baldwin whose 'National' Government (the inverted commas are Collingwood's) he excoriated, singling out 'the empty rodomontades of Ramsay MacDonald and the "con-man" methods of Mr. Baldwin' (AA 162) for special denigration. When these words were uttered in 1938 they were not original as terms of political abuse. A few years or so earlier Churchill had spoken in similar fashion, attributing to Ramsay MacDonald 'the gift of compressing the largest number of words into the smallest amount of thought' (Parker 2000: 32), and Baldwin's bland techniques for inspiring trust were well known. It was the appeasers who were in Collingwood's sights, just as they had been in 1939 and as they were in Cato's *Guilty Men*, the book which, when it was published at the beginning of July 1940, did much to damage the reputations of the politicians it accused. It is likely that Collingwood's remarks on Baldwin in *The New Leviathan* were written after *Guilty Men* was published. The books' attacks on the former British prime minister are similar. Unlike *The New Leviathan*, *Guilty Men* was a polemic written from an explicitly partisan point of view, but in their treatment of Baldwin neither jibs at the selective use of evidence nor at taking his political beliefs out of context. Both look back, from the perspective of the early summer of 1940 some ten months into the Second World War when Britain was facing defeat, to the events of autumn 1936 when debates over the possibility of avoiding war were at their most intense and when British rearmament policy hung in the balance. Both are revisionist in manner and purpose. Indeed, their backward glance is characteristic, since Baldwin's speech in the House of Commons on 12 November 1936, the subject of these often quite bitter reflections, was in intention and delivery a justification for a decision taken in the year immediately before.

The New Leviathan's discussion of these issues (NL 30.41–30.47) reflects the early years of a complex and violent war in which dilemmas of political morality were inescapable. Moreover, by looking back to 1936 Collingwood is necessarily drawn into the attribution of historical blame and so into the questions of truth and falsity which necessarily go with it. *Guilty Men* brought the rearmament policies of Baldwin's pre-war government under renewed scrutiny. Using invective and argument to make its case it fired broadsides at those it considered responsible for British weakness in the face of Nazi aggression. *Guilty Men* alleged that in order to win the General Election of 1935 Baldwin deceived the electorate about the scale of German rearmament and so about the lack of a corresponding need for Britain to arm itself for war. Collingwood too accused Baldwin of putting party before country. Neither Collingwood nor the authors of *Guilty Men* gave any weight to the freedom of a British political leader to choose the timing of a General Election, and neither shows much sympathy for Baldwin's argument that his rearmament proposals required an electoral mandate to make them legitimate. It was Baldwin's frank justification for his conduct in his speech on 12 November 1936, which produced most controversy. Both Collingwood and the authors of *Guilty Men* refer to the same passage of that speech in order to make their case: it is their rendering of this passage which is open to dispute. Common to both is the assertion that when Baldwin referred in his speech to the loss of the election being certain if he had gone to the country with a policy of rearmament he was speaking about the election of 1935. That is why Collingwood in *The New Leviathan* not only quotes exactly the same passage as *Guilty Men* but also injects into it a bracketed comment of his own, one which is not in the original speech, to make his own reading clear. Collingwood's quote from Baldwin's speech reads as follows: '"I cannot", said he, "think of anything that would make the loss of the [future general] election from my own point of view more certain"' (NL 30.43). Collingwood brings Baldwin's speech into his discussion of war as the breakdown of the dialectic which characterizes internal politics. He uses it as an example of a war caused first by the disharmony in government over the best policy to adopt to deal with Germany and second by the influence of a pacifist-minded electorate. Here Collingwood overstates his case. Sharp differences over appeasement were certainly present, but it is hard to see these as the sole cause of war in 1939, especially when it is remembered that at the time there was no obvious road to peace. Further, it is open to question to what degree public opinion was, as Collingwood states, pacifically inclined (for discussion, see Rose 1978: 176). In this context the idea that Baldwin's confession was a myth is pivotal (for the origin of this view, see Bassett 1948: 84–95, and the correspondence which followed in *The Cambridge Journal*, Volume II, Number 4, January 1949 and Volume II, Number 6, March, 1949). This is so much so that when we take it into account Collingwood's treatment becomes close to the left wing polemics of *Guilty Men*. However, not all historians hold the view that the Baldwin confession was a myth (see Parker 2000: 109), and the attacks on Baldwin which used the allegedly corrupted version of this speech are to be found coming from both Left and Right (see, for example, most famously, Churchill 1949: 195).

And yet it has been extensively, if not unanimously, argued that what Baldwin was referring to was not the General Election of 1935 but the state of public opinion in the country between 1933 and 1935. As Baldwin's biographers comment, 'no one *at the time* seemed to have thought that Baldwin meant the 1935 election. The whole web of falsified historiography has risen in retrospect' (Middlemas and Barnes 1969: 972; italics in original). Once this is accepted then the charge that Baldwin put party interest before country loses its force. As John Charmley points out, it is scarcely credible that a British political leader faced with these circumstances 'could have ignored the evidence which June 1935 provided of the pacific mood of the people' (Charmley 1993: 296).

We have seen that Collingwood's fifth question asks how the civilized can respond to barbarism without becoming uncivilized themselves, and it is clear that prohibitions and permissions made imperative by national survival test a democratic society's moral will. What Collingwood refers to as 'the dialectical character of political life' (NL 27.3) is built on a bedrock of human emotional and moral resources without which political morality would make little sense. Collingwood thinks of human communication as resting on agreement, in language and way of life. Discussion which is dialectical searches for a common point of view, whereas that which is eristic merely aims to defeat the opponent, whether an agreed position has been reached or not. However, decisions in political morality signify neither an agreement commonly arrived at nor a victory for one party over the other, but a realization that in politics there are occasions when a political good can be obtained only by setting aside deeply held moral principles. It is true that Collingwood sometimes speaks of political disputes as illusory because they involve 'false abstractions' (NL 26.17), and this certainly can occur, but the issues which characterize political morality are neither false nor abstract and so challenge dialectical reasoning to greater effect.

Not only does Collingwood's answer to the fifth question depend on the arguments of earlier parts; it also shapes his view of what a civilized society's response to barbarism should be and how it can license a suspension of its own principles in order to protect them. Collingwood thinks of civilization as a process, one in which force can never be totally eradicated: 'Circumstances arise in which there is no doing without force; and there are no circumstances in which a certain degree of force, open or concealed is not needed for the very existence of the community' (NL 35.48). Similar remarks are found in Collingwood's discussion of civil peace. He writes, 'Peace is a dynamic thing; a strenuous thing; the detection, even the forestalling, of occasions for quarrels' (NL 40.24). Nor does Collingwood think that peace-keeping is solely the responsibility of the state, believing that those who argue that it is make the mistake of ' "PASSING THE BABY" ' (NL 40.7).

If Collingwood's fifth question concerns the limits of liberalism, it is clear that for him standing above the fray searching for a view from the mountain top is unavailable. There is a strong reason for this. Collingwood envisages the revolt against civilization as stemming from barbarism. The problem facing liberals is then not simply how to talk to non-liberals who just happen not to share their assumptions, but how to talk to barbarians who not only don't share any of their assumptions but with equal certainty also want to undermine and destroy them.

Exactly how much and what kind of force is open to civilized societies when they are faced by barbarism Collingwood says 'must be provided for in the rules of civilization' (NL 35.48), suggesting that this is to some degree an historical question. Barbarism in Collingwood's writings has an actual existence in the form of the fourth barbarism, which he termed The Germans, and an historical existence in the form of the three barbarisms which Collingwood believed preceded it: the Saracens, the 'Albigensian Heresy' and the Turks. It was the job of philosophy to uncover the presuppositions of barbarism both in its contemporary and its historical forms and so by understanding it contribute to its defeat. Since Collingwood thought that no civilization could ever be totally free from assault either from within or without, except as an ideal, the problem of facing up to barbarism is one which never goes away. In Collingwood's eyes this is one guarantee of its importance. Another, of equal weight, concerns the nature of barbarism itself. The principles of civility which drive the argument of *The New Leviathan* forward have something in common with the principles of just war theory. Self-defence together with the doctrine of limited war should be able to tell a civilized society how to behave in the face of a revolt against its fundamental values and way of life. The same argument applies to the problems of political morality which the civilized society will also have to face. The principles of just war set these in context, so presenting a solid obstacle of moral principle to any temptation to bend or break the rules. Now the full complexity of Collingwood's fifth question is apparent. Barbarism lies outside the area of rational discussion on which the derivation and application of moral and political principle depend. If, as we know Collingwood believed, barbarism means the attempt to put the civilizing process into reverse, then no civilized society can assume the truth of its own principles since it is these which barbarism has put in question. Unavoidably then a civilized society which asks how it should face up to a revolt against itself must reach beyond the principles which govern its own existence.

When Collingwood was writing the later sections of *The New Leviathan* Britain was under siege. And yet the political mood was one of determination, despising Nazism and resolving that Hitler must be stopped, even if this meant that Britain would fight on nearly alone. At this point in history Collingwood gave philosophical voice to this mood. He offered a way of understanding the exasperation that often accompanied it. This was not the frustration regularly felt by liberals when they encounter non-liberals who simply do not share their views. The attempts of the British people to make sense of the enemy confronting them and the conduct which was rightfully expected of them in the face of such an enemy are directly relevant to Collingwood's concerns. Collingwood believed that liberalism was the only political doctrine which could unite moral principle and politics in a credible way. And yet his concern in *The New Leviathan* was not with liberalism directly. What concerned Collingwood primarily was civilization contrasted with barbarism. A liberal society and a civilized one are not necessarily coextensive. A society may be counted liberal if its members are free to choose, as long as this does not prevent others from doing the same. Collingwood's notion of civility may well reflect a similar view. But when a civilized society is faced by barbarism the situation is transformed. A barbarist is not someone who merely wants to express dogmatic beliefs or express dogmatic beliefs in a dogmatic way, or even to forcibly prevent others from expressing and holding their beliefs. The barbarist wants not only the freedom to restrict the freedom of others but also the freedom to be cruel to them, to treat them as less than human and to dispose of them as the ruling creed dictates. To answer his fifth question fully Collingwood needed arguments. But, as we have seen, arguments in support of civilized behaviour are precisely what barbarism disdains. And so Collingwood had to tell his readers, perhaps more clearly than they knew themselves, exactly what barbarism was, why it must be fought and why it would lose.

Arguing with Nazism is not Collingwood's strategy. Collingwood thought that barbarism in the form of Nazism would self-destruct because conflict between different barbaric societies or among barbarians themselves was essential to their nature and because barbarism was self-negating, or 'a *will to do nothing*' (italics in original), as Collingwood puts it (NL 36.94). Nor was this position in any sense historicist. Nazism was certainly a form of barbarism, and it was the enemy that the civilized world wanted to see defeated. The defeat of barbarism was assured in the long run but it would occur, Collingwood believed, only under specific conditions. One such condition was that 'there must always be partisans of civilization who are ready to go on defending it, *whatever happens*, until its cause is victorious' (NL 41.74; italics in original,). Collingwood's choice of the evocative term 'partisan' conveys exactly the appeal which Collingwood as an independent liberal wanted to make.

Reconstruction of Collingwood's answer to his fifth question builds on a structured argument thus: the nature of a civilized society's response to barbarism presupposes that we know what a civilized society is, and this presupposes that we know what a social existence is, which in turn depends on Collingwood having answered the questions he raises concerning choice and rational freedom, this latter being the leitmotif of the whole book. Most helpful is a direct connection between Collingwood's fifth question and an answer to an earlier question which clearly satisfied him. When Collingwood asks how a civilized society should behave in the face of barbarism he is not asking for information. He is raising a moral question and in so doing he is pointing his readers in a particular direction. The grammatical form of Collingwood's fifth question is significant. He asks not why a civilized society should respond to barbarism, but how. A civilized society possesses a manner of living which involves deep historical and philosophical roots. Barbarism is civilization's antithesis. A civilized society is one which is inured to the responses which are necessary when a confrontation occurs. As long as the process of mental and emotional habituation described in Collingwood's philosophy of mind is in place then moral scepticism is redundant. There can be no basis for asking why barbarism should be opposed, just as in Collingwood's view there can be no basis for asking why human beings should be moral. Against a different philosophical background, in the hands of, say, Hobbes, this question would make sense, but in Collingwood's mind it does not. This does not, however, mean that moral choice has no work to do. Quite the contrary, in fact, because Collingwood believes that moral freedom is at the centre of a civilized way of living. Nor does it mean that in a civilized society there are no occasions in which choices are unavoidable without moral loss. So Collingwood's fifth question addresses an important additional issue, the resolution of which we need, finally, to reconstruct.

One obvious interpretation of Collingwood's fifth question is that it is a practical one. 'How' questions are to do with the means needed to achieve given ends. For example, how can I get my old washing machine to work or how can I get from Truro to Aberdeen in the quickest and cheapest way. We can be sure that Collingwood's 'partisans of civilization' would need practical intelligence to find the right answers to questions such as how best to counter Nazi propaganda or to military questions such as how to defeat the U boat menace in the North Atlantic. Collingwood's ethics falls short of utilitarianism, but he does find room for utility as one of the forms taken by action in its practical aspect. A slightly different way of answering Collingwood's fifth question about how a civilized society should respond to barbarism may be closer to his meaning. So, he believes, barbarism should be confronted with fortitude – civilization must be defended *'whatever happens'*, he says, until victory is assured. There is no room in this answer for the appeasement of barbarism or for seeking peace terms with it. But even this does not fully capture Collingwood's main thrust. One reason for this is that in *The New Leviathan* the virtues are largely absent from the discussion, even though they do appear elsewhere. Doing one's duty – the fundamental idea in Kant's ethics – does play a part. But Collingwood was clear that this idea is of little help either in general or specifically in answering his fifth question. As reconstructed then his position looks like this. The duty to fight barbarism is an answer to the question why, not the question how. Given that why questions are redundant because, as Collingwood argues, a civilized society displays its answers continually in its way of life and so is able to discard the 'intellectual labour' (NL 41.57) involved in forever worrying about them, and given that moral questions are better construed as how questions, a much more fruitful tactic is to show how civilized societies come to see what is facing them when they find themselves at war with barbarism. In *The New Leviathan* this is surely the approach Collingwood adopts.

Of equal significance to any reconstructed answer is the idea that the moral life is both practical and historical. Thus, Collingwood's answer to his fifth question depends heavily on the answer he gives in Part I to the question what is my duty? It is, Collingwood replies, the act which *'is both possible and necessary: the act which at that moment character and circumstance combine to make it inevitable, if he has free will, that he should freely will to do*' (NL 17.8; italics in original). The welding together of duty and history is one of the key arguments in *The New Leviathan*, reflecting the weight Collingwood attaches to the significance of history for practical life. Any answer to his fifth question would then refer back to his discussion of the relation between history and duty in Part I where he says that 'History is to duty what modern science is to right' (NL 18.51), a statement which is immediately followed by an explicit description of the role of historical understanding in moral reflection. Discovering one's duty is not achieved by syllogistic reasoning but by thinking which is historical in character. Albeit in a highly compressed form Collingwood is here clarifying the kind and degree of consciousness which must be attained for a civilized society to become aware of the nature of any threat that faces it. It is hard not to see this argument as anything other than an essential feature of Collingwood's answer to question five.

What Collingwood is suggesting is a model of moral and political judgement: his model is the historian who notices a pottery shard which others have missed, or the hunter who spots a danger that others were blind to. A civilized society arrives at its response to barbarism by understanding the situation which faces it and then working through the responses available. Coming to see its response as a duty depends on its grasping and accepting a course of action for which the agent, as Collingwood says, 'charactered and circumstanced as he is, he can do no other' (NL 18.52). There is no sense in which responses are predetermined by history – something which, if true, would have undermined the point of Collingwood asking the fifth question – but quite the contrary in fact, since it is implied in his way of speaking about judgement that there can be better or worse ones.

There is then in Collingwood's view no sense in which the historical process exhibits its own internal moral dynamic. The imperative that barbarism must self-destruct derives from barbarism's distinctive logic and not from any determining set of conditions beyond it. Opposition to barbarism remains the major cause of its defeat and that is why Collingwood sees his fifth question as so important. Behaviour in the face of barbarism is to a large degree a matter of judgement, and judgement in turn depends on a grasp of the situation which is historical in nature. In this respect perhaps the philosopher who is closest to Collingwood's views is Alasdair MacIntyre, who writes of the capacity for political judgement, 'Mary Tudor did not, Montrose possessed it, Charles I did not. What Cardinal Pole and Montrose possessed were in fact those virtues which enable their possessors to pursue both their own good and the good of the tradition of which they are the bearers even in situations defined by the necessity of tragic, dilemmatic choice' (MacIntyre 2007: 223; for a brief glimpse of Collingwood's views understood in this perspective, see his discussions of two British prime ministers, Gladstone in his 1940 Lectures, 'Goodness, Rightness Utility', NL 478–9 and Baldwin in the book itself, NL 30.41). As for two other British prime ministers, Lloyd George and Chamberlain, Collingwood's views on their merits and defects are well known. In terms derived from MacIntyre we might say that, for Collingwood, in their broad capacity for political judgement Asquith and Campbell-Bannerman possessed it, but Lloyd George, Baldwin and Chamberlain did not. Collingwood's philosophy lacks the Aristotelian base which is present in MacIntyre's argument, but both see the need for practical insight in dark times and both see that there is no guarantee that a given society, even a civilized one, will be able to provide it.

It is possible, of course, to reconstruct Collingwood's answer to his fifth question differently. It is also possible to charge me with merely rearranging Collingwood's words: of this I am partially guilty. There is no more sense in forever looking outside *The New Leviathan* than there would be in trawling Dickens's other novels for the definitive ending to *Edwin Drood*. Collingwood's words have certainly been used, but they have been arranged as answers to the question he asked. Those have to satisfy several essential requirements, and my argument is not only that these can be found in Collingwood's text but that suitably woven together they constitute the best reconstruction of Collingwood's answer to question five we are likely to have. Collingwood's aim was to construct 'a science of politics appropriate for the modern world' (NL 12.96). The answer to question five is linked necessarily to the discussion which preceded it. Choices made in hard circumstances presuppose the capacity for deliberation and 'extemporary decision' (NL 13.75), the point Collingwood had reached in Part I; collective choice presupposes the possibility of social consciousness, the point he had reached in Part II; social consciousness needs a form of political expression, the point he had reached also in Part II; while the justification for war – 'for the sake of the world at large' (NL 30.92) – is reached towards the end of Part II.

Collingwood's concern with political morality has to do with the area of public life which Aristotle calls law abidingness. Private individuals are not normally burdened with decisions about political morality, but in abnormal times, particularly in time of war, they are greatly affected by them. Collingwood's interest is with conduct in the face of barbarism. It concerns every citizen's everyday behaviour as well as decisions of state. A civilized society operates through self-restraint in minor matters as well as major ones. This is apparent in

Collingwood's discussion of the rule of law which is prefaced by an introduction which shows his readers how civility is related both to its philosophical preconditions and to the kind of behaviour expected of all individuals when a society faces hard times (NL Ch XXXIX, 39.81). Not only does Collingwood's notion of civil behaviour exclude buck passing it also excludes privilege, together with the myriad different forms taken by unfairness and double dealing, many of which were likely to have been unpleasantly familiar to the citizens of the highly regulated society that Britain had become in 1941.

Collingwood's views in *The New Leviathan* concerning a 'True Germany' and the extent of resistance to Nazism within Germany itself are bound closely to many of the political preoccupations in this earlier period in the war. Was Nazism an aberration or were the German people as a whole responsible for German military expansionism and its ruthless policies? Collingwood's liberalism would seem to urge caution. There was a 'True Germany', as he terms it, albeit one he thought too weak 'to sweep the flag of the false Germany' (NL 45.69) from flying over its subject territories. Collingwood's notion of civility certainly sees it as essential that a civilized society at war distinguishes between those among its enemy who support the war and those who do not. Nowhere is this distinction more apparent than in Collingwood's backing for those German refugees who reached Britain. When British expectations of an invasion were approaching their height in June 1940 he wrote to one such, Wolfgang von Leyden, to express his indignation at his internment and speaking of his shame that he had been treated not as a fighter against tyranny, but a supporter of it (Collingwood to von Leyden 6 June 1940, RC 184).

When Collingwood wrote to the Clarendon Press on 11 June 1941 to propose *The New Leviathan*, in the same letter he confirmed what he had probably known for some time – that the book would consist of four parts. He also told them that the fourth part was not yet written. Of the parts which compose *The New Leviathan* Part IV is the shortest and the most contemporary. In an earlier passage in his book Collingwood wrote 'To think historically is to explore a world consisting of things other than myself' (NL 18.52). The sense of Collingwood's writing in Part IV is of things in the shape of situations and events running away from him. The German invasion of the Soviet Union in late June 1941 changed the course of the war and meant it was poised to become global. The universal frame of reference implied by the principles of civilization defended in *The New Leviathan* was threatened but not overwhelmed by these developments, even though the war would reveal levels of evil deeper than anyone knew.

9

Two cheers for Vansittartism: R. G. Collingwood and Germany

Expressive of Collingwood's historical cast of mind in *The New Leviathan* are all the following: bringing Hobbes up to date, the idea of contract, the systematic tracing of the decline of classical politics, the debates with Plato and Machiavelli, the concluding analysis of barbarisms, the digressions in which Collingwood comments on politicians such as Stanley Baldwin, the impingement of events, such as Mussolini's defeat in North Africa early in 1941 and, most contentiously of all, the linking of German barbarism with Germany's inherited past. Nothing in this entails the sacrifice of philosophy to history. The first part of *The New Leviathan* to be written rejects historical relativism and restates his view that without philosophy any illumination of civility would be impossible.

In Collingwood's hands history means the present, and in 1940 the present was England facing invasion and occupation. During the early years of the Second World War, when Britain was engaged in the struggle against Germany almost alone, Collingwood seems to have adopted the persona of the fighting philosopher. The philosopher had become the truth teller, 'in a small way a kind of Edgar on the heath, angry, not mad' (Patrick 1995: 87), exposing in the months before the war started what he felt were the lies and obfuscations behind the British government's policy of appeasement. This is the conventional picture and it is true up to a point, but the historical reality is more complex. The truth is that in terms of their political allegiances Collingwood's later works do not dance to the same tune. As the socialist intellectual Harold Laski wrote in a contemporary review, 'the *Autobiography* suggested that Professor Collingwood was, if not on the road to Moscow, at any rate prepared to consider a ticket for that journey, *The New Leviathan* seems to provide the basis for a sophisticated "Vansittartism" which is asserted rather than proved' (Laski 1942: 98).

Certainly Collingwood felt that his views on Germany and the Germans needed to be stated. For Laski, *The New Leviathan* was 'the catharsis of some angry emotions rather than a detached study of historic experience' (Laski 1942: 98). Was Laski voicing his irritation that what he took to be the socialist promise of *An Autobiography* had turned into a right wing Germanophobia? Collingwood's single cheer for Marx in 1939 struck a note that Laski did not miss. Vansittartism (the doctrine forming the basis for discussion of German as opposed to Nazi responsibility for the war) was of little interest to those who interpreted the rise of Nazism in class or economic terms. So it is significant that *The New Leviathan* rejects Marx not only as the originator of a false economic doctrine but as a loyal follower of 'the German tradition of herd-worship' (NL 33.98). In the late spring of 1941 when Collingwood was hard at work on his final chapters Vansittartism was a topic which divided the nation. Even so, Laski's review of *The New Leviathan* was one of the very few that made any reference to it. Describing Collingwood's Vansittartism as 'asserted rather than proved', he diminishes Collingwood's philosophical arguments by seeing them as 'a complicated preparation for the peroration of the final section with its scornful invective and indignant insult' (Laski 1942: 98). In Laski's view, Collingwood's work was 'a tract for the times' (Laski 1942: 98): less the philosophical basis for Collingwood's liberal counter-attack on Fascism and Nazism than an endorsement of an attitude towards Germany which was current at that stage of the war.

As a work of philosophy *The New Leviathan* reaches beyond its context and therefore beyond Vansittartism, but when Germany occupied much of Europe, and when Churchill's 'long night of barbarism' (Churchill 1941: 212) had to be faced, what was distinctive about the German mind and character was considered in Britain to be a vital question. Laski does not quite bring himself to describe Collingwood's Vansittartism as prejudice, but he does believe that it is an attitude which is not easily justified or proved. Whether intended by Laski or not the effect of this is to detach Collingwood's Vansittartism from his political philosophy, since no unproven assertion, let alone a prejudice, can have a role there. Collingwood has a choice. Either he shows how his Vansittartism can be integrated with his political philosophy, or he accepts that his attempt to tar all Germans with the political brush of Nazi Germany is, as Laski asserts, impossible to prove.

Laski's interpretation of the seminal texts of Collingwood's wartime politics can seem narrow. What Collingwood wanted was neither a single ticket to Moscow nor a return to a liberalism which he thought had failed (MGM 312–18). His aim was to reinvigorate liberalism by anchoring it in a newly revived philosophy of mind and history. And so Collingwood sets Marx aside by rejecting his belief that states are no more than agencies of class oppression, as well as dismissing modern liberal despair that states 'are the chief authors of the evils for whose ending we have made them' (NL 12.93). Collingwood is glancing back to the pessimistic view of the state he himself held in 1936 (MGM 309–12), but in 1940 there was a new dimension to consider. The Second World War was thought of as a war in defence of civilization, and so a distinction between civilization and barbarism is clearly essential to Collingwood's project. Here Laski's charge of 'sophisticated Vansittartism' gains a certain amount of traction. Moreover, the presence in *The New Leviathan* of a Vansittartism which is not proved may be seen to cast doubt on the kind of liberalism which the book seeks to defend. As the authors of a life of Laski point out, 'Laski was worried about the fate in Britain of refugee German socialists, even German Jews, against whom Vansittart's arguments were being used to justify expulsion or internment. He was also concerned that "Vansittartism" might lead to a punitive postwar policy that would make a socialist rebuilding of Europe impossible' (Kramnick and Sheerman 1993: 432).

The war's twists and turns meant that questions which were thought vital at one time later came to be seen as less pressing, in some cases even redundant. New questions emerged as the Nazi enemy made its character and intentions plain. If Collingwood's political opinions did not always sing the same tune it was because the tune had changed and a new song had to be sung. The appeal of Vansittartism crossed party political boundaries, and its popularity rose and fell with the times. In Laski's view, Collingwood in 1939 was a fellow traveller of the Left. No single party line determined his views, and so between July 1939 when *An Autobiography* was published and August 1941 when *The New Leviathan* was completed, Collingwood came to see that a single ticket to Moscow was not worth the price and that Vansittartism merited support. In other words Collingwood was responding to events as they arose. This is surely what a commitment to a blending of philosophy and history means.

Was Collingwood in 1939 really the radical that Laski portrays? *An Autobiography* surely leaves us in no doubt since, as one socialist reviewer said of Collingwood's highly political final chapter, 'It shows a leap from his earlier position of slow philosophical advance to a political standpoint which is not very remote from that of working class socialism. The question remains whether Collingwood will be able to complete the process of allying himself with the progressive class' (Arndt 1940: 444). Collingwood's disillusionment with liberalism certainly left him open to radical conversion, even though his idealist philosophy, together with his rejection of theoretical Marxism, remained formidable obstacles. Like many intellectuals at the time he espoused a political programme that lacked an ideological cutting edge but pointed in the direction that the Left in Britain wished to go. Was Laski's the wishful thinking of a reviewer who wanted to keep the philosopher in the socialist camp? The Spanish Civil War was the touchstone of political allegiance during the late 1930s. What happened in Spain taught liberals that no government, not even one that had been democratically elected, was safe from the Fascist forces within. Collingwood's analysis of British politics in 1938 and 1939 follows this model.

Fierce opposition to appeasement implied robust opposition to Nazism. For many intellectuals who shared this view it was Communism which mounted the only real challenge to the tyrannies of the right, so weakness in confronting aggression in Abyssinia, Spain and Czechoslovakia was a reflection of capitalist perfidy, and no peace would be permanent until the emergence of a form of socialism that was truly international. By 1939 Collingwood had fellow-travelled a considerable distance along this road, although how great that distance was requires caution since it varied with events and ideas. Someone like Orwell thought that Nazism had to be defeated **in order** to bring about socialism (Crick 1980: 277). Orwell saw as well that 'we *could* make a real improvement in human life, but we shan't do it without the recognition that common decency is necessary' (Crick 1980: 261; italics in original). Substitute Collingwood's idea of civility for Orwell's common decency and it looks as if they are making a similar point. The difference between the two points of view is not between Orwell the socialist and Collingwood the liberal, although political beliefs do play a part. Nor is it semantic. The primary difference is philosophical. Whether a human society devoid of civility is intelligible at all is a philosophical question. Whether or not socialism enhances human possibilities is a matter for political debate.

Far from being a liberal half-way house, true in theory but inadequate in practice, Collingwood's politics at that time were, as Laski states, not simply inclined towards the Left but very much of it. However, it was mainly those on the Left who argued that war should be opposed on the grounds that it would erode exactly the liberties it was intended to protect. This was Lindsay's worry, too. In his Election Address he writes, 'Can we rearm on the scale required of us and remain a democracy and preserve our essential liberties? I am confident that we can if we will' (Scott 1971: 249). Collingwood did not go quite as far as George Orwell who in 1939 berated the Labour Party for warmongering. Like Orwell who 'maintained the ILP line of moral equivalence. If Germany had gone bad, the blame was ours, going back to Versailles', he warned with the Independent Labour Party that 'war would lead to the "destruction of the liberties of the people" and the "imposition of totalitarian regimes" in Britain and elsewhere' (Colls 2013: 134–5; for a clear statement of Collingwood's view, see *AA*, 89, 165–6). Just how close Collingwood's position was to progressive left-wing intellectual opinion can be gauged from a circular distributed to members of the Association of Writers for Intellectual Liberty (AWIL), 'these reactionary forces which lead to the open barbarities of Fascism were at work in every country. They are still at work, and they have not changed their character' (Bradshaw 1998: 63). It is true that Collingwood had earlier expressed a willingness to suggest to the Independent Labour Party 'that political doctrines may work in Russia or Germany, and may fail to work in England owing to the Roman element which we still inherit, and that – here I would strongly oppose certain nineteenth century notions, including some of Marx's – there can be no such thing as an international culture, proletarian or any other, that ignores differences of historical background' (R. G. Collingwood to F. G. Simpson, letter dated 17 June 1925, RC: 176). But this was written when Collingwood's confidence in liberalism was as yet undamaged; moreover, as he implies, when the historical background alters, as it did in 1938, then different political needs arise.

Like the Independent Labour Party, which not only warned of the destruction of British freedoms but used this as an argument against war, Collingwood was more concerned to accuse the Chamberlain government of deceiving its own people than of reneging on its duty to prepare for war. During the immediate pre-war period Collingwood's priorities were clear. Defeating the enemy without was the aim, but not at the price of a dictatorship within. If there was to be a war with Germany it would be with Nazi Germany, not the German people as a whole. This political message was shared by a group that held a closely related set of beliefs known as For Intellectual Liberty (FIL), whose aim was, as E. R. Dodds put it, 'to resist any attack from within or without upon democratic freedom and above all to resist fascism' (Dodds 1977: 129. Dodds was closely involved with re-education activities in post-war Germany; see Dodds 1977: 165–6; for a study see Phillips 1983: chapter 2). E. R. Dodds, then Professor of Greek at Oxford, whose political views throughout the Thirties were similar to those of his 'mildly leftist' tutor, E. F. Carritt, had joined FIL in 1936. (For details of the organization FIL I am indebted to Bradshaw 1997: 3–27 and 1998, 41–66. The Papers of FIL are in Cambridge University Library, see Bradshaw 1997: 21, fn. 31; as far as can be ascertained Collingwood was not a member of FIL). Support in British universities for the letters of protest organized by FIL grew from small numbers in 1936 to 375, including six heads of colleges and seventy professors, who in August 1939 signed an appeal to the prime minister, Neville Chamberlain, 'strongly urging' him to include Winston Churchill in the Government (see Swann and Aprahamian 1999: 216; also Gilbert 1976: 1022. Bradshaw 1998: 45 contains useful information on FIL's letter writing activities as well as listing some of their more important signatories). During the campaign to bring Churchill into the Chamberlain government, which reached its height in July 1939, Collingwood was away from Britain, sailing in the Mediterranean on board the yacht, *Fleur de Lys*, returning to Oxford in the last week of August. Collingwood was a supporter of Duncan Sandys, Churchill's son-in-law and fierce critic of Chamberlain and his appeasement policies who, a year or so earlier in June 1938, ran into trouble in the House of Commons over remarks designed to question the Government's record on rearmament (see *AA* 165; and for discussion Johnson 2013: 120–2).

Originally FIL had been concerned to protect civil and academic freedoms but as the Fascist threat intensified it became increasingly political in thought and action. Its predominant tone was one of opposition to Fascism wherever it appeared and to anyone whose policies lent it support whether directly or not. Thus, in February 1938, FIL condemned Chamberlain's appeasement of Mussolini, taking it to be evidence that the British government was a covert friend of Fascism, or, in Collingwood's language, 'a partisan of fascist dictatorship' (*AA* 164).

For one member of FIL, this protest was a step too far. E. M. Forster resigned on the grounds that the purpose of FIL (see Bradshaw 1998: 60) was not to engage in political debate. Collingwood, by contrast, in *An Autobiography* advanced rapidly across this dividing line, scathingly referring to the British electorate as 'dupes of a politician who has so successfully "appealed to their emotions" by "promises of private gain" (the gain of personal safety from the horrors of war) that they have allowed him to sacrifice their country's interests, throw away its prestige, and blacken its name in the face of the world' (*AA* 167). This analysis is not simply left-wing rhetoric. It relies, if implicitly, on something like a notion of false consciousness to make its point. In relation to *An Autobiography* Laski was right. Collingwood was not himself a traveller on Moscow Lines, but he was at least prepared to wave the flag for those who were.

The abandonment of Communism by Western intellectuals is largely explained by the Nazi-Soviet Pact, but there is no trace in Collingwood's writings of any belief in Soviet Marxism. Collingwood wore left-wing insignia as a defaulting liberal in order to criticize the Fascist tendencies of the British government, but he ruled out deep-rooted allegiance to Marxism as much on philosophical grounds as political ones. The key point is not how little Collingwood was attracted by Marxism but how quickly he began to attack it. As the war entered its first full year it did not take Collingwood long to embark on a disavowal of ideologically inspired radicalism. He makes his criticism of Marx (whose credentials as a philosopher and economist he had always doubted) explicit in *The New Leviathan*, and he anticipated it in the letter to his friend Chadbourne Gilpatric on 17 February 1940 (R. G. Collingwood to Chadbourne Gilpatric, letter dated 17 February 1940, RC: 135). A mere five or so months of the conflict had passed when Collingwood turned his back on Marxism and began the process of thought which led to the 'sophisticated Vansittartism' that Laski detects. Such changes of heart and mind lent a tone of urgency to Collingwood's writing which is not easily missed.

After his admission to Gilpatric in February that his earlier enthusiasm for Marx's class analysis was mistaken, Collingwood re-examined his liberal beliefs. And so it was as a reassured liberal that he continued to express worries about the presence in Britain of Fascism within. Collingwood's letter to *The Times* revealing his doubts about the British government's policy of internment and its treatment of refugees (letter dated 11 July 1940) was soon followed by others keen to ensure that liberal principles were not neglected in a time of crisis. G. M. Trevelyan wrote saying, rather harshly it might be felt in the light of the British government's purpose, 'The Nazis keep their concentration camps for their enemies; we use them for our friends' (*The Times*, 24 August 1940). In this Collingwood's awareness of the priority of public safety in wartime is self-evident, but his liberal sympathies are also clearly on display.

Historical context is important. *An Autobiography* was written and published before the Second World War broke out. *The New Leviathan* was written during the war when it was believed with justification that the future of civilization was in the balance. The difference is not merely circumstantial. Liberals want their wars to be undertaken justly and be justly fought. National security in time of war cannot but be a serious consideration, and yet liberals will always argue that justice ought not to be too readily set aside. In Britain public debates about the applications of these principles started early and were extensive and well-informed. The prime minister, Neville Chamberlain, set the tone in a speech delivered the day after the British declaration of war against Germany, 'In this war we are not fighting against you, the German people, for whom we have no bitter feelings, but against a tyrannous and forsworn regime which has betrayed not only its own people but the whole of Western civilization and all that you and we hold dear' (cited in von Klemperer 1992: 154). Public exchange of views about this issue started early and continued throughout the war (see the letters to *The*

Times, 30 October, 1 December, 5 December 1939, in which one correspondent took the view that 'Thirteen million fanatics take a deal of crushing, but until they have learnt their lesson there is no hope of a reasonable Germany. And that is why this war will be long and bitter' (*The Times*, 1 December 1939)). The tone of academic debate was little different. In his foreword to a volume of papers on the German mind which were delivered at a Conference held in London in the summer of 1942 (the period when Collingwood's *The New Leviathan* was first published), the historian G. P. Gooch commented, 'Broadly speaking modern Germany has thought primarily in terms of the might and majesty of the state, modern England primarily in terms of the rights and liberties of the citizen' (Gooch 1945: viii).

Was Britain at war with the Nazi government or with the German people as a whole? Could the internment of foreign refugees be justified when their hatred of Nazism was not in doubt? Such questions were examined in detail at the time both in the British government's discussions of policy and in sections of the British Press. Nor was such reflection always and entirely impersonal. Close friendships like the one between Shiela Grant Duff and Adam von Trott, both of whom Collingwood knew, were tested severely by differences over the issues involved. Sharp and painful disagreements emerged over what Germany stood for, with the one seeing nothing but cruelty and barbarism and the other searching for a way of reclaiming the German soul. For those like Collingwood who came to believe that the German soul, if it had ever existed, was now almost totally broken the war was about saving civilization. German patriotism, even the patriotism of a good German such as von Trott, had no intellectual purchase here.

As events made their impact one view came to dominate. Nazism was not simply an attack on liberal beliefs and values but was evil. Any moral equivalence between Fascism without and Fascism within was unpersuasive. In this new context those who upheld liberal principles of just war struggled to grasp just what was facing them. In what sense satisfactory to liberals could the German people as a whole be described as evil? By the late winter of 1940 Collingwood had seen that this was a question which no Marxist analysis was able to answer. If the answer that Collingwood gave was a 'sophisticated Vansittartism', his liberalism could not remain unaffected. As a liberal Collingwood thought that assertion without reasons is no kind of defence for any political doctrine, let alone one such as his own which looks to philosophy for grounding and support. Did Collingwood tailor his liberal convictions to historical circumstances, however unpalatable to him this might have been? For in the tail of Laski's challenge lies a quite poisonous sting. We saw that Laski describes Collingwood's newly found allegiance as 'asserted rather than proved' (Laski 1942: 98): this requires us to ask what any proof of Vansittartism might amount to.

When Laski's review appeared in *The New Statesman* in 1942, some two years or so after battle had been joined, debates over appeasement had little relevance. Laski draws a connection between *An Autobiography* and *The New Leviathan* to make a highly partisan political point. He wants his readers to see the opinions contained in *An Autobiography* as signs of the times rather than derived from conviction. When the times changed, Collingwood's opinions changed with them. By writing *The New Leviathan* Collingwood, the socialist manqué of 1939, had revealed his true colours. The flag of Vansittartism was not one of convenience. Nor, although there is stronger justification for this, was it solely the doctrine the times needed. Laski is telling his readers that Vansittartism is intrinsic to what Collingwood in 1941 wanted to say.

To appreciate the seriousness of Laski's point we need to understand Vansittartism and why it provoked such acrimony. Angus Calder captures the strangeness of public debate at the time, 'Even if Vansittart had been retailing truths, instead of half-truths, it was bizarre that he should have been allowed to make these, and later, broadcasts at a time when political circles in Britain quite seriously hoped for a rising of the German people' (Calder 1992: 490). Throughout the writing of *The New Leviathan* Vansittartism was at its peak in terms of dissemination and public debate. The views of the high-ranking British diplomat, Sir Robert Vansittart, had appeared extensively in the British press and in BBC broadcasts which, in January 1941, were published as a pamphlet entitled *Black Record* (Vansittart 1941. The pamphlet was reprinted four times within the month of its first publication.). This provoked a number of publications arguing for or against its main thesis (see Rose 1978: 247–8 and 252 fn. 111). Vansittart had been one of Nazism's fiercest critics in England, and he became implacably opposed to appeasement and to the defeatism which he associated with the Chamberlain government's foreign policies. Hatred of Nazism raises the question of who was responsible for it; so when Vansittart identified the German people as the source of everything that was barbaric in Nazism, many liberals in Britain were affronted. Nazism may have been contemptuous of everything that liberals stand for, but one of the principles that liberals stand for is that the responsibility for a crime belongs to the individual who commits it. Reservations about the concept of collective guilt were at the heart of the liberal view that, contra Vansittartism, not all Germans were evil.

A common response to Vansittartism was to reject it as a piece of crude Germanophobia, a state of mind which is based neither on facts nor logic. As John Colville, private secretary to the prime minister, Winston Churchill, noted when discussing Vansittart's thoughts on dealing with Germany, 'Hatred and harsh words are the methods which he prescribes' (Colville 2005: 345). In his diary entry dated 6 January 1941 he also records Churchill's disagreement with a paper by Vansittart, quoting the prime minister as saying, 'I contemplate a reunited European family in which Germany will have a great place. We must not let our vision be darkened by hatred or obscured by sentiment. The expressions to which I attach importance and intend to give emphasis are "Nazi tyranny" and "Prussian militarism"' (Colville 2005: 282).

There is no evidence that Collingwood read Vansittart or listened to his broadcasts, but the remarks on Germany in *The New Leviathan* left Laski in no doubt as to their political provenance. *The New Leviathan* has its own structural logic but Collingwood's Vansittartism is present from the start; even earlier on 18 July 1939 during his voyage around the Aegean Collingwood was rehearsing some of its arguments (see FML 72). Beginning with scattered references to native German belligerence in its early chapters, moving on to the charge that 'the introduction of classical politics into Germany fell as flat as the introduction of a treatise on love into an audience of eunuchs' (NL 33.52), an assertion Collingwood glosses with Freudianism, 'The Germans made nonsense of the classical politics because they feared and hated the freedom of social life' (NL 33.52), and concluding with the analysis of German barbarism, written around the time of the German invasion of the Soviet Union, which ends the book, what is surprising about Collingwood's Vansittartism is that it was noticed by so few.

Defenders of Vansittart argued that the charges he lays against Germany of an historic militarism and of a violently unquenchable territorial ambition were based on evidence. Collingwood too promotes a discussion of German history which, like Vansittart's, has every appearance of following the historical facts. But after digesting some of its passages not a few readers of *The New Leviathan* might be forgiven for believing that Collingwood's view of the German psyche was, like Vansittart's in many people's eyes, simply an unbalanced expression of national dislike.

Was Collingwood's view just basic Germanophobia? When we take Collingwood's personal sympathy for and the help he gave to refugees from Germany the answer seems clear. Similarly, when we take Collingwood's investigations of German thought into account in, for example, his studies of Hegel the answer is obviously no. However, *The New Leviathan* does mark a different approach. For example, Kant's moral philosophy, Collingwood writes 'is characteristic of the German he was' (NL 16.75 fn. 1). And there is much more in the same vein, as when Collingwood talks about Nietzsche or the German school system (for Nietzsche see NL 12.4–5, and for the German school and university system see NL chapter XXXIII). Much of this reflects Collingwood's need to understand how, as happened to Germany during the 1930s, a whole nation can become galvanized by a single will. This question worried many at the time, especially those who were not unfriendly towards Germany. It is his answer, however, which is contentious. Germany exhibits an historical predisposition to 'herd-worship', Collingwood asserts, defining herd-worship as the individual's 'feeling of powerlessness in the grip of a non-social community, a community he did not help to create and cannot, however slightly, alter by deliberate or voluntary action' (NL 33.36). Collingwood's use of this term in 1941 reflects his generation (see NL 30.7, also Boucher 1992: xlix ff.); and his diagnosis of the failure of German political philosophy to account for the state understood as free activity is surely one of the reasons for Laski's description of Collingwood's Vansittartism as 'sophisticated'. Variants like 'herd-worship', 'herd-sense' and 'the politics of the herd' were commonplace descriptions of political behaviour in Germany during the rise of Nazism. William L. Shirer, an American journalist who lived and worked in Germany throughout these years, described in the diary he kept at the time the huge crowds of people he observed at rallies enthusing over Hitler and being 'merged completely in the German herd' (Shirer 1985: 124).

What are the differences between Collingwood and Vansittart? Differences are not at the level of national stereotyping, nor at the level of history. Both see Nazism as contiguous with the main thrust of German geopolitical history, most noticeably with the Prussianism which preceded it. But whereas Vansittart denies that he is speaking theoretically at all (Vansittart 1941: x) Collingwood is full of theory. Thus in early 1940 Nazism is explained by Collingwood as the survival of a pre-Christian paganism (EPP 168–76; for discussion see Gilman 1986: 111–21). A little before writing this Collingwood berated race theory saying that in supporting it Nazism was flogging a dead horse (see 'Untitled Fragments on Barbarism', Bodleian Library, Oxford, 24/6), and in *The New Leviathan* itself, in a manner which indicates that his immersion in psychoanalytic theory in the mid-1930s was still influential, he talks of Nazism as an ideology, the historical roots of which are to be found in religious millennialism, and as a wish-fulfilment fantasy which expresses itself through 'the Messianic pretensions of its leaders' (NL 26.94 and for discussion see Paylor 2015).

We saw that after the Saracens, the 'Albigensian Heresy' and the Turks, Collingwood defines the Germans as the Fourth Barbarism (NL 45.1), so unavoidably raising the question of German responsibility for Nazism. For one historian, 'However manufactured the image was, there can be no doubt of Hitler's genuine and immense popularity among the great mass of the German people down to the middle of the war' (Kershaw 2011: 13; for a measured view of the historical issues at stake, see Evans 2015: especially chapters 7 and 8).

During the time Collingwood was writing *The New Leviathan* the few dissenting voices in Germany were being rapidly silenced. Collingwood and Vansittart both make this point in remarkably similar language. For Vansittart German liberalism belonged to a 'weak minority' (Vansittart 1941: 15). For Collingwood, speaking of the 'True Germany', 'there are not enough of them' (NL 45.69). Collingwood's contemporary view is at one with that of a later historian, 'although "good" Germans were brave, sincere and individually admirable there were simply not enough of them' (Roberts 1991: 108). Vansittart and Collingwood give parallel accounts of how this situation has come about. Vansittart adopts the metaphor of the butcher bird to convey German rapacity (Vansittart 1941: 1–3). Both follow Tacitus in his claim that Germans think with their blood (Vansittart 1941: 19–20, NL 45.28). Collingwood's view that Germans were historically predisposed to 'herd-worship' certainly looks like Vansittart's, although he additionally explains 'herd-worship' in philosophical terms (NL 33.36).

The New Leviathan is neither a mirror of its times nor separate from them. In its more universal tone it links political philosophy with the philosophy of mind, but in a narrower focus it also addresses concerns which, for a Britain at war with Germany, were of practical relevance. Vansittart's argument seeks to persuade the British government and people of the truth of a point of view. Neither Collingwood nor Vansittart portrays the German nation as a totally undifferentiated whole. Neither argues that German barbarism is innate (Vansittart 1941: 55; 'The soul of a people *can* be changed.' NL 45.13). At the time, however, Vansittartism was taken to defend both these standpoints, and moreover, both were taken to threaten the liberalism which Collingwood defends.

Critics were not slow to indict Vansittartism with inconsistency and illiberalism (for discussion see Goldman 1979); inconsistency because treating the entire German people as responsible for the rise of Nazism appears little different from the Nazis holding the Jews responsible for the world's ills, and illiberalism because demonizing Germany neglects not only the tradition of liberalism within Germany but also ignores those good Germans who opposed Nazism, a significant number of whom lost their lives fighting against it. Among these 'good Germans' we should include Adam von Trott who was feted in Oxford when he arrived there as a student in the early 1930s. As well as giving a party for him in Oxford in May 1933 Collingwood wrote enclosing one of his own books as a gift, inviting von Trott to get in touch whenever he was in England and assuring him of his particular friendship and welcome. A few years later, however, during the summer of 1939 with war against Germany thought to be unavoidable, a number of von Trott's friends in England found their original sympathies hard to reproduce.

Collingwood's account of barbarism is a philosophical one and no more depends on the reduction of the notion of the 'True Germany' to the number of honest Germans than it does on the reduction of its opposite to the number of German liars. When Collingwood was writing *The New Leviathan* the case against Vansittartism was made in the strongest possible terms. There was simply no basis to the claim that the German people were either historically or psychologically predisposed to Nazism. To defend such a claim results only in using the German people as a scapegoat. No liberal would want to be associated with a proposition which tarred a whole people with the Nazi brush.

Collingwood is clearly sensitive to the issues involved. The charge against Vansittartism was that it treated the German people as a whole as scapegoats for the rise of Nazism (see Russell Wallis, 'Good Germans, Bad Nazis', I.B. Tauris Blog, 9 April 2014). Collingwood had read at least one work by a German author in which this issue is discussed (NL 45.75), and so when somewhat out of the blue he asserts the importance of Greek verb endings we can be sure that an important bee has begun buzzing (NL 41.13; Collingwood's reflections on barbarism can be dated to 1939/1940, in particular the unpublished manuscript 'Untitled fragments on Barbarism' (1939/1940, Bodleian Library, Dep. 24), in which the distinction (see below) between 'not being an x but behaving like an x; often, though not necessarily, without being one' is made, see Connelly 2003: 268).

The short section on scapegoatism in *The New Leviathan* (NL 41.1–18) is written in the clipped manner which characterizes much of the book. Together with the earlier '*Untitled Fragments on Barbarism, 1939–40*', it is, nevertheless, important because it tells us much about Collingwood's way of thinking about the war and some of the issues it involved. The idea Collingwood wants to illuminate is barbarism. Barbarian originally meant not-Greek. Peoples who did not speak Greek were called 'barbarians' since that is how their language sounded to the Greeks (ba-ba-ba). Over time not-Greek came to mean not just different from but inferior to Greek in lacking the basics of civilization as the Greeks understood them.

Collingwood now introduces a further distinction. To the difference between Greek and not-Greek (barbarian) he adds the difference between barbarian and savage, the crucial distinction being that whereas the savage lacks civilization the barbarian is in revolt against it. Now comes the most important point. Since in order to revolt against something it is necessary to have at least a rudimentary understanding of what it is, the barbarian must possess a level of understanding which the savage cannot possess. From this it follows that barbarism consists essentially in **behaving like** a savage rather than in **being** a savage (although the outward behaviour of each may appear to be exactly the same to the outside observer). Collingwood adds that his warrant for saying this is that Greek words ending in 'x-ism', such as barbarism, 'signify not being an x, but behaving like an x, though not necessarily without being one' (as cited in Connelly 2003: 268).

This distinction between being something and behaving like that something is important. As an example Collingwood speaks about Hellenism which means 'not being a Hellene but behaving like a Hellene'; as he says, 'You would never ascribe Hellenism to a Greek' (as cited in Connelly 2003: 268). Or we might talk about someone behaving like an idiot without being one (which does not rule out, as Collingwood says, being one as well).

Applying this way of thinking to Collingwood's Fourth Barbarism, The Germans, we can interpret him as saying that the Germans did not behave **like** barbarians but that they **were** barbarians. By contrast, von Trott's view was that the Germans were not barbarians, even though they behaved like them. To the Good German like von Trott, someone who was as unrelenting in their opposition to Nazism as they were passionate in their patriotism, Collingwood's standpoint might well have lacked appeal since it would have communicated precisely the spirit of 'blind denunciation of Germany's ills' that von Trott had complained about in a letter to Shiela Grant Duff in the autumn of 1938 (Adam von Trott letter to Shiela Grant Duff, 10.8.1938, as cited in von Klemperer 1988: 317). But we should not be too critical of Collingwood. According to his analysis civilization is different from and deeper than its appearances. Its agencies more commonly take the form of sentiments than conscious policies and aims. By contrast, barbarism can have only one aim, and it can only pursue that aim consciously. Barbarism is not savagery but it is like it. The difference is that its defining purpose is the overthrow of civilization. In all other respects it is no different from savagery. This Collingwood believes is barbarism's Achilles heel since the barbarian, as Collingwood writes, 'plays a losing game. The cards are stacked in favour of civilization, and he knows it' (NL 41.65). In other words, barbarism in Collingwood's usage is not simply defined by a deficiency of liberal attitudes and values, or even by an excess of nationalism, but by the distinction between savage and barbarian with which his argument originates. Similarly, it is this distinction which supports Collingwood's belief that the barbarian is infinitely worse than the savage.

Collingwood focuses on the intransitive sense of 'to barbarize', that is, 'to behave like a barbarian'. However, English allows us to use the verb transitively too, such that 'to barbarize' means 'to render someone (or something) barbarous'. Similarly, a ruler who is said to brutalize his people might mean either that he is behaving like a brute towards his people or that he is turning his people into brutes (transitive). Collingwood's focus, in largely following the original Greek, is on the intransitive form of such verbs. This focus helps to explain Collingwood's deliberate use of 'barbarist' (where we might say 'barbarian'): he wants to remain close to the Greek use of '-ist' for a concrete substantive, 'denoting an imitator' (NL 41.16).

In the light of this we can now see more clearly why Collingwood objects to the use of the term scapegoatism, relevant here to his view of Vansittartism. For him the use of this term would have to place the focus on the intransitive sense of scapegoating – behaving like a scapegoat, imitating or modelling one's behaviour on that of a scapegoat, rather than on its transitive sense of scapegoating as the practice of making a scapegoat of someone or of a whole people. The oddity involved in this way of speaking suggests that Collingwood is not trying to wrench the meaning of scapegoating into something it is not meant to be but rather he is complaining about an author who uses the word scapegoatism to provide his work with an academic gloss, whereas if there was such a word (it is not clear whether Collingwood thinks there is) it would need to follow what Collingwood sees as the original Greek model for words ending in –ism. In fact no one uses the word to mean what he says it would have to mean according to his logic. So when he uses scapegoat himself he is not being self-contradictory but is using the term in its normal English sense. When he says, rather dramatically, that the author's use of the word scapegoatism may lead to the collapse of the English language it is likely he is just complaining about writers who drag invalid words into their work to give it respectability but without any notion of what actually makes them invalid.

Collingwood follows the English usage himself when, like Chamberlain, he tries to blame 'the old scapegoat' (Roberts 2006: 250) Versailles for what followed rather than the guilty party, Hitler (AA 89), or when in the same book he tries to make Chamberlain the scapegoat for 'everyone else, including liberals and the British Left in this period'. As Bernard Crick says, 'That Chamberlain misled an innocent and unwilling British public about Hitler is as great a political absurdity as to think that Hitler alone misled an innocent and unwilling German public about the Nazis' (Crick 1964: 19). In fact, Collingwood thought that the first of these claims was true but that the second was, if not straightforwardly false, then superfluous to the issues at stake.

The goat in the Bible (Leviticus 16) who was allowed to escape once the sins of the people had been laid upon it had to be believed in as carrying blame which should properly have belonged to the people themselves. However, scapegoating understood as the deliberate tendency to treat people as scapegoats, as Hitler did the Jews or Stalin the kulaks, to take Collingwood's examples, attempts to hide 'motives of sectarian loyalty' (NL 16.11), as Collingwood puts it, behind a screen of false empirical evidence. And so it is important that Collingwood allows for the possibility that the attempt always to shift blame elsewhere – on an individual or an event – does not mean that that is where it is necessarily to be found.

Collingwood's rejection of any scapegoating of the German people is important for political as well as etymological reasons. Like all liberals Collingwood took the view that culpability belongs primarily to individuals rather than collectivities. There were some Germans who opposed Hitler just as there were many who supported him. Indeed, any opposition to the British policy of internment, like Collingwood's in 1940, must depend on such distinctions, or something like them. And yet Collingwood never believed, as a number of senior figures in the Church of England certainly did, that links between resistance to the Nazi regime in Germany and the regime's opponents in the world outside Germany could be made politically effective or even morally obligatory. His reasons for this are clearly spelled out in *The New Leviathan*: first, because 'there are not enough of them' (NL 45.69) and second, because the duty of resistance belongs in the first instance to the resisters themselves (NL 45.7–72). The British government itself reached this view. In a speech delivered on 16 May 1942 the Foreign Secretary, Sir Anthony Eden, came close to paralleling Collingwood's argument (NL 45.73), when he said, 'If any section of the German people really wants to see a return to a state which is based on respect for law and for the rights of the individual, they must understand that no one will believe them until they have taken active steps to rid themselves of their present regime' (as cited in von Klemperer

1992: 278–9). Variations in estimations of the practical viability of opposition within Germany crossed political boundaries. Stafford Cripps, on the Left of the Labour Party, thought that 'a German revolt was less likely' (Burridge 1976: 26), the longer the war lasted, even though he was, like his son John who was at Balliol College Oxford at the time, a friend of Adam von Trott and admired his decision to return to Germany to oppose Hitler from within (von Klemperer 1992: 279). Collingwood's pessimism in mid-1941 about the potential of the anti-Hitler movement within Germany can be read in the same light. In the summer before the outbreak of war Cripps was hopeful that 'that ordinary Germans could be disabused of their support for the Nazi regime'. Cripps, like Collingwood, thought that the Versailles Treaty had been a 'humiliation' (EPP 194), but Collingwood, unlike Cripps, thought that Versailles could not explain everything about German political developments, arguing that 'The spark in a fuse is not the sole cause of an explosion' (EPP 194), and he went much further towards Vansittartism than Cripps felt able to do. At the time when Collingwood wrote *The New Leviathan* he was convinced that any negotiations with Hitler for a compromise peace would lead nowhere and that, with military success in Europe, the German people were overwhelmingly behind their Nazi rulers. Collingwood was, in a phrase used by Leonard Woolf, a 'bitter-ender' (Leonard Woolf to William Gillies, letter dated 3 April 1942, as reprinted in Woolf 1990: 431). The war would have to be fought to a finish.

Collingwood was adapting his thinking to events. By the summer of 1941 the German grip on the mainland of Europe seemed unbreakable. German military success abroad confirmed and expressed unanimity of purpose in Germany itself. In this context the distinction between the Nazi regime and the German people as a whole, which many in Britain clung to at the start of the conflict, became increasingly difficult to maintain. The belief that the Nazi regime was a government which lacked popular support and so could be undermined from within, in these new circumstances appeared not only as hopelessly impractical but as an appeasement of Germany as a whole. As we have seen, in 1938 Collingwood was a vigorous opponent of the Chamberlain government's policy of avoiding war with Germany by appeasing its rulers. In 1940 Collingwood opposed the compromise peace which some in the British government thought unavoidable. In 1941 Collingwood warned against the defeatism involved in the belief that Germany was invincible. By mid-1940 Collingwood had come to see, with Anthony Eden, the British Foreign Secretary, whose words these are that 'Hitler is not a phenomenon but a symptom, the expression of a great part of the German nation' (as quoted in Glees 1982: 62).

Collingwood's views on the German question altered as people gradually learnt more about what they were fighting against. Collingwood associated German aggression with Prussianism, with those he called the 'ring of German war-lords' (AA 90); in the summer of 1939 he spoke of mendacity as a German trait (FML 186); in the winter he followed Chamberlain by arguing that in Germany, as in Italy and Spain, 'the vast majority of the population is sympathetic to liberal-democratic ideals and hostile to the Fascist or Nazi minority that has seized power' (EPP 191). Even so at the same time he argued alongside Vansittart (see Black Record, 6 and 9) that Nazis "'think with their blood'" (EPP 192), and that the historically weak liberal tradition in Germany had become ossified and easily broken (EPP 194), and in a lecture given on his behalf in Cambridge in May 1941, he spoke of 'the poison of Pangermanism' ('The Three Laws of Politics', EPP 222). Harold Nicolson, in a lecture he gave in London on 14 November 1939, stated that Pan-Germanism meant the doctrine that 'Germany ought to rule the world and that she would do so by the use of force' (*The Times* 15 November 1939).

After many years of thinking differently Neville Chamberlain, the political bête noir of *An Autobiography,* came to believe this too, saying that responsibility for the continuation of the war 'was now as much the German people's as their rulers' (as quoted in Glees 1982: 62). During the Blitz and while living in London, and when Chamberlain was no longer prime minister, Collingwood wrote to his wife, arguing that it was the Germans themselves who had maintained Hitler in power. He writes,

> This war, I now think, will go on until Hitler is smashed. I never believed that Hitler could long survive his first public and notorious failure. He has now had it. The attack on London is a public and notorious failure. Hitler is done for. It may be a long time before his corpse is thrown out into the street for the dogs, because the Germans are too cowed to rise against him even now when every German must know that he is heading for a crash: they are a pack of good-for-nothings, anyhow, or Hitler would never have been able to stay in the saddle since 1933: ten good Germans, if there had been ten good Germans, would have shot him years ago. I hope myself that they will go on backing him up until we drive our tanks into Berlin and dictate terms of the armistice in Potsdam or wherever you do dictate terms in or near Berlin.
> (R. G. Collingwood to Ethel Collingwood, letter dated 1 October 1940, AWOW 392)

This was a widespread view. It meant the end of any negotiation with the 'Other' or 'True' Germany, as von Klemperer writes,

The Battle of Britain ... only strengthened the determination of the new government, as well as the population at large, and had the effect of playing down the 'search for the "Good German"'. Although in the summer of 1940 Lord Halifax still presented the War Cabinet with the proposition that, with the French out of the picture, Britain could safely return to the policy line that Germany, once rid of Hitlerism, could 'take her place in a new and better Europe', ... one by one all distinctions between Germans and Nazis faded.

(von Klemperer 1992: 218)

The key issue is the allocation of blame to collectivities. In Britain at the start of the war the general belief was that the fight was with Nazism, not the German people, and that attempting to transfer responsibility for the war from Nazism to the German people as a whole was scapegoatism. When it became clear that the German people were fully involved in pursuing the war effort, then excusing them from the actions of their rulers meant little. With the focus on collective culpability some relied on metaphor, as the anti-Nazi German patriot, Adam von Trott, did on his return to Oxford, saying 'My country is very sick' (as reported in Berlin 1986: 61–2). The issues dividing von Trott from his Oxford friends were both personal and political. Von Trott's letter to *The Manchester Guardian* in February 1934 minimizing the persecution of the Jews caused great distress. The Saar plebiscite of December 1934 was also a source of division with Shiela Grant Duff arguing that it was an opportunity for expressing opposition to the German government while von Trott saw the Saar as an essential and non-negotiable part of Germany. However, when Collingwood wrote to von Trott in May 1935 after having spoken with him early in the month his tone could scarcely have been more effusive. It seems that on this occasion at least any political disagreement was playing second fiddle to friendship.

Collingwood remained in contact with the troubled German intellectual whose efforts to avoid war continued throughout the 1930s. It can be persuasively argued that Collingwood's account of duty in *The New Leviathan* embraces the search that one in von Trott's position would have to undertake. Collingwood says that the question 'what is my duty?' does not admit of an answer which is 'either conclusive or unequivocal' (NL 17.81), but which is '*morally* certain' (NL 17.81, Collingwood's italics). This might be taken to imply sympathy on Collingwood's part for someone in von Trott's circumstances, even though Collingwood's pessimism about the future of opposition to the Hitler regime from within Germany was explicit.

The affinity between Collingwood's view and the British Government's position of 'absolute silence' on any negotiation with Germany is clear. As Klemens von Klemperer explains, 'The great divide in the attitude towards the German Resistance was thus between the policies of the Chamberlain and Churchill governments. Chamberlain was still hoping for that internal stirring in Germany to allow for a negotiated peace with the "other Germany"; Churchill's preference from the very start was "absolute silence"' (von Klemperer 1992: 236), hence Collingwood's continued distrust of Chamberlain in 1940. When von Trott visited Oxford in the early summer of 1939 the terms he offered for the avoidance of war struck at least one of his old Oxford friends, Maurice Bowra, then the newly appointed Warden of Wadham College, Oxford, as asking for nothing less than appeasement, and so, in the words of his biographer, he 'chucked him out'. This was a reaction Bowra later regretted, although his rejection of von Trott's proposal was unalterable (see Bowra 1966: 305–6; Mitchell 2009: 214–18, and Inglis 2009: 207–8).

The difficulty with von Trott's proposal is explained by one recent historian of the German resistance. Talking of Ulrich von Hassell who, like von Trott, was executed by the Nazis in 1944, Richard Overy writes, 'He was one of a number of resisters who thought that Germany should be allowed to keep some of the spoils of the Hitler regime, including union with Austria, the annexation of the German-speaking areas of Czechoslovakia and a revised Polish frontier.' As a result British support for the German resistance was thought by many to be highly undesirable. Overy comments, 'It was this insistence on retaining a strong, sovereign German state that made it so difficult for the Allies to take very seriously the idea of supporting the German resistance. The Allied commitment to unconditional surrender left the German opposition with few easy options' (Overy 2011: x). Von Trott's dilemma has been well put by Patricia Meehan, 'Many of his Oxford friends expected him to repudiate his country simply because it had been taken over by Hitler's evil regime. Any right-thinking person, it was felt, would withdraw from all contact with Germany. Voluntarily to live under the system would be to endorse it. But to exile oneself from Germany unless actually in danger of death from the regime, was to stand aside from the fight merely to prove one's own integrity. The battle could not be fought from the outside: the impotence of émigrés was to become all too obvious' (Meehan 1992: 212–13).

Once war had broken out the sickness or otherwise of the German people was a less than helpful notion, with many, including Collingwood, worrying about its applicability to a country where intense patriotic feeling was widespread.

In general Collingwood's references to collectivities are unreserved, when, for instance, he talks about the Romans in Britain, or the Saxons, or, again, more contentiously, the Turks in *The New Leviathan*. However, discussion of the 'True Germany' is different. Collingwood argued that, in wartime political debate, such terminology was not descriptive but animated by 'motives of sectarian loyalty', the aims of which were to change opinion both inside and outside government. Just how disputed the meaning of 'the German people as a whole' had become is clear. Political differences over its sense and terms of reference were implicit in debates in Britain over policy towards refugees, towards peace negotiations with Germany, and, after Collingwood's death in early 1943, towards the war's conclusion and the conditions of any post-war settlement.

Collingwood believed, as Vansittart did, that the key to twentieth century German political psychology was history. But Collingwood's account of German political history in *The New Leviathan* is linked to philosophy and so operates at a level that Vansittart's polemic does not reach. Collingwood's argument is less a sophisticated version of the same position than a different kind of analysis altogether. If he had been content to say nothing more about it Collingwood's use of the term 'herd-worship' would sound a lot like Vansittartism. For Collingwood, however, though clearly not for Vansittart, terms like 'herd-worship' are used as shorthand for what is a philosophical and historical interpretation of German social and political life in its inherited and contemporary form. Central to this is the view that German political culture lacks a concept of free will (NL 19.94). Collingwood claims that no such concept exists in the German language (NL 19.94). Added to this historical thesis is the view that the German inability to develop a free civil association derives from repression. He says of the Germans, 'it is not that they lacked experience of free will; it is that they had repressed that experience ever since at least the fifteenth century at the bidding of their most popular leaders' (NL 33.58). Ripples of Collingwood's reading of Freud remain in *The New Leviathan* and operate, possibly inconsistently, alongside its historical and philosophical claims.

The New Leviathan is a philosophical account of a liberal political community which recognizes that, as an idea which is historically instantiated, the state exhibits varying degrees of estrangement from this theoretical ideal. With assistance from psychoanalysis, Collingwood's account of German politics is, in essence, the application of this way of thinking to the condition of Germany in 1941. None of this intellectual apparatus is to be found in Vansittart. What does bring Collingwood close to Vansittartism is not theoretical at all. It is a common approach to the political dilemmas existing at the time.

Read in this light the weaknesses in Laski's association of Collingwood with Vansittartism become apparent. For in describing *The New Leviathan* as an exercise in 'sophisticated Vansittartism' Laski surely wants his readers to believe that the doctrine on offer in that book remains essentially Vansittartism, as opposed to being converted by its sophistication into something else. And yet if the common ground between *The New Leviathan* and Vansittartism is not Germanophobia but a way of addressing a number of intractable political problems as they existed in 1941 then Collingwood's views can be shown in a more revealing perspective.

Many thought Vansittartism totally unacceptable no matter how sophisticated its defence, but when the view took hold that Britain's enemy was barbarism Vansittartism regained its relevance. Collingwood's belief that barbarism was doomed from within (NL 41.73) and that all barbarisms eventually turn in on themselves rests on the view that, unlike civilization whose purpose is peace, barbarism's sole aim is to use the language of Hobbes which Collingwood often deploys himself, quarrel (NL 41.76). The measures necessary for the effective prosecution of the war transfer this argument to a different stage because at issue are the permissible and practical means available to a liberal civilization when it is attacked by a state which is neither liberal nor civilized. Vansittart had clear and rather surprising views on this. Moreover, they were views which Collingwood shared.

Unlike Vansittart whose career as a high-ranking civil servant in the Foreign Office gave him a platform for his views and brought him close to the centre of government, Collingwood had no direct involvement in the making of public policy. Nor did Collingwood debate his views in public as Vansittart did extensively before and throughout the war, in the House of Lords after his elevation to the peerage in 1941, in the national press and elsewhere. One of Vansittart's more notable adversaries was Bishop George Bell, Bishop of Chichester, with whom he debated the issue of support for anti-Nazis within Germany on a number of occasions during the war. Bell argued that there are some situations in which the defence of human rights overrides the sovereignty of state boundaries. As we have seen, Collingwood disagreed, arguing that the principle of minding one's own business, as he terms it, is one 'which I, like other people, neglect at my peril' (NL 45.73).

Vansittart's views on Germany were at odds with those of the Chamberlain government, which led in January 1938 to his dismissal from the senior Foreign Office post he had held since 1930. While Vansittart was given another position he knew that he was being deliberately shunted to the margins. Even so he continued to expound his hatred of Nazi Germany together with his refusal to recognize the distinction between the German people as a whole and the Nazi movement, and he developed a wide range of contacts in the German resistance movement and among German refugees in Britain (Rose 1978: especially chapter X).

As I pointed out, common political ground with Collingwood is striking. Both held that Nazism had to be snuffed out. Both believed that this meant totally defeating Germany militarily and that there could be no compromise peace. Collingwood argues that war is justified when it is the only means to peace (NL 30.99). Such was the mass appeal of Hitler in Germany during the early years of the war, and such was the political evil at the heart of that appeal that nothing other than complete victory would do. Both saw that the anti-Nazi opposition inside Germany was too feeble to form any meaningful resistance to the regime, and both believed that German political exiles in Britain had their own political agendas and were not to be trusted. Collingwood's opinion of defeatism derives partly from the time of appeasement. In a letter to his wife, Ethel, he writes of some people he had met while in the Dutch East Indies, 'They are fascists and Hitler-worshippers, not out of conviction but out of defeatism: they are sure Hitler is going to conquer the world, and think only fools will try to stop him' (R. G. Collingwood to Ethel Collingwood, letter dated 31 December 1938, AWOW 546, RC 104).

Philosopher and politician agree that many German refugees were merely masquerading as liberal democrats. For Collingwood they represented the defeatism that threatened the British cause. For Vansittart they were anti-Nazi out of convenience while retaining the expansionist aspirations that had characterized German political thinking since before the First World War. Given Collingwood's agreement with Vansittart that opposition to Nazism within Germany is symbolized by position not mass, it is clear where he stands. This is Vansittart's application of Euclid's definition of a point to the number of 'good Germans', as he said in a debate on Germany and the Hitlerite State in the House of Lords in 1943, 'They have position, but no magnitude' (*Hansard*, HL Debates 10 March 1943, Volume 126, cc535–82, 550). Modern historians who ask why resistance to the Nazi regime was not widespread within Germany when its evil became known are rightly sceptical of what Richard J. Evans calls the 'Older explanations which looked to stereotypes of the German national character for an answer-militarism, love of violence, willingness to obey authority, desire for strong leadership, civil passivity and similar clichés of dubious validity' (Evans 2008: 118). As Evans points out, in addition to the Jewish community, there were a number of groups in Germany for whom Nazism was anathema, social democrats, communists and Catholics being especially prominent. Laski, however, calls Collingwood's Vansittartism 'sophisticated', and he is right because German barbarism is, for Collingwood, 'something historical, not something that "is" but something that "becomes"' (NL 45.22) and so in this form admits varying degrees of instantiation.

If Nazi rule appeared invincible then this was because the support of the German people made it seem so. German exile politics was, in Collingwood's phrase, a wine that does not travel (NL 45.76). Suggestions by German political exiles in Britain that 'the Germans, with the exception of a small number of fanatics, only sullenly and grudgingly accepted the regime in Berlin and would do away with it if they could', as Aaron Goldman (1979: 155) puts it, revealed for Collingwood a basic misunderstanding, he says, of 'the conditions under which that tyranny can be exercised' (NL 45.74).

Collingwood's remarks on German political refugees in Britain reflect a debate about their influence on British policy. In line with Vansittart, whose criticisms of the German Social Democratic Party in exile went deep (Goldman 1979: 171), Collingwood thought that exiled German politicians 'did a very ill service to their hosts' (NL 45.74). Such debates were often acrimonious especially in the Labour Party which, on this issue and others connected with it, was divided into pro- and anti- Vansittartist camps. William Gillies was one senior figure in the Party who adopted the Vansittartist view, at one point asking substantively, 'Why do we still make such pathetic efforts to distinguish between good and bad Germans? Surely anyone who knows anything of European history and politics must be aware that this distinction is a sheer impossibility' (Glees 1982: 34). So, as has been pointed out, 'Vansittartism split the Left' (Kramnick and Sheerman 1993: 432), with Gillies and Hugh Dalton on one side and Laski on the other. In the summer of 1941 Collingwood had come to think, as Vansittart always had and Gillies slowly and reluctantly did, that 'the Germans, as a people, were incapable of democratic behaviour' (Glees 1982: 129), and that if a civil way of life was to be brought about at all in Germany it would be only after a lengthy period of enforced tutelage. While Collingwood was writing *The New Leviathan* it was Labour Party policy 'that there was a fundamental distinction between the German people and their Nazi rulers' (Glees 1982: 106; see also 'The distinction between the Nazis and the German people remained a cardinal tenet of all official Labour pronouncements on the war until 1943, and was never relinquished by the Left wing' (Burridge 1976: 24)). As this policy came under pressure from the impact of the war the doubts about German politicians in exile which Collingwood had expressed in the summer of 1941 grew, and it was thought by a number of influential figures in the Labour Party that the views of these exiles were too nationalistic to be trustworthy.

Does this mean that on this issue we should consider Collingwood as a Labour supporting Vansittartist? Vansittartism certainly crossed party political boundaries. As one writer on the German exiles in Britain says,

> Vansittart's supporters continued to maintain that while the émigrés might well claim it was unjust to identify the German people with National Socialism, the successes of the German army and the absence of opposition to Hitler showed that the Nazis had a broad popular base and that it was a myth to make out that a handful of Nazis were subjecting the German people to a bloody dictatorship. If the 'other Germany' existed, where was it?
>
> (Palmier 2006: 614)

This was Collingwood's question exactly. Another left-inclined intellectual, one who knew Gillies well, was Leonard Woolf who, like Collingwood, was a liberal internationalist in 1914–18, and who, in the Second World War, again like Collingwood, remembered the anti-German sentiments expressed in Britain during the First World War. Woolf was never a full-blown Vansittartist, thinking, as many did, that it dealt only in half-truths, but he was prepared to agree with Collingwood, and, indeed, Vansittart, that, as he wrote in a letter to H. N. Brailsford, 'the communal psychology – and therefore history – of the German people has presented a problem since 1848 which is different from all other peoples' (Leonard Woolf to H. N. Brailsford, letter dated 17 October 1943, see Woolf 1990: 433).

In early February 1942 Vansittart laid down the principles which he believed should govern policy towards a future Germany. These included 'a prolonged occupation by the allied forces; the complete destruction of the German army; drastic control of German heavy industry; the total disarmament of Germany; and the re-education of the German people' (Rose 1978: 260). As his biographer states, 'this was the essence of Vansittartism' (Rose 1978: 260 and Collingwood follows the same political logic. And so *The New Leviathan* defends the destruction of Nazi Germany 'as a body politic, not the destruction of all its members, many of whom in spite of their political incompetence might prove capable of a useful life under the shelter of men more intelligent than themselves' (NL 30.93).

We can take Collingwood's point further. It has been argued that the Allied post-war reconstruction of Germany was based on justice, as Michael Walzer writes, 'Pending the establishment of a post-Nazi and an anti-Nazi regime, the Germans were to be placed in political tutelage: it is a consequence of their failure to overthrow Hitler themselves, the chief of the ways in which they were collectively held responsible for the injuries he and his followers caused to other nations' (Walzer 1977: 115). As Collingwood says himself, such tutelage was to be limited and temporary, its aim being, as the prime minister, Winston Churchill, emphasized at the time, the restoration of peace and German democracy. The concept which drives Collingwood's argument in *The New Leviathan* is civility, not justice, but there are occasions when their demands coincide. One such was the restraint imposed on the Allies by the policy towards Germany of 'unconditional surrender'. Essential to this, as both Churchill and Roosevelt understood, was the requirement, as Michael Walzer puts it, 'that the German people, the greater numbers of them, at any rate, must be included under the rubric of "civilization". They were entitled to the protection of civilized norms and could never have been entirely at the mercy of their conquerors' (Walzer 1977: 112). Collingwood's purpose in *The New Leviathan* is to clarify what civilization means and to ask what obligations it imposes when, as in this case, standard social and political conventions are of little use. Historical circumstances are the factors which govern Collingwood's philosophical purpose here (for the prime minister's own view of unconditional surrender see Churchill 1951: 612–19).

Unlike Laski for whom close involvement in politics was almost life itself, Collingwood's swing to radicalism in 1939 fell short of joining a political party and with it the opportunity to influence policy. His was primarily an academic voice and, as concerning public events, largely muted despite the intensity of personal feeling which marked, for example, his sympathy for China in the Sino-Japanese War (see Johnson 2013, 149–50 for discussion). Throughout the 1930s liberalism was a discredited creed. For Collingwood liberal ideals were inviolable, but something more than a shadow of this loss of faith is to be detected in his political conscience. Collingwood had never been a pacifist, but in 1936 he came to believe that the terrors of modern war were so great that few causes could justify it. The resulting dilemma was all too obvious. Collingwood's quandary was not that of Bertrand Russell who as a pacifist thought that the appeasers had a strong case (for discussion see Monk 2000: 241–2), but it was a version of it. Communists attempted to square the circle by seeing war as a function of capitalism, offering a socialist future as one worth fighting for. (As A. J. P. Taylor remembers it, in Oxford student politics during the 1930s it was the red flag which ruled. He writes, 'The university labour club, being at the time under communist domination, opposed support for Finland and was duly disaffiliated from the national Labour party' Taylor 1983: 151.) Collingwood, however, though at one time prepared to voice a brief supporting cheer, soon set these views aside. Indeed, as the evil of Nazism became apparent Collingwood came to see, as Russell did in the summer of 1940 (Monk 2000: 241–2), that the war was necessary and, given the nature of the enemy, would have to be fought to a finish.

In *The New Leviathan* Collingwood re-examines the Peace Ballot organized by the League of Nations Union in June 1935, and he rejects, as the great majority of its responses did, both militarism and pacifism, together with the wished for, but hardly practicable alternatives of world disarmament and internationalism. At that time Collingwood had little faith in the League and he thought rearmament was less a sensible political policy than a sign of madness. In 1940, however, with all the advantages of hindsight, Collingwood accused Baldwin of having 'steered the country into a war which he rightly regarded as the inevitable outcome of his action' (NL 30.45). But the circumstances of 1940 in which Collingwood was writing were not at all those of 1936. In 1936 it was the strength of France (whose defeat in 1940 no one, including Collingwood, expected) which acted as an obstacle to accommodation with Germany. Baldwin's strategy during the mid-1930s for dealing with the dictators can be credibly presented as both rational and coherent. That it crumbled to pieces had more to do with 'Germany's "mad-dog" threat to European peace' (Kershaw 2004: 187); as Baldwin said in April 1936, 'With two lunatics like Mussolini and Hitler you can never be sure of anything. But I am determined to keep the country out of war' (as quoted in Kershaw 2004: 187).

Collingwood's accusation that Baldwin lacked leadership was similar to the charge Churchill made at the time. But there is an important difference. Collingwood, unlike Churchill for whom, as a practical politician, this way of speaking would have been political suicide, came close to saying that in 1935 it was the pacific instincts of the British people which undermined policies to stop the dictators in their tracks (NL 30.4). No one in Britain in 1935 wanted war. Both main political parties went to considerable lengths to tell the people the obvious untruth that collective security was able to stop war while at the same time preventing territorial aggression. The British Labour Party, in Piers Brendon's words, wanted 'Britain to act as a policeman of the world while refusing to provide either helmet or truncheon' (Brendon 2000: 360). Collingwood's views on rearmament at that time were little different, leaving him with the worst of both worlds, accepting in Hobbesian fashion that all states had the right to arm themselves against attack, but then describing the armaments themselves, in the psychoanalytical language favoured by progressives at the time, as a sure sign of neurosis. There is no doubt that Collingwood understood the weaknesses of internationalism, but when others in Britain, particularly after 1936, were coming to the view that whatever the risks, an increasing pace of British rearmament was unavoidable for strategic reasons, if not for all-out war, he held back.

Vansittart, like Collingwood, had little faith in the League, and he thought that British indecision served merely to encourage German expansionism, but, unlike Collingwood, he did speak plainly about the need for rearmament in Britain, particularly air power. As British policy in the late 1930s foundered in the face of German duplicity and intransigence Vansittart's public warnings increased, even as his governmental influence weakened. By the time of the writing of *The New Leviathan*, with the failure of appeasement now complete and with Germany under Hitler revealing its monstrousness, Vansittartism came to mean not merely a set of personal political beliefs but a doctrine that many in Britain, including Collingwood, thought true.

Does Collingwood's Vansittartism weaken his liberalism? Liberalism establishes human rights and duties independent of race, nationality and history. National stereotyping should be anathema to liberals, even if, as Collingwood clearly thought, there was evidence for it. At the time *The New Leviathan* was being written we saw that the German people showed little dissension from policies that supported the glorification of the Reich and the extension of its rule across Europe. However, what was at issue in the Second World War was the protection of a liberal way of life, not just from those whose background, upbringing and training might have made them incapable of that life or even antipathetic to it, but from evil. And Collingwood believed that evil must be resisted, even if, in the course of that fight, 'hard choices between relative evils' (Reynolds 2004: 110) have to be made.

It can be argued that Collingwood's terminology in *The New Leviathan* undermines his liberalism. Just war theory enshrines just practice as well as just cause. Just practice requires that a state at war makes every reasonable effort to distinguish between combatant and non-combatant. A civilized state should follow these norms. But this cuts across the distinction between civilized and barbarian. We pointed out earlier that Collingwood saw the Germans as the Fourth Barbarism. Does this mean that all Germans were combatants and so from a military point of view to be treated indiscriminately? Or does it mean that in facing up to barbarism no civilized state can abandon the just war distinctions on which liberalism depends? I think we know where Collingwood stands. He writes 'A degree of force is inevitable in human life; but being civilized means cutting it down, and becoming more civilized means cutting it down still further' (NL 39.15).

War did not, Collingwood believed, abolish liberal values, even though it permitted their temporary suspension. In his Hobhouse Lecture, still banging his anti-Chamberlain drum, he accused the former prime minister of having lied to the British people so as to avoid a war which might easily be lost (TLP 214). In this Collingwood was being provocative. The facts about the existence of concentration camps in Germany, together with the persecution of the Jews and opponents of the regime, were at the time Collingwood was talking about extensively publicized in the press and elsewhere; also any concealment of the truth by the Chamberlain government would then have served little purpose, and in fact when in power Chamberlain did have a policy of rearmament. On hearing that Arnaldo Momigliano had been forced from his Professorship in Turin for being Jewish, Collingwood wrote from the Dutch East Indies to his wife, Ethel, asking, 'How long will it be before Hitler tells Mr. Chamberlain that all Jews must be driven out of jobs in England?' (R. G. Collingwood to Ethel Collingwood, letter dated 27 January 1939, James, AWOW 546, RC 104; for further evidence and discussion of Collingwood's view, see Johnson 2013: 149). A slightly more sympathetic view of Chamberlain states that 'his concern with Anglo-German relations shaped his response to the persecution of the Jews. He was not averse to showing the Germans that their policies were isolating them, but he wished to develop good relations with amenable elements in Germany. He was prepared to show distaste for anti-Jewish persecution' (London 2000: 106–7).

When the Soviet Union became an ally in the war against Germany yet more severe moral compromises were called for. In his lecture Collingwood agreed with Laski over the causes of liberalism's decline (TLP 213). Laski's lecture does not refer to Green's famous description of the Russian state under the Tsar as a state 'by courtesy only' (EPP 213, where the reference in Green is to be found), a point of view which Collingwood in his Lecture analyses at some length (TLP 212–16). Nevertheless both take issue with the optimism they find in Green's philosophy of history and both claim that the main weakness of liberalism is that, as Laski puts it, 'When Green rejected the view that force is the basis of the state, he refused to look the facts in the face' (Laski (1940), 13) or, as Collingwood puts it, 'Freedom is certainly part of the name "body politic". But it is not the whole of it. That is what is wrong with Liberalism as a political doctrine' (TLP 214). Collingwood goes further than Laski by charging Green with confusing practical with scientific terminology. Collingwood also says that he wishes to explain the decline of liberalism in his own words but he has his own reasons, and these are sometimes quite different from Laski's, most notably when Green is rebuked for following the purportedly German practice of identifying the state with the 'body politic' as a whole.

Laski believed that the war was fought not against the German people as a whole but against their Nazi rulers, believing that Vansittartism was unable to supply the imperative the times needed. Collingwood was a defender of Vansittartism in all but name. However, while the war remained to be won such differences over the nature of the German national character appeared to at least one significant figure as secondary. As the prime minister Winston Churchill said in a letter to Laski in the spring of 1942, 'we ought to win the war first, and then in a free country the issues of Socialism and Free Enterprise can be fought out in a constitutional manner' (Martin 1953: 153).

Vansittartism certainly troubled people in Britain during the early years of the Second World War, but when it was realized that Britain's fight was not against the Nazi Party alone then judgements about collectivities such as the German people became unavoidable. Collingwood was never a secular liberal, for whom religious beliefs have no automatic priority. Like that of the Old Testament prophets who were unafraid of castigating whole peoples as warlike or sinful Collingwood's language is often robust. When the Assyrians are described in the Bible as barbarians, having destroyed 'all lands utterly' (Isaiah 37, 11), it is not totally impossible that amidst the violence there were a few good Assyrians trying to make their protests heard. The first of the four epigrams which the historian William L. Shirer chose to preface his book, *The Rise and Fall of the Third Reich*, is taken from Goethe. It reads, 'I have often felt a bitter sorrow at the thought of the German people, which is so estimable in the individual and so wretched in the generality' (Shirer 1960: preface). Collingwood believed that with such a people as your enemy it is the rule and not the exception that counts. 'War', he writes, 'serves the cause of peace, and is therefore politically justified, when it is the only available method of discouraging a people from pursuing abroad an aggressively belligerent policy, the natural extension of the tyranny to which they are accustomed at home, and forcing them to realize that the only way to prosperity at home is through peace abroad' (NL 30.99).

Part Three

A new beginning

10

Civility and the claims of justice

War is the immediate context for *The New Leviathan*, but even when peace was far from assured a demand for social justice was emerging in Britain which, with the war's end and a Labour government in power, would transform the British way of life for generations to come. For a state facing barbarism, Collingwood thought that civility is a bedrock value, but for aspirations of a very different order it seemed that a political standard with greater imperative power was needed.

It is more than tempting to interpret *The New Leviathan* as reflecting the liberal aspirations of its age. Questions such as whether or not its arguments fall short and if so by how much, or whether they lag behind such aims and ambitions, follow naturally from this way of thinking. I have asked similar questions myself on more than one occasion. But Collingwood thinks of the history of philosophy as a conversation. Theories of justice are one of the many topics which the conversation is about. From this perspective Collingwood's idea of civility is a voice in its own right, one that stands to other theories as an intelligible and credible alternative, one which can be accepted, corrected or rejected, but not ostracized solely because it belongs to the past. In this sense Collingwood's arguments concerning civility and social justice are contemporary with ours, as his conception of history teaches and his conception of philosophy always maintained, and my discussion of social and economic equality follows this general view. In this chapter I look in close detail at Collingwood's defence of civility, particularly in relation to the idea of social justice.

Contemporary liberals argue that a community cannot be counted liberal if it practises civility in the absence of justice. And yet in *The New Leviathan* Collingwood barely speaks about justice. Is Collingwood saying that a society that practises civility does not need a concept of justice? Or is it that a society that lacks civility cannot be just? There is a straightforward answer if what Collingwood means by civility is good manners. A society that places a high value on civility as politeness may also be exploitative, unjustifiably discriminatory and indifferent to the existence of wide inequalities between rich and poor. Similarly, it would be odd to think of an occasional incivility, say, showing off and thereby causing embarrassment to others, as a serious obstacle to justice.

So if civility is understood as a feature of good manners liberals do not need to apologize for elevating justice above it. However, civility as Collingwood understands it has an importance that takes it beyond courtesy or politeness. To treat another with civility, Collingwood writes, 'means respecting his feelings: abstaining from shocking him, annoying him, frightening him, or (briefly) arousing in him any passion or desire which might diminish his self-respect' (NL 35.41). It is, Collingwood writes, 'respect for others as shown in demeanour towards them' (NL 37.15). So, to treat others with civility means, in a positive sense, to attend to them, to notice or to take consideration of them; in a negative sense, to refrain from interference, insult or harm.

It is instructive to compare Collingwood's views with those of influential liberals. For example, John Rawls, like Collingwood, understands civility as a species of respect. Individuals in a just society have a duty to 'treat each other civilly and to be willing to explain the grounds of their actions, especially when the claims of others are over-ruled' (Rawls 1973: 179). Civility for Rawls, however, is a natural duty and not a reliable model for justice as Rawls portrays it. He writes, 'Whereas there are various principles of natural duty, all obligations arise from the principle of fairness' (Rawls 1973: 342–3). The principles of justice create obligations because individuals freely choose them as rational ways of distributing primary goods, whereas natural duties 'apply to us without regard to our voluntary acts' (Rawls 1973: 114). And yet in Rawls' account, civility understood as respect for others is not a contingent consequence of justice as fairness. It comes about necessarily through the description of individuals as free and equal and through the requirement to actively acknowledge the self-understandings of those who do not share a single conception of the good. There is, in other words, a close connection between justice and civility that is not found between, for example, justice and affection. So for Rawls, in the absence of justice civility must lose its status as a virtue.

For the Rawlsian liberal, civility and justice differ in terms of both subject and scope. For example, Rawls considers that caste societies are morally anachronistic because their lack of justice undermines their civility. Treating another civilly hardly qualifies as a virtue when it derives from the belief, as Rawls writes, that each person 'is held to be equally fated and equally noble in the eyes of providence' (Rawls 1973: 547). Similarly, civility by itself cannot guarantee that a given distribution of resources is just. To say that force and fraud play no part in the ways resources are distributed falls a long way short of demonstrating that such ways are just.

In Rawls's view a commitment to justice as fairness arises in order to satisfy the requirement of impartiality: the need, in other words, to remain neutral between different conceptions of the good. Moral philosophy, in Rawls's understanding, aims to construct a 'social point of view that all can accept' (Rawls 1980: 519). Rawls thinks of individuals as bound in two main ways: either by self-incurred obligations or by natural duty. The natural duties of civility apply to all individuals irrespective of their consent. Thus I could not defend myself against a charge of cruelty by saying that I had never agreed to abstain from it. For Collingwood, civility means refraining from diminishing another's self-respect. Civility prohibits the unconditional use of force: it encompasses the need to respect others and the projects they pursue, in addition to the mutual recognition of rights and duties. Civility, too, implies a willingness to reach agreement, a preparedness to conciliate and adjust in contacts with others. However, in the vocabulary of Rawls's liberalism it is hard to see civility in either of these senses as being anything other than a restraint rather than an injunction. To the Rawlsian liberal, a commitment to fairness means even-handedness in the derivation of the principles of justice and in their application. For Rawls, the principles of justice derive from a notional agreement entered into under conditions which 'situate free and equal persons fairly and must not allow some persons greater bargaining advantages than others' (Rawls 1973: 139). This kind of liberal will think of civility as a moral disposition that is of vital assistance in the execution of justice but as no substitute for the principles of justice themselves.

Collingwood does not recognize the concept of natural duty. This means that he cannot use natural duty as a basis for putting civility and justice in different logical compartments. More importantly, Collingwood describes injustice as a wrong because it is a breach of civility. Thus he writes of a particular case of economic injustice that 'the existence of a contrast between rich and poor is an offence against civility' (NL 38.74). Rawls insists that civility alone cannot generate principles of justice. Collingwood understands civility as an ideal to which existing societies are always approximate. So, while a specific economic injustice may be thought an offence because it breaches civility as an ideal, for Collingwood, 'it is not necessarily an offence against a particular civilization' (NL 38.75). It is precisely to avoid this state of affairs that Rawls understands the business of moral philosophy as the construction of a 'social point of view that all can accept' (Rawls 1980: 519).

Collingwood's writings on politics and economics are safely thought of as liberal, but they are not libertarian. Collingwood wishes to give priority to freedom, but he does not do so in the name of justice. It is civility which sustains a liberal way of life. Civility prohibits the unconditional use of force so encompassing the mutual recognition of rights and duties which liberalism values. Whereas libertarians argue that civilly conducted economic transactions are automatically just Collingwood wishes to qualify the market's freedom, but how can he do this if he has nothing but civility to fall back on?

Libertarians argue that justice in buying and selling, saving and investing, employing and being employed depends entirely on their voluntariness. Once force is excluded from the market, including the force involved in the redistribution of resources from rich to poor, then the market's internal logic can be left to operate on its own terms. Market relationships are self-regulating. Any imbalances will work themselves out.

Against libertarians Collingwood separates civility from justice. Civility serves to prohibit force and fraud (NL 35.41) and excludes the forms of disrespect. By contrast, justice is a distributive virtue. Civility and justice differ both in subject and scope. To say that force and fraud play no part in the ways resources are distributed is a long way short of saying that such ways are just. Similarly, societies that value civility can be to various degrees unjust. What this means is that Collingwood cannot speak about justice under the rubric of civility. Is there, then, in Collingwood's liberalism a compelling means of judging economic and social relationships in terms of justice?

A first thought is that the understanding of justice which best fits Collingwood's inquiry is justice as fidelity (I take this classification from Barry 1989: 466). The keeping of agreements freely entered into and the exclusion of force and fraud are commonsense requirements of justice understood on the model of promise-keeping or law-abidingness. So when Collingwood wishes to condemn the wages of 'sweated labour' on the grounds of their injustice he does so not by a theory of a social wage but by asking the law to erase the circumstances in which 'sweated labour' arises. In other words, Collingwood's first move is towards a theory of the state and a theory of political obligation rather than a theory of justice which sets principles for institutions and individuals to follow. However, justice as fidelity is no guarantee of justice as fairness since it is not difficult to think of agreements freely made which are nevertheless unfair. Collingwood himself speaks of bargains which although freely struck are best not entered into. Civility, in other words, is not sufficient protection against injustice. Hobbes who is Collingwood's guiding hand in *The New Leviathan* is made of sterner stuff.

For Hobbes, the idea of justice as fidelity – the keeping of voluntary agreements – is the only possible conception of justice. So commutative justice requires that exchanges between individuals concern items of equal value, but in Hobbes's view there is no judge of value beyond the appetites of the parties to the exchange. Hobbes writes, 'the value of all things contracted for, is measured by the Appetite of the Contractors: and therefore the just value is that which they are contented to give' (Hobbes 1651: 98). So market value is the only possible value, and economic justice is reduced to the price that the respective parties are willing to pay. Similarly, Hobbes denies that distributive justice can be understood independently of the market. He writes, 'the Value or Worth of a man, is of all other things, his Price, that is to say, so much as would be given for the use of his Power' (Hobbes 1651: 57). Any actual distribution must be just as it stands because there is no test of worth in economic relations outside the market.

Both Hobbes and Collingwood stress justice as fidelity, but Collingwood rejects Hobbes's stark individualism, so implying that there must be more to the measure of value than simply the verdicts of the market. Collingwood defends the distinction between economics, morality and politics as different spheres of activity and, by contrast with Hobbes, he does not believe that appetite is the sole determinant of value. His problem arises because the conception of justice as fidelity is not an adequate test of the just exchange and distribution of goods. This means that Collingwood needs a conception of justice which does not merely validate existing distributions of opportunities and resources but assesses them in the light of principles independently agreed.

In short, Collingwood needs a theory of social justice (for material on social justice relevant to this chapter I have used Miller 1976; Miller and Walzer 1995; Boucher 1998 and Barry 2005). He does so because no liberal theory of justice can address the distribution of human resources in economic terms alone. On this account the goods distributed by justice include the economic goods of income and wealth, but they also include educational opportunities and welfare provision neither of which can be explained solely in the language of supply and demand. However, Collingwood's stress on civility as the absence of force makes it look as if he is unwilling to give human opportunities and powers the same priority as human rights and duties, a move which, if true, would heavily circumscribe any construction of a theory of social justice, one which is consistent with civility but also covers substantially different ground. Similarly, it would be hard for Collingwood to repay his debt to Ruskin without acknowledging the role of many-sidedness in human self-development, in art and craft as well as in agriculture and industry, in the construction of social ideals.

Where, then, in Collingwood's political philosophy are we to look for a theory of social justice? Collingwood wrote no single treatise on justice. Discussion of Collingwood's own political opinions is a poor starting point because in none of these are the principles of social justice laid out in a consistent form, nor do they address the questions of method that the construction of a theory of social justice must involve. Thus, Collingwood's support for the social legislation of Asquith's first administration (see *AA* 156; for discussion see Cowling 1980: 184–8 and Collini 2006: 344–7), New Liberal though much of its legislative programme was, tells us little about how a philosophical justification for social justice might be mounted. Can we draw from Collingwood's liberal political philosophy enough by way of argument, subject matter and method to say that it contains the theory of social justice that his rejection of libertarianism requires?

In looking for a theory of social justice we are asking for a concept of justice that is more demanding and more contentious than the usual sense of justice as the fair or balanced treatment of different and often competing claims. Social justice concerns the distribution of benefits and burdens in society in accordance with principles agreed under conditions of impartiality. Whereas our ordinary conceptions of justice apply readily to individuals and their actions in treating like cases alike and in prohibiting contract breaking, the aim of social justice is more comprehensive. The principles of social justice are formulated neither as a response to egotism nor saintliness but to the need for fairness in the distribution of the goods we value. Social justice concerns the distribution of benefits and burdens among individuals and groups of individuals in a given society where no deliberate wrongdoing is involved. A theory of social justice takes a considered view of the nature of the goods to be distributed together with the method of their distribution. So, in the liberal formulation of John Rawls, principles of justice as fairness express our respect for each other as equals in the distribution of basic social goods. Civil and political liberties are to be distributed equally so that each individual enjoys the most extensive liberty compatible with the liberty of others. Opportunities are to be open to all on the basis of merit. Income and wealth are to be distributed equally, unless an unequal division can be shown to provide maximum benefit to the least well-off (see Rawls 1972, hereafter referred to as TJ), and see the useful summary of the whole argument in Rawls 2001 (hereafter referred to as JF).

While it would be a mistake to think of Collingwood as labouring in Rawls's shadow there are aspects of Rawls's theory which Collingwood would surely have found appealing (for discussion of points of contrast and comparison between Collingwood and Rawls, see Vincent 1995: 134–5; McIntyre 1996: 118–23 and Boucher 1992: xli–xlii, where Boucher writes, 'Collingwood's understanding of the social contract is set in the context of a theory of society and civilization which precludes gross disparities in the riches of individual members. In other words, the principles of sociality and civility, which are one and the same, *entail* a socially just distribution of wealth;' my italics). Rawls does not think of the basic structure of a fair society as the best deal available to rational calculators who each seek as much as they can get. Collingwood would have agreed. Rawls seeks to counter the social damage produced by envy and free-riding by linking basic social goods with respect. Collingwood would have agreed with that too, but where Rawls moves on to argue for the distribution of basic social goods in line with principles of justice Collingwood's focus of attention is civility. Collingwood and Rawls are also at one about the priority of politics over economics. 'Civilization in the economic sense, therefore, whether the economic activity in question is production or exchange, is not definable in economic terms', Collingwood writes (NL 508), a distinction that is heavily reinforced by the theory of practical reason that Collingwood defends. Rawls, if not in quite the same manner, also distinguishes between the workings of just constitutions and the processes of the market. Economic theory is not a good model for political philosophy. Matters of political economy are subject to the criteria embodied in the basic structure of justice as fairness (TJ 360–1).

We should not think that whereas Collingwood's liberalism is grounded in civility and not justice Rawls, by contrast, says a great deal about justice and nothing about civility. The principles of justice that Rawls defends are addressed to individuals who do not share a single conception of the good. Primary goods which are essential to the quality of life are distributed in accordance with the principles of justice as fairness. But some goods take the form of ideals which are irreducibly plural and so do not attract automatic or universal assent. A forum is needed in which such commitments can be discussed, and Rawls argues in defence of a domain of public reason in which individual citizens and legislators have a 'duty of civility' to address fundamental issues in ways that satisfy the requirements of openness and reciprocity (JF 90–2; see also Rawls 1993: 212–20). But civility understood as a natural duty does not displace the obligations derived from the principles of justice as fairness. Quite the opposite, in fact, since civility in the absence of justice would scarcely qualify as a virtue at all.

The stress on agreement reached by reasonable individuals through open and free discussion is common to both Collingwood and Rawls. Indeed, Collingwood makes much of the idea of a well-ordered society in which individuals engage in dialectical debate (NL 24.59 and 28.18). But the acid test of liberalism is not the erasure of force alone. What is important about justice is that the removal of force is not always sufficient to achieve it. Thus, there is a recognizable sense in which contracts freely entered into may still be thought unfair even though the parties to them have given their agreement voluntarily (see Barry 1989: 467). Further, we should not think that principles governing the allocation of social goods simply fall out of the descriptions we give of them (I owe this felicitous expression to Brian Barry; see his 'Spherical Justice and Global Injustice', in Miller and Walzer 1995: 72). While a great deal can be said about the character of healthcare or education as individual goods their just distribution covers different and independent ground.

A test for the existence of a theory of economic justice in Collingwood's writings should reflect the kind of priority Collingwood as a liberal political philosopher gives to economics, morality and politics understood as distinct activities, each operating under the appropriate terms and constraints. A theory of economic justice, then, presupposes a theory of social justice, and a theory of social justice presupposes a theory of entitlement. For liberal political philosophers entitlements stem from agreement and agreement flows from individuals whose status as free and rational beings qualifies them uniquely for a communal life. To find the theory of economic justice we are looking for we should expect from Collingwood, first, an account of the distinguishing features of economic activity in order to give the theory distinctive subject matter; second, a theory of justice expressed in moral as opposed to economic terms, and, third, an account of the principles which would make specific allocations just.

The term which best captures the nature of economic activity, in Collingwood's view, is exchange (EPS 8 and EPP 95-6). By exchange Collingwood does not simply mean the exchange of this for that, say, of a loaf of bread for a glass of beer. What Collingwood stresses is the relation between means and ends that exchange involves. Thus, exchanging the bread is the means of obtaining the beer. Further, it is only because I specifically want the beer that I am prepared to give up the bread. Equally, I would not specifically give up the bread unless by doing so I received the beer. Economic activity is end directed. Means are important only insofar as they deliver the end in the most economical way. Thus, if I could obtain the beer by cheaper means I would do so by exchanging something I valued less. Collingwood thinks of exchange as the essential vehicle for economic relationships, but reciprocity too figures, although only through the relation between means and other people's ends. Thus, when I exchange my bread for your beer the bread which is a means to me becomes for you the end to be satisfied, and this is also true in reverse; the beer which is a means to you becomes for me the end (EPP 64–6).

Economic relationships involve cooperation, but it is not the cooperation of friends. My reciprocation of the exchange is bound up with the value I place on wanting the beer, as your reciprocation is with wanting the bread. If one or other of us decides that the means of obtaining the end we want is too expensive then the transaction either does not take place or we search for a new basis on which to conduct it. In other words, for Collingwood, economic value is determined by the market (EPP 67). What individuals are prepared to pay emerges from the exchanges they engage in. At this stage Collingwood has said nothing about how goods might be distributed independently of voluntary transactions. Utility value is understood entirely in individual terms, and Collingwood makes no attempt to assess outcomes either by aggregation or by testing them against an ideal pattern of distribution. Economic motivation is confined to instrumental gain. Where moral considerations enter in, as they might when you need my bread rather than choosing to exchange your beer for it or settling for such an exchange then, as Collingwood comments, it is open to me to give you the bread as a free gift (EPP 68). But then all issues of relative cost drop out since with gifts nothing is purchased or sold, and so there is no price. And yet the language of gifts does not square with the language of need since need is suggestive of entitlement, whereas gifts are gifts because all sense of entitlement is lacking.

Collingwood's stress on the voluntary character of economic exchange tells us a great deal about his liberalism. Some cases of economic exchange are about indifference as well as the satisfaction of desire. Thus, while you may specifically want my bread I may be indifferent between the beer and the cider that you are willing to trade for it. Equally, you may be indifferent between beer and cider as a means so long as one or other delivers my bread. In Collingwood's understanding of economic transactions the presence of indifference does not affect their character. It is sufficient that exchange is conducted civilly, that is in the absence of force. But in distributive exchanges where issues of justice are at stake we do not treat indifference as a reasonable option since their treatment in relation to others matters to individuals and justice is stringent in its demands. The differences between justice and civility are now readily apparent. Whereas I can be indifferent in my choice of goods and in my treatment of others and remain civil, indifference and a sense of justice do not sit easily together. We expect just treatment and just distribution to be impartial, but we do not expect either to be indifferent to the outcomes they produce.

Collingwood discusses economic justice under the headings of just price and the distinction between riches and wealth. Both owe a debt to Christian and British Idealist views (for discussion of British Idealism and Christianity in the period see Sell 1995). In defending the idea of just price in modern market conditions Collingwood again tells us much about the liberalism he supports (EPP 68–71; NL 38.65). From the start Collingwood's defence is less to do with the injustice of the price than with its incivility. Thus, an unjust price is not one that is disproportionate to the value of the goods exchanged, as the medieval doctrine of the just price requires, but one which the purchaser is forced into accepting. However, prices can be disproportionate to the seller's costs, and even to the value of the goods, without purchasers necessarily feeling constrained into paying them. In other words, the distinction that Collingwood is most concerned to protect is not between a just and an unjust price, or a willing seller and an unwilling buyer, Collingwood's 'pseudo-bargain' (NL 38.67), but between the domain of the market price and law. So when Collingwood speaks about a just wage, wages, in Collingwood's view, being a special case of prices, he limits control of wages by law to ensuring 'fair bargaining' and 'amending the condition of society' (EPP 69–70).

Traditional theories of just price are relatively narrow in scope, but they do contain the elements of proportionality that the common sense understanding of justice requires. A just price should reflect a balanced distribution of gain between buyer and seller as well as producing a benefit to the community affected by the exchange. Raising prices to take advantage of a temporary scarcity would be judged unfair. However, in Collingwood's interpretation it is not the unfairness itself which is the basis for law, but the restriction of freedom involved. Just price theory operates on the borders of more entrenched systems of value. It asks that gains be moderate in relation to the standards of the community, but it tells us little about what these should be. Collingwood expresses just price theory in terms of his account of civility, but he is aware that in communities marked by severe disparities between rich and poor just price theory is insufficient.

Collingwood's discussion of wealth is a part of his account of civilization, and so a civilized economy will aim at a balance between production and consumption. It will not attempt to artificially stimulate demand nor will it treat money as a commodity which causes financial instability and lack of trust. It will be as much concerned with balanced distribution as with production, and it will not allow private overconsumption to displace a proper concern with the public good. How, if at all, does Collingwood's distinction between wealth and riches meet the requirement that in a just society wealth, as a primary good in Rawls's terminology (TJ 90–5), should be distributed in accordance with principles of justice?

Collingwood's distinction between wealth and riches is set out in *The New Leviathan* and 'What 'Civilization' Means' (NL 38.3–4, 503–9). There are discrepancies between the two accounts, and so I shall describe both before moving on to an assessment. What we find is a double distinction. First, wealth is a comparative term, riches a relative one. Second, wealth is primarily a feature of communities, riches of individuals. Thus, if communities are wealthy then individuals are wealthy, but only as members of the community. By contrast, if individuals are rich then the community can be rich only in relation to poorer communities.

Collingwood amplifies both distinctions. Comparative terms involve an independent standard which may be met or not. Thus, 'this dinner is good' or 'this community is wealthy' is decided by reference to the appropriate standard. A relative term, by contrast, can be defined only in relation to itself. Thus, 'this car is fast' does not imply that a standard speed has been met, only that the car is fast in relation to others which are slower. Some terms can be both comparative and relative, but wealth necessarily involves a standard and so is exclusively comparative. In any given community it is the level of wealth which forms the standard. Thus, it is perfectly possible for the standard to be reached by every individual member of the community, if, for example, wealth is distributed evenly between them.

Collingwood thinks of riches as a purely relative term. Thus, an individual is rich only in relation to others who are poor. Moreover, a relation between rich and poor is an economic relation. So rich and poor stand to each other as buyers and sellers. But buyers and sellers form a single community; therefore, Collingwood argues, in that community riches will always be unequal, the rich being rich in the same degree as the poor are poor. In this relation the rich get richer in proportion to the poor becoming poorer. Thus, the relation between rich and poor is one between the strong and the weak. It is, in Collingwood's words, 'a relation of power' and, as such, undermines civility.

In 'What "Civilization" Means' the account of riches is substantially the same as that in *The New Leviathan*. However, wealth in 'What "Civilization" Means' is not defined as a comparative but a relative term (NL 504). So both wealth and riches are relational, but whereas riches are a relation between a dominant economic force and a weak one, wealth is a relation between expenditure and needs. To be wealthy 'is to be in possession of the means to satisfy your needs'. Wealth implies that a balance exists between income and the satisfaction of need. Relationships involving wealth, therefore, are distinct from relationships involving riches since they lack the element of compulsion that the latter necessarily involve. Further, if it is this element which makes relationships involving rich and poor unfair, and relationships based on wealth necessarily lack it, Collingwood concludes that free exchange must also be fair. So, Collingwood sums up his argument, 'riches imply poverty, but wealth does not' (NL 505).

The distinction between wealth and riches is important because Collingwood believes that it allows him to combine Adam Smith's laissez-faire economics with Christian theology as applied to economic life. Smith's optimism derives from his talking not about riches but wealth, and the Christian condemnation of avarice derives not from the pursuit of wealth but of riches. Camels do not pass through the eyes of needles any more than the rich have a place in the Kingdom of God. On the other hand, the wealthy through productive manufacture and exchange enhance the wealth of all. Theft, misappropriation and games of chance may deliver riches to some, but they can never be sources of wealth.

What should we make of the distinction between wealth and riches? It looks as if Collingwood is attempting to have the best of both worlds by describing the Marxist analysis of economic exploitation in terms of riches and the capitalist theory of economic growth in terms of wealth. However, Collingwood's problems begin at a much earlier stage of his argument. In fact, they start with his terms and definitions. A relative term requires only a contrast with its own correlative. On this basis we can say, for example, computer B's speed of access to the internet is fast only in relation to computer C's which is slower. If computer A's speed is greater than computer B's then the same analysis applies. And, yet, it would be odd to say that computer A's speed of access was the cause of B's being slower or of C's being slower still. In other words, we can talk about relative speeds without talking about cause and effect. Further, there is nothing in Collingwood's terminology which would prevent us averaging speed of access, so computer B could then be described as fast in relation to computer C and slow in relation to computer A, but average in relation to all.

Collingwood's point is that the rich are rich only in relation to those who are poor, but this is very far from saying that the poor are poor only because of the rich. Similarly, Collingwood is favouring his own case by saying that the rich are rich only in relation to the poor because the poor might be poor only in relation to the average. In other words, the language of relative terms lacks a normative reference and is, in any case, highly equivocal.

Here we can help Collingwood's argument out a little. In 'What "Civilization" Means' Collingwood describes both riches and wealth as relative terms. But what is clear is that on Collingwood's own account of wealth it is not a relative term like riches. Wealth, Collingwood says, 'is the possession of means to satisfy your needs' (NL 504). Rich is a relative term which is assessed along one axis, so car A is fast only in relation to car B which is slower. Individual A is rich only in relation to individual B who is poor, and so on. And yet, in Collingwood's account of it, wealth is not assessed on one axis but two, possessions and the needs they satisfy. Thus, unlike riches, it is not only in relation to others that wealth is assessed. Collingwood is right to distinguish wealth from riches, but his description of wealth as a relational term weakens his case. There is a relational sense of wealth which we apply by means of the adjectival description 'wealthy' to those whose command over the resources needed for the achievement of their ends is very great. Used in this way, 'wealthy' is a relational term like 'rich' so that one is wealthy only in relation to those who are less so, but it is clear that there is a meaning of wealth which rises above this relational sense, and it is this that Collingwood is trying to capture when he describes wealth as a comparative term, that is one involving a standard.

Collingwood's distinction between wealth and riches expresses his belief that wealth is essentially communal in character. By this Collingwood does not mean that the wealth in a community needs to be owned communally. Almost the reverse is true since Collingwood describes an individual as wealthy when 'income, be it large or small, balances his expenditure' (NL 504–5). Mr. Micawber would have approved. In much the same vein Collingwood identifies wealth creation and fairness with free exchange. In the light of this, Collingwood's downgrading of public and associational sources of wealth seems less strange. For Collingwood's working assumption is that voluntary economic exchange is wealth creating and so benefits all. By contrast, riches 'constitute a kind of force exercised by the rich over the poor' (NL 503), and so benefit only the rich.

Inequalities in wealth and riches are subjects of a theory of social justice, but in Collingwood's treatment wealth and riches relate to justice in different ways. In Collingwood's picture riches necessarily produce poverty, but they are an affront not to justice but to freedom. Wealth creates more wealth but gives justice no work to do. In other words, Collingwood's account of riches links him to Marx while his account of wealth protects his liberalism. However, social conflict arises from the unequal distribution of riches and wealth, a point which Collingwood's definitions obscure. So when Collingwood asserts that the distinction between wealth and riches holds independently of the levels of each he is, in effect, evading the issue since it is with the nature and extent of such discrepancies that a theory of social justice is concerned.

When we ask Collingwood for a definition of wealth then the assumptions that guide his liberalism become even clearer. We can think of wealth in broad terms as the possession of the means necessary to the achievement of ends. Collingwood speaks about wealth as a balance of income over expenditure, but income is only one form of wealth. Ownership of material goods in the form of property, share ownership, machinery and equipment is another. Similarly, rights which confer benefits such as rights of access to goods and services also constitute wealth. Further, by associating wealth closely with income Collingwood understates the role of money as a source of wealth. Money, as Collingwood understands it, is not only the means of facilitating exchange but is bound up with the character of economic activity itself. Money, as Collingwood writes, 'has the peculiarity of being earned to be spent; or rather, whatever is earned to be spent is money' (EPP 73). Thus, it is essential to money that it not be treated as a commodity and that its value remains stable. That is, it belongs to the idea of a bank note that its role is that of a currency, not, as Collingwood puts it, an exchangeable commodity for lighting pipes (EPP 75; NL 40.89). Limitless hoarding of money is as much an economic evil as the unlimited printing of it. Money, however, can also be understood as a stock or asset as well as a flow. So there is no necessity that money is automatically earned to be spent. Rather money can also be thought of as an asset to be kept as prices unfold. None of this requires us to treat money as a commodity to be bought and sold like any other.

In Collingwood's liberal economics justice enters only in a commutative rather than a substantive form. Justifiable interference with the freedom of production and exchange is limited to the prohibition of force in the shape of theft or the expropriation of property. Collingwood does not play down the competitiveness of economic life, but his response to the often arbitrary distributions of benefits and burdens which result does not derive from a theory of social justice. Property obtained lawfully through inheritance and income accrued legally but not earned do not fit easily into Collingwood's definition of riches and yet both contribute to the material inequalities which a theory of justice is concerned to address. Collingwood does not exactly rule out making the rich less rich through a system of progressive taxation, but then he does not explicitly rule it in either.

Collingwood talks about wealth, as opposed to riches, as involving a standard. The standard is stability of value. Wealth understood as a legal command over the means of production and exchange derives, in Collingwood's view, from the free activity of free agents. While Collingwood does not, as Keynes does explicitly, condemn 'the love of money' as a neurosis (see Skidelsky 1992: 236), he remains committed to his excoriation of the rich. To Collingwood the distinction between wealth and riches is more than semantic. However, Collingwood fears instability more than he does inequity in the distribution of wealth, hence his stress on sound money and opposition to financial speculation. And yet such fears are minimal since Collingwood understands riches to be a relative term, one which is assessable only in relation to its opposite. On Collingwood's account, the very existence of riches entails the domination of the poor, but is this simply a reflection of what economic life is like – reducing the gain of others to a minimum and maximizing your own – or is it that the rich are just better at being rich than anyone else? Collingwood wishes us to think of the condition of the poor as alterable. He speaks of a community proposing to narrow the gap between rich and poor, but 'without a greater inroad on its income or capital than it can afford' (NL 38.8). However, what a community can afford requires an estimate of its riches as well as its wealth. Collingwood's caution reflects his unwillingness to contemplate social reform in the absence of cost, but he tells us little about how cost should be distributed. In Collingwood's picture, the King's Peace protects life, liberties and possessions, and it guards against attempts to obtain money by threats or by false pretences. The King's Thrift ensures sound public finances, and the King's Plenty is the balancing of saving and investment, of production and consumption which, according to Collingwood, is the aim of civilisation in its economic aspect.

A theory of social justice stipulates conditions apart from which questions of justice in the distribution of resources cannot be said to arise (TJ 126–7). One such circumstance of justice is moderate scarcity. If resources were abundant a scheme of cooperation to mitigate conflicts of interest would be unnecessary. But conflicts of interest arise because resources are scarce in relation to wants. Wants are best understood as a species of desire, so principles of justice will assume a picture of human psychology in which individuals are motivated by the satisfaction of their desires and also possess sufficient rationality to enable them to find the best means of doing so. Interestingly, Collingwood does not equate plenty with abundance. It is not 'a life of full bellies and soft sleep' (NL 40.81). And Collingwood describes economic rationality in terms of instrumental rationality. It is a matter of finding the most cost effective means for the achievement of ends. But, for Collingwood, economic rationality is simply one stage in the development of human rationality. And while human rationality in its moral expression includes justice in the sense of law-abidingness that is all the significant work Collingwood gives justice to do. Yet Collingwood understands wealth creation in terms of striking a balance not simply, in the case of consumers, between more consumption rather than less, but between more and less in relation to their aims, in Collingwood's words, to 'carry on his business, keep his health, bring up x children, or the like' (NL 40.84). Resources are scarce, therefore, not only in relation to desires but, more importantly, in relation to the ends and purposes that human beings share. Collingwood's terminology of 'balance' and 'mutual adjustment' points towards the language of social justice, but it is absent the principles that a theory of social justice requires. It looks as if Collingwood's stopping point in his argument is arbitrary and that something like a theory of social justice is still what his argument needs.

One might reasonably argue at this stage in the construction of a theory of economic justice that all Collingwood has to show is that economic activity has its own rationale, achieved by distinguishing economic action from impulse and morality. In separating the different forms of practical life Collingwood repays his debt to T. H. Green and the broad tradition of British Idealism, especially its denial that moral action is explicable in instrumental terms alone (AA 48–50). Green rarely speaks about social issues in terms of justice, preferring instead to talk about the common good and self-realization. Where Green refers to justice as a 'habit of mind leading to respect' (see Nicholson, below, 284 fn. 22), he is closer to Collingwood's understanding of civility, but in my interpretation civility and justice are conceptually distinct (for a discussion of Green on justice, see Nicholson 1990: 159 and 284 fn. 22). Of all the British Idealists it is perhaps in Bernard Bosanquet that we find a discussion of justice in terms which most address the requirements of social justice (see Bosanquet 1917: 195–211).

But when Collingwood tells us that an act performed on impulse lacks the distinction between means and end he is telling us as much about impulse as he is about economics and morality. So an 'impulse buy' in which an exchange of money nevertheless takes place cannot be economic action proper and, equally, an impulsive act of charity cannot be a moral act proper, even though the benefit has been transferred. Collingwood's point is that impulse cannot explain utility any more than utility can explain duty, but if we reverse the argument we reach the same conclusion. Duty cannot explain utility any more than utility can explain impulse. While Collingwood has found a determinate subject matter for economics he has not yet shown why economic action should be subordinate to morality.

How does Collingwood square his defence of the autonomy of economic activity with his willingness to see it superseded by morality and politics? For Collingwood the contrast between utility and duty is basic (NL 16.23). Economics as an empirical science has as its business the construction of laws, or of law-like generalizations, concerning, say, the relation between supply and demand or between means and ends. It is morality which asks whether or not the end should be pursued at all. Morality establishes a framework of principle within which economic activities take place. Economic laws tell you what will happen (Collingwood may well have been a little over-optimistic about this feature of economics) but not whether it should rightfully happen. But, and this is Collingwood's difficulty, if economics has its own logic then any intrusion of a different logic will change the nature of the issue. Thus Collingwood writes that 'as soon as any moral motive is imported into an economic question the question ceases to be an economic one' (EPP 68), so our difficulty (and Collingwood's) remains.

Collingwood's solution is to switch descriptions. The description 'theft' fits a given economic activity better than 'moneymaking', or, to take a slightly different case, 'sweated labour' fits better than 'low wages' (EPP 68–9). But this move creates an obvious difficulty since Collingwood still has to explain his choice of new descriptions; why, for example, does 'theft' fit better than, say, 'fraud'? Collingwood imagines a copper dealer who buys cheap in one country and sells dear in another (MM 11). So far so good, both economically and morally, Collingwood believes. But then imagine that the dealer has acquired a monopoly in copper so that it can be sold only at the dealer's price. In this case, Collingwood argues, it is 'theft' rather than 'highly profitable' which suits. So Collingwood's monopolist in copper is 'guilty of a crime against society, as if a pig-dealer should make pigs dear by poisoning everybody else's pigs' (MM 11).

This subordination of economics to morality is also present in Collingwood's discussion of the ethics of labour (EPP 69). The wages of 'sweated labour' are exploitative because the worker has no choice but to accept them. A choice between work and starvation is no choice at all. But from an economic point of view low wages equals higher profits and so is beyond criticism in economic terms. So, Collingwood argues, morality requires either that low wages be replaced by charitable giving or we look to the state to rectify the circumstances in which the exploitation has arisen.

Some evils are better described as public evils. The monopolist and the exploiter enjoy private gains but at public expense. Not all goods are private, and so there are some goods which only the state can protect and advance. When Collingwood defends the displacement of economics by morality it is in this liberal direction that he is heading. And yet economics, morality and politics constitute different spheres of activity, so, in Collingwood's view, it is a confusion of mind to justify one frame of conduct by reference to another. The political good is order, not efficiency or prosperity, although both of these may result indirectly, and the expression of order is law, not moral worth, although, again, this may well be encouraged as a consequence. In broad terms Collingwood wishes to separate the state from the moral and religious beliefs of its citizens, and so he limits justifiable state interference in their lives to the removal of disorder. Thus Collingwood restricts state interference to the maintenance of political goods such as promise-keeping and civil peace. Queuing too Collingwood identifies as a political good even though it may seem strange to include it as one of the concerns of the state (EPP 95–6).

Nowhere does Collingwood's philosophy influence his liberalism more than in the distinctions he draws between different modes of activity. In his political philosophy this leads him to think of the political good as 'orderliness, regularity, submission to a rule which applies equally to all persons' (EPP 100). So when Collingwood includes slum clearance as a political good he follows the distinction between moral and political activities on which his liberalism rests. Decent houses are desirable as a political good not because they make their inhabitants happier or even less wicked. This argument seems open to extension. For if decent housing is to be thought of as a political good, but not a moral one, then a number of welfare goods might be justified on the same basis. So we should think of medical care as a political good not because a healthy body means a healthy mind but because medical care which is provided in a disorderly, irregular or unequal manner would scarcely be care at all.

What is striking about Collingwood's account of justifiable state interference is how little it depends on a theory of justice. The specific business of the state is law. The state's concern is with the maintenance of the conditions of civil peace, by which Collingwood means security and the reduction of conflict. Justice only enters this picture at the level of law-abidingness. So when Collingwood describes slum clearance as a political good he is a little hazy about whose responsibility it is to deliver it, as he also is on the question of rehousing. More importantly, Collingwood's account of the political good as orderliness leaves open its connection with rights, opportunities and resources. Civility may well promote stability, but it may also promote it in the absence of justice. Medical care, for example, distributed civilly may still be available only to those who can pay for it. Outside the law which guarantees property rights, including the rights of the rich and powerful, redress of social deprivation depends on charity and an appeal to the compassion of the well-off. Certainly we should not think of irregular health care as true care, but it does not follow from this that the source of its provision is irrelevant to justice. Formal equality before the law

(Collingwood's 'rule which applies equally to all persons') is one of the basic values of liberalism, but it may also exist alongside substantial inequalities in opportunities and the exercise of powers.

We have discussed Collingwood's account of economic activity, his defence of the just price doctrine, together with his distinction between wealth and riches as components of a theory of economic justice and his view that economics is secondary to morality and politics. We must now ask whether a theory of social justice can be drawn from his arguments. Theories of social justice aim to correct the idea that the distribution of opportunities and resources will be automatically just if that distribution excludes force and fraud. Thus a well-ordered society is as much dependent on principles of justice as it is on a sense of civility deriving from law and from the natural duty of cooperation. A well-ordered society advances the good of its members when it is 'effectively regulated by a public conception of justice' (TJ 453). It is a feature of Rawls's version of liberalism that it focuses not on the state but on the 'basic structure of society' (TJ 7), so the primary subject of social justice is the just distribution of rights, opportunities and resources rather than the institutions of democratic society themselves.

What becomes immediately apparent is the lack in Collingwood of any extensive discussion of how independently agreed principles of justice might be derived and what their character might be. Without such a discussion, justice, in Collingwood's understanding, is a virtue applicable to individuals rather than institutions and societies. It would call for equality before the law and it would reject arbitrary treatment, but it would say little about the fairness or otherwise of a society's way of life and the distribution of opportunities it contains. Profiting from deliberately contrived scarcity or need would be condemned, but the solution found in legal redress rather than a theory of justice in which need acts as a moral criterion for a redistribution of resources. However, while it is true that Collingwood does not address questions of distributive justice he does speak about fair division. Moreover, the discussion of fair division suggests that Collingwood thinks about the just distribution of resources not in terms of principles but procedures. Collingwood seems to be suggesting that in a society characterized by the principles of civility, given fair procedures, then the outcomes of transactions will be just. Clearly this is something of a departure from Hobbes, but it remains a long way short of Rawls in whose hands matters of procedural justice are important only after the basic structure of justice as fairness has been agreed (TJ 86–7).

Collingwood's discussion of fair division in *The New Leviathan* has been rather neglected (NL 19.65–8). Its interest here lies in Collingwood's apparent aim to include both freedom and justice in his account of what a society is. What marks a society is the free engagement of its members and a *'suum cuique'* ('to each their due') (NL 19.64; see Connelly 2003: 210–12), which gives the society its particular way of life. At least in part then a society is defined in terms of justice. Each society will be marked by a distributive scheme which allocates benefits and burdens to individuals according to their due. At best, however, it is only justice in its formal sense that we can glean from this argument. We should certainly accept that the idea of justice as *suum cuique*, to each their due, implies uniformity of treatment. If two individuals are the same in the relevant respects then they should be treated in the same way. Equals should be treated equally. But we do not know what due refers to, nor are we told what might constitute relevant grounds for discrimination.

Against a background of civility Collingwood argues that there is a reasonable expectation of economic prosperity. Justice as fidelity encourages the virtues of partnership which Collingwood takes as distinguishing features of social existence. But civility lacks the imperative power of justice, and justice as fidelity is only a limited check on severe disparities of income and resources. Collingwood's response is to look to procedural justice for a solution. A fair division of shares offers a way of ensuring that economic exchanges satisfy the need for reciprocity. By the same token there are some goods which would not remain goods if thought of exclusively in terms of private satisfaction.

Collingwood gives two examples of sharing; in the first, dividing an apple, division is appropriate, in the second, sharing an umbrella, it is not. Clearly it is important to Collingwood that these represent goods of a different kind, but do they provide the account of distributive justice that Collingwood is looking for? At first sight Collingwood's example of apple division looks promising. Perfect procedural justice occurs where we have an independent standard for estimating a fair distribution and a secure means of delivering it (see Miller 1976: 43–5 for discussion; also Barry 1965: 97–106). Thus, four children sharing an apple will divide it fairly so long as the independent standard is understood and so long as the child with the knife is to receive a segment herself. The problem is that perfect procedural justice has only a limited range. It applies very well to a restricted number of goods but not at all to others. It makes no reference to claims for special consideration on grounds of need or desert. Similarly, fairness in procedures is more readily guaranteed than fairness in acts of exchange because all that is required is that each receives the same or is treated the same as the others. Collingwood's second example is of a good where division is not appropriate. So what is shared in sharing the umbrella is not the actual segment of the umbrella but the benefit the whole umbrella gives. Since to separate the segment from the whole would be to destroy the benefit, it follows that any benefit to you has also to be a benefit to me. Or, to put the point differently, a decision to take your part of the umbrella would not only lose any benefit to me it would also lose it to you. In other words, there are some goods which are goods only because they are indivisible. Problems arise because of the restricted range of this example. The indivisibility of umbrella sharing is true almost by definition whereas many of the goods that most interest theories of justice are not only divisible but are so in different and contestable ways. Moreover, the near complete lack of cost in, say, taking turns to carry an umbrella means that successful umbrella sharing is all benefit and little burden. What concerns theories of social justice, by contrast, is not a highly efficient joint enterprise involving little cost, but how the burdens involved in a particular good might be shared when there is a strong possibility that some will receive the benefits while avoiding the burdens. We can say, therefore, that while Collingwood's example is not explicable in terms of private goods it is equally unable to explain public ones, even though public goods are to various degrees characterized by indivisibility. In the case of a public good such as street lighting we recognize that once available it has to be available to all. It is to that extent indivisible. But public goods also involve costs, and principles of justice are required in order to assure individuals that those who benefit from public goods are also playing their part in maintaining them. It may be the case that the removal of street lighting because some are avoiding their share of its costs would make everyone worse off, but individuals will have a stronger motive for sharing the burdens when they know that some are not playing their part if they have the assurance that free-riding is unjust and that there is an agency for proscribing it.

The close association of justice with equality is a key feature of theories of justice. In Collingwood's liberalism civility is linked with respect, and respect would do little normative work if it was not connected with equality. Potentially then we have a route to a theory of justice, but Collingwood is not the kind of liberal who wants to elevate equality above freedom. The consciousness of oneself and others as free participants in a social existence is the mark of a liberal society. It is not equality as such that liberals like Collingwood value but equal liberties (NL 21.6). Equal liberties alone, however, are no substitute for justice, so liberals will look to justice to show them the proper boundaries of equality. But justice means treating individuals equally, so we need to ask equality in what? Collingwood understands equality of respect and equality of consideration under the rubric of civility, but civility and justice bear on politics in different ways. Treating individuals equally in respect of their basic rights would certainly forge a link between equality and justice, except that Collingwood says little about rights independently of law. Collingwood does, however, speak of justice in terms of desert (justice renders each their due), so justice requires that individuals equal in merit should be rewarded equally, that those equal in guilt should be punished equally and so on. But this does not address the question of unjustified inequalities. Two equally skilled flautists should receive the same treatment in terms of opportunities and advancement, but if one has battled against prejudice and scarcity of resources then there are broader issues for justice to consider. From the point of view of social justice then the concerns of liberal justice look relatively narrow.

A theory of social justice has to cover undeserved natural inequalities in addition to inequalities deriving from income and social position. Here Collingwood is concerned with inequalities in natural endowments and the sort of response they merit (NL 21.61–4). Leaving aside (as Collingwood does) the problem of separating natural inequalities from those of social origin, the question is the status of natural endowments when seen from the perspective of justice. Collingwood identifies three responses. One, natural inequalities in ability may be compensated for by the stronger making up for the deficiencies in the weaker. So, to use Collingwood's examples, the stronger walker carries the knapsack, the stronger chess player grants the weaker a pawn. Two, a society can turn natural inequalities into assets to further the pursuit of the common end, so the best map reader carries the maps. Three, natural inequalities in, say, personality may be treated as resources which are of value to everyone. So the possession of initiative by one can be identified and made use of by others.

Any comprehensive liberalism has to address the question of inequalities of natural endowments. While Collingwood talks of natural as opposed to socially determined endowments he speaks about them only from the perspective of an elementary theory of justice. Clearly compensation implies the rectifying of an inequality, so when compensation is given for a loss of earnings, say, the amount received matches the loss. But when we try to compensate the weaker chess player the player's abilities do not remain static. Natural endowments are not fixed, so compensating the weaker chess player may easily diminish their skills further. Equally, handicapping the stronger player can have the same effect.

The difficulty facing Collingwood is that he is speaking about natural, and possibly undeserved, differences in ability, but in the absence of principles of justice which would give a focus. Collingwood, like Rawls (JF 74–7), tackles the problem of inequalities in natural endowments by turning them into common assets, the best map reader, the person with initiative, imagination, etc. Collingwood, again like Rawls, draws on the notion of reciprocity to describe what is due to others when natural assets are unequally distributed. What Collingwood's account lacks, however, is a principle of justice which gives the better endowed (whose talents are undeserved) an obligation to assist the poorly endowed (when their lack of talent is also undeserved). Rawls, in the derivation of the principles of justice as fairness, ensures that individuals are ignorant of whatever natural assets they might possess (TJ 137). But once the principles are formulated then they offer 'a way of seeing nature and the social world as no longer hostile to democratic equality' (JF 76). In other words, it is the distribution of natural endowments which is the common asset, not the natural endowment itself. And yet Collingwood's choice of activities to illustrate his points is significant. All depend on cooperation and the coordination of different skills for their success. As examples of cooperative activity, games, navigation, project instigation, all show how human differences can complement one another when mutually aligned. 'Complementarities between talents' is the phrase Rawls uses to describe this (JF 76), but, unlike Collingwood, he uses it in conjunction with a theory of justice that specifies entitlements obtained under fair conditions.

Collingwood not only sets questions of social and economic justice aside but in terms of his own position is mistaken in doing so. One defence against this accusation is to say that questions of social and economic justice are simply matters for a given society at any particular stage of its development. Collingwood's distinction between the philosophy of economics and economics as an empirical science reinforces this point (EPP 58–9). Economics in its philosophical form aims to establish the differentiae of economic activity, whereas in its empirical form it aims to explain economic events through the construction of laws or empirical generalizations. Money, for example, introduces a genuine difference of meaning into the concept of economic action as instrumental and so is a part of a philosophy of economics proper. Money understood as an empirical fact, however, belongs to the empirical study of economics, and so questions of money supply and rates of exchange, for instance, are matters of policy but not philosophy.

However, the distinction between philosophical and empirical understanding also applies to justice. We can picture justice as an empirical fact in the sense that it is a feature of the laws and practices of any given society, and we can picture it as a subject to be grasped conceptually through the methods of moral and political philosophy. So when Collingwood speaks about a 'just wage' or a 'fair price' he shows how the distinction between philosophical and empirical understanding can be made to work. Arguments for economic justice which attempt to extend the formal requirements of justice to wealth, income, levels of savings and investment become proper subjects of philosophical scrutiny. They attempt to find a workable sense of justice for economic relationships. They are not simply descriptions of economic facts or regularities. In other words, there is nothing in Collingwood's conception of philosophical method which would block a discussion of social and economic justice. We cannot defend Collingwood's inattention to social and economic justice by defining it away. Equally, however, without such a discussion Collingwood's liberal economics looks fragile.

Collingwood might argue that his critics have simply misunderstood his concerns. His central interest is derived from Hobbes. Justice is vital in economic life mainly as a protection for contracts, and this could not be achieved in the absence of civility. Collingwood's operating contrast is not a just society as opposed to an unjust one but a society that is civilized as opposed to one that is barbaric. In economic terms the contrast is between plenty and waste. Overconsumption is as much a sign of a barbarous economy as impoverishment. So Collingwood associates plenty with civility because civility requires both abstention from force and a mutual and balanced adjustment between production and consumption (NL 40.82). None of this, however, tells us how plenty is to be procured. Nor does it tell us how plenty, if procured, is to be shared. Collingwood speaks of obtaining plenty by 'canalizing' production, distribution and exchange into public benefit, and he repeats his injunction against the practice of artificially keeping prices high by restricting supply and that of treating money as a commodity (the bank notes used for pipe lighters, again). The term that Collingwood uses to describe this process of commodity production is thrift (NL 40.92). And yet it is surely the case that the model of thrift is not frugality alone, for if it was we could be thrifty by simply not spending. Equally, thrift does not simply imply saving but prudent saving, a setting aside of immediate satisfaction against the possibility of unavoidable expenditure in the future. However, like charity, thrift derives much of its moral value from its being engaged in voluntarily. So if one is lucky enough to have thrifty parents who set funds aside for the future then all will be well, but if not then trusting to one's own resources, and possibly fate too, may be the only response remaining.

Justice, by contrast with thrift, is stringent. Justice creates a sense of entitlement and with this a sense of obligation. From Collingwood's viewpoint in moral philosophy, however, entitlements and the recognition of obligations are signs that the civilizing process is well advanced. Civility certainly accompanies civilisation, but as a moral state which is more basic than justice it also sends the civilizing process on its way. What interests Collingwood is the difference between a flourishing economy and no economic life at all. Take away civility from society and economic life vanishes. Thrift is important, therefore, because it represents a method of containing economic excess for societies which lack agreed principles of justice. Learning to be civil is separate from learning to be just, and so thrift stands to civility as justice does to a sense of obligation.

A society that saves out of thrift, however, is not one that saves out of justice. A concern for thrift is not wholly a matter of sentiment, but it lacks the sense necessary to justice that each is receiving what is their due. Thrift too, like justice in the economic sphere, is a response to relative scarcity. But, unlike justice, thrift responds to scarcity by trying to protect the thrifty from its effects. So the thrifty, by means of good housekeeping, avoidance of wastefulness, cutting back on luxuries and so on aim to minimize any harm in bad times by restraint in good. But setting resources aside for a rainy day is not an adequate principle of social justice since it leaves substantial inequalities untouched. Similarly, saving out of thrift is scarcely an acknowledgement that we have obligations to those who follow us in time. Generations that follow us may well resent our lack of thriftiness, but they will not feel that they have been unjustly treated, as they would be entitled to feel had they been bound to us by mutually agreed principles of justice.

Utilitarianism values principles of justice because of the goods they lead to. Welfare, security and prosperity are each desirable human states which are hard to visualize in a society lacking justice. Collingwood does not value justice because of the benefits it produces (NL 40.14). Indeed, if justice were to be valued in this way then Collingwood argues it would not be valued at all. Collingwood is here talking about justice under the law. There is a significant respect in which the sense of justice as valuable in itself is the only sense in which Collingwood uses it. When Collingwood censures riches he does so because he thinks of riches as inherently unjust. Making the rich less rich will simply make others rich. Since riches are a relative term (x is rich only in relation to y), transference of riches will not remove their injustice. Further, the direction of Collingwood's argument is determined less by inequality of income or property than the inequality of power that riches signify. Collingwood is not a doctrinaire egalitarian. He does not want to diminish the harms suffered by the poor, the needy or the dispossessed solely in the name of equality, but he does wish to diminish them nevertheless.

It is here that Collingwood's arguments seem to fail him. For the only room to manoeuvre Collingwood has left is provided by his distinction between riches and wealth. And yet when this is introduced in order to address the gap between rich and poor the result is unimpressive. Even a slight contrast between rich and poor indicates the presence of force, but Collingwood says that this contrast may be justifiable so long as it is 'sufficiently paid for by the service done to the whole community by the rich as the class charged with maintaining the communal wealth' (NL 38.77). But, as we have seen, Collingwood thinks of riches and wealth as conceptually distinct. As a relative term, riches make sense only in relation to more or less rich. Thus any transfer of riches to wealth or use of riches to maintain wealth means either redefining riches as wealth or dropping the distinction completely. Clearly, redefining riches as wealth is not a persuasive option since it would mean losing the connection with force that Collingwood thinks is specific to riches, and this would mean in turn that Collingwood could no longer claim that it is riches alone that are inherently unjust. Dropping the distinction completely is surely the better alternative, for this would make both riches and wealth (each appropriately understood) open to the scrutiny of principles of justice. Or to put this argument more succinctly, Collingwood by losing his half-way house version of Marxism could then reinforce his liberalism and push it closer to a liberal theory of social and economic justice.

Dropping the distinction between riches and wealth is desirable for another reason. Collingwood's remarks on thrift rightly associate thrift with responsibility (NL 40.95–40.97). Opponents of social justice will argue that issues concerning poverty cannot be addressed without considering the responsibility that individuals must bear for their own choices and way of life. From this perspective it is not difficult to attribute large differences in material inequalities not to luck or circumstances but to unequal merits. The rich are rewarded for industry and hard work while the poor receive what their laziness deserves. But in Collingwood's view, riches are straightforwardly unjust. They are unjust because they are uncivil, and they are uncivil because they involve the use of force. Poverty, therefore, comes about not from the fecklessness of the poor but from the exploitation of the poor by the rich. And yet Collingwood denies that law can be effective in challenging this state of affairs: 'by what legal reformation it can be made illegal to buy labour for less than its just price by taking advantage of one's own economic power and the unemployed labourer's economic weakness I do not know' (NL 38.69).

Thrift, by contrast with riches, is necessarily wealth creating and is also a matter of private and public responsibility. Unlike opponents of social justice

Collingwood does not lay all social irresponsibility at the door of individuals and none at the public associations designed to protect them. Neither does Collingwood deny that there are some choices that individuals cannot sensibly be asked to make. But whereas defenders (and opponents) of a theory of social justice operate with a conventional distinction between rich and poor Collingwood's division between riches and wealth cuts across this, so producing results which, in terms of social justice, can seem anomalous. Thus, someone who is industrious but poor and uses their limited means thriftily, in Collingwood's distinction possesses wealth, whereas someone who is idle but rich and uses their extensive resources without a care for the future is conspicuously lacking wealth. If Collingwood's denial that wealth is not open to transfer is added to this argument (which owes something to Ruskin, and beyond Ruskin to the Christian parables. For Ruskin's economics see Batchelor 2000: 209–11), then we can readily see how difficult it is to express Collingwood's viewpoint in terms of social justice.

As a liberal Collingwood sees clearly how the often 'morbid symptoms' (SM 173) of economic conflict require a theory of politics. He sees too that the state in its historical reality cannot be defined as a business concern without losing the King's Peace that guarantees legal rights and freedoms. But unlike at least one contemporary theorist of social justice Collingwood does not separate entitlements from desert. One of Rawls most notable contributions to the theory of social justice is his sharp separation of justice and merit. Life is too chancy, economic outcomes too unpredictable and social circumstances too arbitrary to permit social goods to be 'distributed according to moral desert' (TJ 310; see the discussion by Joshua Cohen and Thomas Nagel in Rawls, 2009: 1–24). Hence the need for a theory of justice which satisfies legitimate expectations through social institutions rather than personal worth. However, in Collingwood's formulation justice is restricted to law-abidingness, and it is hard to think of thrift as praiseworthy without thinking of the thrifty as morally admirable too.

We must allow Collingwood the thought that justice is a state of mind leading to respect for others and for the circumstances in which they live their lives, but in Collingwood's philosophy respect is understood under the rubric of civility not justice. Collingwood's liberalism is not wishful thinking or a thinly disguised conservatism, but it is hard to avoid the conclusion that it is a liberalism that is looking for a new stimulus. Collingwood is neither an economic liberal nor a defender of social justice. A liberalism couched in terms of civility lacks the normative power needed to respond effectively to the substantial inequalities which a theory of social justice seeks to rectify. Collingwood thought that 'there will always be one law for the rich and another for the poor' (NL 38.71); by contrast, a theory of social justice must claim that this is neither a necessary truth nor a wry defeatism. Not only does Collingwood's political philosophy lack a theory of social justice, it is surely the case, as we have shown, that his liberalism needs one.

Civility plays a far-reaching role in Collingwood's account of political education, and it is not difficult to see how and why it is also vital to the processes of public reasoning on which many contemporary theories of social justice depend. However, none of this permits us to equate civility with justice or to regard civility as a virtue when justice is absent. If Collingwood's liberalism had started and ended with civility then we would have a clear picture of the kind of liberalism he wished to defend but, as we have seen, it is hard to evaluate the rightful distribution of private income and public goods in terms of civility alone. And so Collingwood does allow justice an appearance, explicitly in his accounts of economic justice and procedural fairness and implicitly in his distinction between riches and wealth. Both manoeuvres leave supporters of social justice short changed. Collingwood is not exactly an opponent of social justice, but neither is he a fully paid up defender of it. It is rather that without a concept of social justice Collingwood's arguments will not work.

11

Civility and economic licentiousness

Collingwood's interest in political philosophy, like that of his predecessor, Thomas Hobbes, is with the conditions of civil peace. If order is the distinguishing feature of political activity understood philosophically, then civility is its moral face. Through civility human beings who often disagree and are prone to be troublesome to each other find, if not total harmony, some degree of mutual accommodation and peace. Civility prohibits the unconditional use of force, and it enjoins respect for others and the projects they seek to further. Civility, however, operates better as a restraint than an injunction. It tells us what conduct we should refrain from but less clearly what we should do. Moreover, human beings who value their freedoms as well as their virtues should find civility congenial, since it protects expectations without making excessive demands.

It is civility's lack of imperative power relative to justice which alerts us to its weakness as a sovereign political value. For civility by itself is no guarantee that a given distribution of economic resources in a society is just. To say that force and fraud play no part in the ways resources are distributed tells us little about whether or not such ways are just. Further, we may well feel that there is something amiss with a society in which individuals treat each other civilly and yet also spend much of their lives accumulating unnecessary economic goods. With equal force we may feel that there is also something wrong with a society in which civility goes hand in hand with massive public and private debt. The forms of economic licentiousness – overconsumption in the shape of the pursuit of luxury and greed, and indebtedness without the assets to support it – are well-known to liberals as the unlooked for consequences of the freedoms they value. Is civility alone sufficient to identify what has gone wrong? In this chapter I look in close detail at Collingwood's economic thought, particularly in relation to its capacity to deal with economic intemperance and excess and in the light of the demand for social justice that was emerging in wartime Britain.

Collingwood, while being fully supportive of liberalism in principle, frequently attacks liberals for failing to apply their ideals in practice. Liberals cannot be wholly neutral between the goods they value, and yet Collingwood is no perfectionist for there are some requirements, civility being the most obvious one, which apply to all irrespective of status or desert. Collingwood decries the shallowness of liberalism, and he opposes the picture of human goods common among political economists as functions solely of appetite or desire, but he is committed to civility as a fundamental political good – one, moreover, which is a good precisely because it avoids substantive judgements on the many and varied goods that individuals pursue. Indeed, it is this feature of civility which makes it attractive to individuals who are determined not to live in each other's pockets but who are equally aware that they cannot adequately exist wholly separately from each other either.

Modern liberals, like Collingwood, are political philosophers before they are economists, but Collingwood, unlike many modern liberals, makes no attempt to construct principles of justice which enable individuals to rank the goods they value. So for a modern liberal such as John Rawls, the procurement of income and wealth is a primary good, but the degree to which the acquisition of such goods is justified is determined by principles of justice independently derived and agreed. Rawls famously allows for economic inequality in society so long as liberal political institutions are in place and the resulting distribution of resources benefits the least well off (Rawls 1999: 65–70). As at least one critic of Rawls has pointed out, the resulting division between political egalitarianism and the private freedom of wealth accumulation may well be morally unsustainable (see Cohen 2000). But what is noticeable about Collingwood is that he does not speak in these terms at all. What interests Collingwood is the contrast between a civilized and a barbaric way of life. It may be the case that political egalitarianism fits uneasily with the facts of economic life in modern acquisitive societies, and it may also be the case that liberals who are egalitarian across the board do not fit at all, but Collingwood's interest is not in social and economic justice but civility, and so it is necessary to ask if the economic excesses that justice condemns would also be rejected in a society based on civility alone.

We make Collingwood's task more difficult than it need be if we assume that greed necessarily implies unfairness. For example, feeding Kahishi, the Sumo wrestling champion, twenty eggs a day certainly gives him more nourishment than a beginner, but this does not make Kahishi greedy. Nor is the practice unfair so long as resources are available and wrestlers of equivalent rank receive the same. We can describe Kahishi as greedy when he wants more for himself than he needs (even when he needs a lot compared with others) or when he takes what others need or when he wants only what others want because they want it. Kahishi acts greedily if he continues to eat more than he needs when all the other wrestlers are replete, but he also acts unfairly and uncivilly if he grabs an excessive share of the eggs before the others have finished. In this way civility can restrain competitive impulses where injustice is involved and where it is not. But equally, some impulses should not go unrestrained even though we would not count them either uncivil or unjust.

We are looking, therefore, for some method by which Collingwood can curtail economic excess given that he has no understanding of justice beyond fidelity in the form of law-abidingness and the keeping of promises or contracts freely made. Clearly, commutative justice acts as a restraint on the pursuit of unrestricted appetite, but it says nothing about the size of the appetite itself. So when the non-wrestling painter and decorator, Mashimi, contracts with Kahishi to take all the wrestler's surplus eggs because he enjoys gorging himself on them and is willing to incur debt to pay for them, all that matters is that the agreement is upheld. Similarly, contractually agreed vast pay increases are defensible even though the economy is in bad shape, and the increase is massively disproportionate to the rate enjoyed by everyone else. In other words, we are asking Collingwood for a source of economic restraint distinct from law, justice or promise-keeping.

We should notice first that Collingwood does not consider economic relations to be wholly self-regulating. In Collingwood's humane Hegelianism, economics is an activity which points beyond itself to the more complete forms or moral and political action. But even if we grant Collingwood the truth of this picture we should not conclude that acts of economic exchange have no independent work to do or that it is a straightforward matter to decide under which rubric – excessive profit or necessary investment, overconsumption or fuelling demand – a given piece of economic behaviour is best placed. Further, while Collingwood thinks of economic activity as a rule-governed practice which is, in its own way, as necessary to the civilized life as morality and politics, it is also his view that, like all human practices, economics is subject to disorder and excess. 'The Yahoo is always with us,' Collingwood writes (NL 30.8), suggesting either that economic rationality is simply another name for Yahoo want satisfaction or that outbursts of imitative economic behaviour are in some way a regression from civilized economic life.

We can be reasonably sure that Yahoo commercial acumen, such as it is, will never act as a model for *homo economicus* for, although economic action may be prone to the unceasing satisfaction of wants, this is not a necessary feature of it. In Collingwood's view, the essence of economic activity is exchange, and exchange implies reciprocity and hence the notion of a limit (EPP 95–6). Indeed, the very idea of economic excess suggests that some norm of economic behaviour has been transgressed. It is not, however, a norm of reciprocity that Mashimi breaches when he tucks into the eggs he has received from Kahishi. Both are satisfied with the exchange. Kahishi has received payment for goods that would otherwise have gone to waste, and at least one egg eater's appetite has been assuaged. The relationship involves neither force nor fraud and hence satisfies the standards of civility as Collingwood understands it; and yet we still want to say that something is amiss. What we have here, therefore, is not the unrestrained Yahoo pursuit of appetite. The relationship between the economic agents involved is not a free for all. But equally it is a relationship which can just as well facilitate avarice as obstruct it, hence the difficulty of explaining quite what is wrong with avarice in purely economic terms. Or, to put the same point slightly differently, what is wrong with promoting unlimited consumption if it takes place civilly and makes no one worse off?

Whereas the Yahoos in Swift are stuck at the level of gross experience, pre-social individuals as Hobbes understands them, whose fears are at least as important to them as their appetites, are able to construct a civil peace which allays the former thereby easing the pursuit of the latter. So for Hobbes, without the security provided by the state there will be 'no place for Industry; because the fruit thereof is uncertain; and consequently no Culture of the Earth' (Hobbes 1651: chapter XIII). But this picture of public institutions framing private desires runs into severe difficulties not least in economies where massive overspending is the norm. First, the state may be even more profligate with expenditure and with debt accumulation than the private individuals and their enterprises it is designed to protect. Second, if the sole function of the state is to enforce promise-keeping and the integrity of contracts then the degree of overconsumption becomes irrelevant unless it threatens civil peace. In fact, Hobbes does not visualize the state as guarding the pursuit of unnecessary wealth. He condemns covetousness and regards the accumulation of riches beyond what is reasonable as unnecessarily troublesome to the civil order. Wealth beyond what is required for self-preservation is simply superfluous, possibly a reflection of human vanity and certainly a vice which rational and moderately self-interested individuals should strive to avoid. As Keith Thomas remarks of Hobbes's views, 'endless acquisitiveness is bad in itself because it serves no useful purpose' (Thomas 1965: 217).

Hobbes does not picture money supply as unlimited, and hence he has little conception of a market economy as self-regulating, open to expansion and correction as desires wax and wane and as new desires are stimulated with new investment, together with the risks that go with it. However, Hobbes does understand human life to be competitive. Human desires, as Hobbes sees them, are not essentially sinful, and so they can serve as much as engines of the economy as restrictions to it. Covetousness, as Hobbes sceptically reminds us, is both a sin and 'the root of men's estates' (cited in Thomas 1965: 217). Nor, famously, does Hobbes believe that there is a single, over-riding good at which human action is aimed. Collingwood, however, does distinguish between true and false desires, and he rejects both Hobbes's stark individualism and his view that appetite is the sole determinant of value. There is then the possibility of finding in Collingwood what is so conspicuously lacking in Hobbes, namely, a substantive conception of the good life and hence a perspective from which economic excess can be located and defined. It is exactly such a conception that Collingwood seems to offer when he writes, 'the best life, and what every sound man wants, is to be a complete man, *teres atque rotundus*' (NL 23.79).

It is as well to remember that this phrase of Horace's does not refer to a life which has everything, for then the standard of completeness would simply be the satisfaction of wants, and the difference between the best life, the good life and the worst possible kind of life could be assessed along a single scale of value. Rather, Horace is pointing to a life of a certain kind or, more exactly, one which is lived in a certain kind of way. Thus the complete life will be one in which economic goods are valued, but not to the neglect of goods whose value cannot be expressed in economic terms alone. By a complete life, therefore, Collingwood, in drawing on Horace, may be understood as meaning one which is both rounded and polished, in the sense that the individual living that kind of life will move smoothly from one activity to another, deriving the appropriate level of satisfaction from each activity and also matching the satisfaction to the kind of activity it is. The model of completeness, in other words, is not that of arithmetic but geometry.

It's worth stressing one significant difference between Collingwood and a modern liberal such as John Rawls. Rawls certainly speaks of primary goods, for example, rights and liberties, income and wealth and the social foundations of self-respect, as necessary for citizens living a complete life. But a complete life is defined in terms of the principles of justice which make up the basic structure. As a liberal, Rawls is not specific about individual conceptions of the good. Rather, individual flourishing will best take place against the background provided by the principles of justice themselves. But Collingwood's political philosophy lacks a conception of distributive justice, which means that whatever role completeness has in establishing the best life it is not one that derives from justice. A complete life would be impossible in conditions of incivility. But what still remains to be seen is how the complete life excludes unnecessary consumption when Collingwood offers civility, but not justice, to ground his case. To justify and hence limit economic inequality Rawls offers the need to appeal to the least advantaged. While the merits of this as a method of curbing extremes of wealth are open to debate, what is clear is that for Rawls the 'equality in the social bases of self-respect' (Rawls 1999: 478) manifest in a just society serves to control envy and so to restrict damage caused by preoccupation with relative economic position. Certainly Collingwood associates civility with self-respect, but even though he thinks of self-respect as a good it is not the kind of good which is open to distribution by reference to distributive principles of justice. When we realize that Collingwood is not the kind of liberal whose confidence in the market is unbounded then we begin to appreciate his difficulty. Like Rawls, Collingwood does not wish to eliminate the hope of economic gain as a legitimate motive for action, and, again like Rawls, neither does he wish for social arrangements to be judged by reference to economic efficiency alone. In the absence of a conception of distributive justice and, indeed, of the state as the practical agent of such a conception, what in Collingwood's view is the best method of keeping extremes of economic behaviour under control?

His answer looks back to Christian restraints on economic consumption in the form of charity and thrift and forward to secular economic scepticism about the utility value of limitless expenditure. Avarice is not a characteristic of the economic life as such but only of the pursuit of riches rather than wealth. Christian moral theology is entirely consistent with economic civilisation as Collingwood understands it, hence his comment that 'St. Joseph is not held up as an example of avarice because he made his living by carpentry, nor St. Paul because he made his by tent-making' (WCM in NL 507). Just as modern economists warn against the assumption that increased riches bring increased happiness Collingwood counsels against the pleasures of material reward and the unrestricted pursuit of desire satisfaction. And yet without a net balance of income over expenditure charity and thrift would be impossible, and so Collingwood's aim is not to curb economic activity, or even to level out its results, but to discipline it, first, by means of a distinction between wealth and riches; second, through a classification of public and private goods; and, third, by an account of the best life for human beings in which goods are understood not as creatures of desire but the expression of a picture of the best life which is independently derived. So the distinction between wealth and riches points towards a theory of the common good, and the classification of public and private goods rejects the idea that maximizing individual interest satisfaction necessarily carries a public benefit. Collingwood's liberalism enshrines the prohibition of force and fraud as the primary source of political order. What this means is that it is not self-enrichment itself that is the law's direct concern, but the disorder which follows when it is the result of force or fraud. Collingwood needs an account of the role of civility in economic life, and the distinction between wealth and riches is his first move in this direction.

The distinction between wealth and riches is in fact threefold (NL 38.3–63). First, wealth is a comparative term, riches a relative one. Second, whereas a comparative term is one in which reference is made to an independent standard which may be either met or not, a relative term is judged only in relation to itself. Thus, whereas the judgement, 'this wine is good' is decided by reference to the appropriate standard, the judgement, 'this car is fast' is relative to those which are slower, as we saw in the previous chapter. Similarly, 'this community is wealthy' is decided by reference to a standard, whereas 'this individual is rich' is decided by reference to others who are poor. Third, wealth is primarily a feature of communities: if communities are wealthy then individuals are wealthy but only as members of the community. So if individuals are rich then the community is rich only in relation to other communities which are poorer. Collingwood looks to the distinction between wealth and riches to distinguish between economic activity which leads to the general benefit (wealth) and activity which benefits one only at the expense of others (riches). 'Riches', Collingwood writes, 'imply poverty, but wealth does not' (WCM NL 505). Moreover, as the relation between rich and poor is an economic relation, then the rich become richer as the poor become poorer. Further, a relation in which the stronger benefits at the expense of the weaker is a relationship of force and as such undermines civility.

In Collingwood's liberal economics, wealth implies a balance between income and the satisfaction of need. However, Collingwood is suspicious of too readily accepting a distinction between necessities and luxuries, arguing that, as economic civilization develops, what is counted as a luxury is often switched into the category of a necessity, and also that new luxuries are in constant supply (NL 35.57). Indeed, Collingwood does not explicitly associate wealth with necessities, nor does he identify riches with superfluity; rather he claims, in a manner reminiscent of Hobbes's account of value, that 'a thing which a community is able to produce creates a demand for itself by the mere fact of being produced' (NL 38.25). Much more important to Collingwood is the idea that relationships involving wealth lack the exploitative element present in relationships involving riches. In this light what Collingwood needs to show is how his conception of wealth implies moderation and mutual benefit, whereas his conception of riches does not. Certainly Collingwood speaks out against what he refers to as 'pseudo-bargains' (NL 38.67) in which the poor may be compelled out of weakness to pay more than a fair price or receive less than a fair wage, as he also condemns the production of apparent but unreal wealth by artificially stimulating scarcity in order to maintain prices or by devaluing money so that it ceases to be a unit of account and is treated as a commodity like any other. But neither of these has a direct bearing on the definition of wealth as opposed to riches. Collingwood argues that so long as the 'possession of three motor-cars or the command of one good meal a day' (NL 38.55), for example, is the standard of wealth in a community, then individuals in that community can be judged wealthy by reference to that standard. This means that an individual whose ownership of three cars is at the expense of others who either own one, two or no cars at all can be counted rich but not wealthy, whereas an individual whose ownership permits others to own the same is wealthy but not rich.

At least some of the problems that Collingwood faces arise from the restricted range of his examples. We do think of wealth as involving legal command over the means of exchange, but legality is only one of the tests involved, and Collingwood's definition neglects wealth derived from inheritance, to which there is a legal entitlement but which also carries with it substantial inequality of distribution. Further, whether or not multiple car ownership is a sign of an unwarranted gap between rich and poor (quite independently of being considered the cause of one) is heavily bound up with cost relative to earned income and, therefore, points more to inequality in economic opportunities than the absence of force and fraud. Collingwood does not reduce the desire for wealth to the desire to be wealthy, but the absence in his argument of any clear-cut separation of necessities – what Hobbes thinks of as the means of self-preservation – from luxuries means that at least one route to the identification of economic licentiousness is closed. Certainly, Collingwood's example of one good meal a day suggests, if rather quaintly, a level of diet without which survival might be considered difficult, but deprivation here is surely best thought of as related to economic and social opportunities in addition to the sources of incivility which are at the heart of Collingwood's analysis. We can allow that Collingwood does speak of wealth being distributed so that few will be too far above, nor many below, the appropriate standard (NL 38.77). But the difficulty is to see how this can be achieved by reference to civility alone. Further, as both Collingwood and Hobbes acknowledge, it is hard to diminish the competitive element in riches without also reducing the social benefits which result.

The idea that wealth, unlike riches, is measured by reference to a standard which applies to communities rather than individuals is one which points towards a conception of the common good. In this respect Collingwood's political philosophy mirrors T. H. Green's denial that 'all "goods" were private' (*AA* 49; for discussion of T. H. Green see Nicholson 1990: 54–82), even though Collingwood does not provide a full consolidation of Green's insight. For when we move from wealth as the means of procuring goods to a discussion of the goods themselves we are entering territory to which Collingwood is often thought a stranger, either because his thought is closely associated with liberal neutrality towards the goods that individuals actually choose or because he says little beyond the fairly non-controversial claim that not all goods are private. However, the distinction between wealth and wealthy does suggest an understanding of well-being which takes into account logical differences between goods, and this in turn suggests not only that some goods are incommensurable but that understood solely in economic terms they could not be intelligibly pursued at all. In other words, there are some goods which are disqualified as goods when they are pursued in excess. With these kinds of goods it is not simply that additions to already substantial stocks yield only a small amount of extra happiness. It is rather that they are goods for which assessment along a single quantitative scale is wholly inappropriate. If Collingwood's political philosophy can be made to yield an account of different kinds of public good, then we should be in a better position to see what Collingwood means by the complete life and why it excludes excess.

When Rawls develops his idea of primary goods he does so with a view to their distribution by principles of justice. Collingwood's thought lacks such a distributive principle, but this does not mean that he has no conception of goods independently of wants and desires. Both Rawls and Collingwood understand the need for liberals to develop a classification of goods. Rawls makes this explicit (Rawls 2000: 368). In Collingwood it is less so, but no less important for that (*NL* 21.6). The principles of justice as fairness are ordered lexically because Rawls wishes to resist the possibility that prosperity can be balanced against civil rights and freedoms (Rawls 1999: 378). Collingwood too sees the importance of this, and he blocks it by constructing an account of the political good the value of which cannot be expressed in economic terms.

When we link Collingwood's denial that all goods are private with his understanding of the political good as 'orderliness, regularity, submission to a rule which applies equally to all persons' (EPP 98), we can see more clearly why Collingwood argues that a scheme of free institutions subject to laws that it initiates itself has an intrinsic value. What concerns us, however, is not the institutional expression of civility but the role civility has in curbing economic excess. It is in this respect that Collingwood's thought points towards the idea of a public good. Such goods derive their significance because their value is not reducible to the private good of individuals. Indeed, in the case of a public good such as street lighting its value (as we saw earlier) is such that to remove the benefit it gives to one is also to remove the benefit from all. Collingwood does acknowledge that political goods defy explanation in utilitarian terms. To take just one of Collingwood's examples, queuing represents orderliness but it can also be costly in time and self-discipline, and it does not serve the interests of all equally (EPP 97–8; I should emphasize the contrast between Collingwood's discussion of queuing and that of Cohen 2008: 350–1, which makes justice explicit. Cohen writes, 'You need not queue in an orderly way if nobody else does: justice then releases you from that obligation. But orderly queuing surely remains the system recommended by justice.').

Queuing is one way of distributing scarce goods when demand outstrips supply. It is a practice which gives the appearance of benefiting all equally so long as each is self-restrained but which also requires that those with the strongest desire exercise the greatest degree of self-control. However, the rule 'first come, first served', on which queuing depends, may be highly unfair when, for instance, those at the back of the queue are in greater need than those at the front. Neither is queuing an adequate response to greed since it is not unknown for people to queue for goods they do not want or for goods they do want but only because they wish to sell them at a profit later. It is true that many political goods do not follow the model of public goods, just as many private goods do not follow the model of individual desire satisfaction. Insofar as civility can be invoked to recognize this then, Collingwood must surely argue, it will not act as a screen legitimizing the unceasing acquisition of consumer goods.

The problem that Collingwood faces is that when separated from justice civility is as able to promote economic excess as to restrict it. Imagine Collingwood making the same point but substituting politeness for civility. Good manners and mutual respect do not merely smooth the civilizing process; they are also the necessary impulse to encouraging commercial instincts on their way. At issue here is the disparity between goods and wants. Some goods are public goods because their benefits are necessarily shared. We saw that street lighting cannot benefit me without also benefiting my neighbour. But it is equally true that street lighting gives me what I want. The fact that it also gives my neighbours what they want is not incidental to me. For if lighting was taken away from my neighbours, then it would also be taken away from me. Not all public goods follow this model. Art and science might reasonably be thought public goods, even though there are many who are indifferent to them. Both types of good resist explanation along one scale, but in the first this is because the good involved is indivisible, whereas in the second it is because the good involved is quite independent of the satisfaction of wants.

So while Collingwood's liberalism recognizes the importance of public goods it falls short of a complete account of them. Moreover, Collingwood denies that the value of an increase in the production or consumption of a given commodity is something that can be settled theoretically (IH 324). This is surely right if we approach the issue of what value more or less of a particular item has in the abstract. But in the example he discusses Collingwood is quite specific. We are asked to imagine a fish-eating community which discovers that the daily catch can be doubled by the adoption of a new and more efficient method. Why should we not straightforwardly consider this an improvement? But, Collingwood asks, from whose point of view is it an improvement? The older generation may well not be willing to gain extra leisure when in order to do so they have to give up treasured customs and beliefs. Equally, the younger generation are unable to judge because they are not in a position to compare one way of life with the other. What is excessive and superfluous to one generation is thought of as highly advantageous by the other. However, as a liberal, Collingwood clearly cannot leave the matter there. And so he suggests that a given way of life, one which embraces, say, the economics of capitalist individualism, will see its life improved only when the removal of its weaknesses does not undermine its strengths. Now we can be sure that one of the strengths of an individualist economics, as Collingwood sees it, is the premium it places on free economic exchange. Indeed, Collingwood sometimes writes as if this is all that is needed for the production of plenty (NL 40.82). But plenty is a term marked by ambiguity for it can mean either that I have quite enough or that I have everything I desire. To the moderate, plenty means one meal a day; to the immoderate, plenty means eating all you desire.

Insofar as economic agents are free, rational and capable of disciplining their desires, characteristics which are present in Collingwood's philosophy of mind, then all will be well. *Homo economicus* can be accommodated by *homo politicus*. Reference to public goods modifies private interest because public goods would not be the goods they are unless they were shared. But

Collingwood's method of maintaining a balance between buyers and sellers is to draw on the idea of a just price, an idea which can be traced to Aristotle and which has only a limited application in modern acquisitive societies. Certainly Collingwood condemns bad economics, for example, treating money as an exchangeable commodity like any other or artificially manipulating demand to keep prices high, but in the context of modernity bad economics begins to look like the norm, and capitalism promotes not freedom of choice but acquisitiveness for its own sake.

Collingwood's reflections on capitalism are sometimes more sympathetic than liberals might wish to allow. The capacity to create demand is a feature of capitalist economics that Collingwood admires, and he is critical of those who 'blame it on the cupidity of capitalists marketing trash for their private ends' (NL 38.26). That, Collingwood says, 'is demonology, not economics' (NL 38.26). But, as we have noticed, capitalism creates both wealth and riches and, in Collingwood's account, riches is necessarily marked by force and force necessarily marked by poverty. Collingwood seems to want the best of both worlds: wealth defined as civilized production and exchange as the agency of the good life, riches its unfortunate side effect. Whereas Ruskin, to whom Collingwood is indebted for aspects of his economic thought as well as much else, condemns capitalism without qualification as inherently oppressive (see Batchelor 2000: 209–10); Collingwood adopts a half-way house, warming to its wealth-producing endeavour, but condemning its tendency to competition and risk-taking.

Nowhere perhaps are the characteristics of Collingwood's economics more apparent than in their implications for the economics of taste. One way of setting the boundary to acquisitiveness is to point to objects which can be appreciated only through their distinctiveness. When it is realized that the poem or the painting or the piece of music can be understood and enjoyed only by recreating what each uniquely expresses, then it becomes impossible to think of the art work as a product open to unlimited reproduction and consumption. This leads to Collingwood's denial that art is 'a quality of objects' (PAE 195) which can be attached to any object at will, simply to satisfy a demand. Lying behind this view is the argument advanced in *Speculum Mentis* that economics is not a description of one type of action but an abstract account of all action (SM 173). So when art is approached from the standpoint of economics the artist becomes a producer, the work of art the product and the audience the satisfied (or dissatisfied) consumers. The error which results is to understand art not as it should be understood, as an activity of collaboration between artist and audience, but as the means to a state of affairs external to itself, for example, excitement, stimulation or distraction.

In a society in which each 'regards everyone else as a means to his own ends' (SM 173), then, as Hobbes famously argues, market value is the only possible value. Self-restraint comes about only because individuals discover that they have priced themselves too high for what the market will bear or that their appetites outreach their resources. Collingwood does not share Adam Smith's confidence that the satisfaction of private ends leads necessarily to public contentment, but the lack in Collingwood of a conception of distributive justice means that he has to look elsewhere for an alternative. A stable economic life involving sound money, responsible wealth creation and civilly conducted commercial dealings should prove self-regulating, but, as Collingwood's experience of inter-war economics might well have taught him, capitalist economies are heavily prone to crisis in which trust in the state's guiding hand is not always sufficient to find a way through.

As it did for many liberals, the English industrial revolution and its effects test Collingwood's resolve. While wealth increased through exploitation of mineral resources and improved communications, so did riches, massively for the few, but also gradually and more widely for the consuming many. The poor remained, of course but, as Collingwood a little pessimistically remarks, 'there will always be one law for the rich and another for the poor; for that is what being rich and being poor are' (NL 38.71). Moreover, exploitation of land brings wealth as a communal good into conflict with nature, so forcing Collingwood to make hard choices between competing goods. In Collingwood's liberal economics, ownership implies responsibility but, we might ask, to wealth creation or to landscape? Further, ownership does not always imply appreciation, just as, with possibly greater force, appreciation does not necessarily require ownership. With some goods, however, Collingwood sees the threat posed by greater dissemination of wealth in more intractable terms. Wealth more widely dispersed means greater freedom, and greater freedom challenges liberal values through speculative economic development and what Collingwood calls, 'the invasion of the country by petrol-driven hordes from the towns' (MGM 333).

Here Hobbes's view of value as a function of appetite is less appealing. For, as Collingwood is surely acknowledging in his plea for the protection of landscape, in addition to the countryside, there are some goods which can be made accessible to all only by destroying their standing as goods. A public good such as security or health cannot be removed from one without harming all. We may think of the publication of a work of literature as a public good, not because all should read it (many may be indifferent) but because no one will be penalized if they do. But, as Collingwood is surely telling us, an area of landscape – say the Lake District – one distinguished and advantaged by literary association as well as possessing a unique natural beauty, is not a public good in either of these senses. It is not an amenity like a playground, but neither is it ideal-regarding as we might think a work of art to be.

Modern liberals who speak about the quality of life in terms of justice do so because they wish the goods essential to life to be distributed fairly. Like modern liberals, Collingwood proscribes economic obesity in all its forms but, unlike them, he argues not from the standpoint of justice but civility. Like modern liberals, Collingwood wishes to remain neutral regarding the substantive choices individuals make but, unlike them, he does not offer an account of basic goods which it is assumed that all will want. *Speculum Mentis* is not a guide to life, but it does provide a description of a life in which the forms of experience, art, religion, science, history and philosophy make up a unity which aspires to completeness. No one way of life is sufficient, but all are, in some sense, necessary if diversity and comprehension are to be embraced together. Collingwood's economic writings are eclectic. And the potential failure of eclecticism is that in appealing to everyone it satisfies no one. By giving priority to civility, Collingwood enshrines freedom above equality: private choices about how we should dispose of our income should remain private and out of range of redistributive public policy. By giving priority to wealth above riches, however, Collingwood's economics points in a very different direction. There is nothing wrong with people being acquisitive so long as they are industrious as well. Collingwood's connection between wealth and civilisation looks back to the eighteenth-century Scottish school of political economy (see Hont I. and Ignatieff M. 1983), but shorn of its emphasis on profitability. For Collingwood, wealth production in order to benefit the rich at the expense of the poor is barbarism, the active attempt to put the civilizing process into reverse. In our world, however, liberals will argue that civility is a poor substitute for justice. This means that Collingwood's economics is left awkwardly stranded between two allegiances: to Hobbes who sees worth as a function of cost and to Ruskin who absolutely does not. *The New Leviathan* was written to bring Hobbes up to date. In terms of contemporary liberalism, Collingwood's economic thought, specifically his attempt to deal with economic intemperance, is perhaps simply not new enough.

Afterword

Few philosophers have been more aware than Collingwood of the historical dimensions of politics. Politicians too have felt the inescapability of history. Winston Churchill who was British prime minister during much of the time Collingwood was writing *The New Leviathan* believed that whatever he had done in the past, and no matter what choices he made or might have made, his elevation to the leadership of his country through the struggle to come was providential. There is in this a great deal more than mischievous self-promotion. Churchill thought of his political role as pre-scripted. It is destiny which decides. Collingwood's philosophy of history told him otherwise. As the agencies of human character and choice the Fates belong to mythology, not history. In dangerous times historical knowledge might well help to spot the tiger in the grass, but deciding what to do about it is a different matter. To think otherwise is clairvoyance, not history as Collingwood understands it.

The New Leviathan was written as a defence of civilisation against barbarism. In 1940 barbarism took the form of Nazism and its onslaught cut deep. It is no accident that the engine which drives *The New Leviathan* is philosophy nor is it incidental that the concept which it defends as the mainstay of any human life worth the name is civility. Collingwood's arguments are tailored to his purpose. Civility is the moral imperative of civilisation. It is grounded in a philosophy of mind which provides the foundations for the argument and shapes the kind of politics that the book defends. Throughout his working life one of Collingwood's main concerns was to reach a rapprochement between philosophy and history. *The New Leviathan* can be read as the exemplification of this. In this guise the book is an attempt to crystallize its times in thought. It can be argued that in this Collingwood is only half-successful. From one perspective Collingwood's touch is sure, and he shows why civility is basic to human societies and what occurs when it is lost or is forcibly and contemptuously taken away. And yet from a different perspective – the development of a liberalism that is adequate to the social and political aspirations of the age – the feeling persists that Collingwood does not quite achieve his purpose. The encompassing in thought which Collingwood values as the book's driving methodology does not quite live up to the times in which it was written. Something important has been omitted.

Read in this perspective *The New Leviathan* is less an articulation of liberalism in the abstract than of the British way of life in particular. The question which arises from this is both hard and necessary. It is hard because in this instance we seem to be asking more of political philosophy than it is able to provide. It is necessary because the author of *The New Leviathan* never wanted a philosophy which was adrift from history. Civility is the key, but for many in Britain, increasingly so as the war progressed and particularly on the Left, it was an ideal which fell short of its time. It is no answer to argue, as Collingwood might have done, that what is true of civility is true of all ideals. In the crisis of 1940 he looked to essentials, but as the burdens of war increased the popular mood was otherwise. Civility may well be the basis for any human life worth the name but, if it is unaccompanied by principles of social justice, too many questions are left unanswered and too many legitimate demands are set aside.

It is not difficult to imagine Collingwood's reply to this criticism. The point of philosophy is not simply to reflect the problems of the age but to scrutinize them. A political society with civility at its core gives peace and security to free relationships, including the free exchange of goods, without imposing on its citizens a specific conception of distributive justice. Collingwood was convinced that justice was sought through law, whether criminal or civil, and he thought too that the concept of justice expressed by legal judgements concerned rectification not distribution. Not only does Collingwood say quite explicitly that 'a society and a civilized society are thus the same' (WCM NL 509), but also, again quite explicitly, that the notion of a fair price is 'merely the application to exchange of the distinction between free action and forced action' (WCM NL 505), the very distinction which explains the essence of civility as he understands it.

Contemporary reviews of *The New Leviathan* read the book as a work of political philosophy (for these see RC: 215–16). They did not see it as a political programme or policy. In this respect the early reviewers were surely right. While it is possible to extract practical conclusions from Collingwood's arguments these are not his primary purpose. And yet it is surely the case that such arguments, together with the often highly original and innovative concepts that inform them in *The New Leviathan*, can revitalize our understanding of particular human practices. An example might be education. Collingwood is not directly concerned with the education system itself, but rather with the human capacities which have to be in place for there to be a system of education at all. But this does not rule out interconnection between a given practice and the presuppositions which inform it. In fact, it encourages it. So in the case of education a discussion of the concepts of re-enactment and imagination can show why history and art are necessary in education (see Hughes-Warrington 2003).

In works written around the same time as *The New Leviathan* Collingwood defended Christianity as the living faith which he argued is a necessary condition of a liberal society and the civility which he argued was its mainstay. He writes, 'The doctrines concerning human nature on which liberal or democratic practice was based were not empirically derived from research into anthropological and psychological data; they were a matter of faith; and these Christian doctrines were the source from which they were derived' (FN EPP 190). For Collingwood, as we know, a society without civility is scarcely a society at all. And yet it is not difficult to think of a way of life which is civil but also substantially unjust. The Antebellum Southern States of America might be a defining example. Another might be Germany under the Third Reich, before impending defeat changed the basis of human relationships. Certainly these are dramatic and possibly extreme cases, but they express the important point that without justice civility loses much of its moral force. But this is not quite what *The New Leviathan* teaches. In Collingwood's view, all societies are approximations to an ideal. He writes, 'What is called a society never altogether deserves the name' (WCM NL 509). Restlessness when an ideal continues to serve its particular purpose but no longer covers new expectations is one indication of this.

In this respect, Collingwood's 'What Civilization Means', a work written towards the end of 1939 and not published in his lifetime, but which sets much of the agenda for *The New Leviathan*, reflects the preoccupations of the time. Whether or not a more just society was a utopian or dystopian dream or an achievable object of reform was a contemporary question of both theoretical and practical interest. Indeed, during 1941 when in the first six months of that year much of the second half of *The New Leviathan* was written, calls in Britain for a new social order, one based on justice and equality, including extensive redistribution of wealth and state provision of welfare, were pressing and hard to ignore. Social justice may not then have been given the philosophically sophisticated treatment it would receive in later liberal theories of justice, but in content and sometimes in name it was asserted as a principle that no programme of reform could do without. Liberalism allied with a Christian social message, in the shape, say, of William Temple's *Christianity and the Social Order* (1942), a book which at the time gained a significantly large readership, seemed to reflect the kind of society the British people wanted after the war was over. A work published by the Ministry of Information in February 1941 said of these general and wide-ranging aspirations, 'It is hoped that the extremes of wealth and poverty will be swept away, that there will be a greater degree of social security for all and that what is loosely termed "privilege" will also be got rid of' (see Todman 2016: 645). Although Collingwood does not ignore the relation between a just society and a civil one since he does distinguish between wealth and riches, nevertheless he states his own view very clearly: the first imperative of civilization is that of Hobbes, 'Seek peace and ensure it.'

It is apparent then that civility in the absence of justice leaves too many legitimate claims unaddressed. In addition, civility cannot be completely disassociated from cost. It is said that behaving civilly to others costs nothing. That may be true when we think of civility as an aspect of good manners and compare it with other values which place a greater strain on human interests and capacities. But the defence of civility as a practice against an enemy determined to destroy it required much by way of sacrifice of life and effort and was hugely draining of material and economic resources. If philosophy is to bear upon life, as Collingwood insists, then it needs to say something at least theoretically about the distribution of the burdens involved. Philosophical scrutiny has a place here because there are many different ways of adjudicating between benefits and burdens, and because the standard chosen will affect the distribution which results; most importantly of all perhaps because the reasons lying behind a government's choice of standard are not always made explicit.

For many in Britain when *The New Leviathan* was being written, as T. D. Burridge puts it, 'It was not enough to want victory; it was essential to want victory for ends which would make possible an enduring peace' (Burridge 1976: 54). One of these ends was social justice. Collingwood gave reasons for what many in Britain saw instinctively, that without civility the British way of life is shorn of its most distinctive and essential feature. But for an increasing number of those who were seeing the war through, and were looking for a fairer distribution of economic and social goods, civility without social justice could never deliver the imperative the times required.

Although Collingwood did not live to see the Allied victory which concluded the end of the war in Europe, he did experience the general will to resistance during the war's early years when the British way of life was imperilled. As a philosopher who was more than ordinarily aware that moral concepts are not just given in theory, but follow, and sometimes change, trajectories in life, Collingwood knew that what might be a sufficient description in one context in another may well be inadequate to, or misrepresent, possibly even falsify, the issues at stake. Strains within a way of life are not worked out at the level of theory. Responding civilly when what is demanded is justice is surely productive of exactly the kind of strain-causing dissonance that occurs when a way of life is changing, perhaps coming to an end, and when one concept is stretched beyond its limits and another scarcely formulated.

The job of principles of social justice is to provide an impartial arbitration between demands. It is not the philosophy of mind grounding Collingwood's liberalism that blocks him from adopting this point of view. Nor should we think that Collingwood's contractualism, with its emphasis on the move from non-agreement to agreement, is in any way unsympathetic. Supporters of social justice argue that it promotes a wider measure of agreement than can be achieved by civility since it helps to minimize envy, dilute feelings of social exclusion and grounds a framework of legal principle through which grievances of various kinds can be addressed. It is hard to think of Collingwood not welcoming these as desirable social goods. Whether grievances are real or fanciful, justified or merely self-serving are appropriate questions for social justice to answer. Leaving them unexamined or describing them in terms which understate what they are about are surely to be considered omissions of political rule, as Collingwood understands it. And, yet in *The New Leviathan* the principles governing this process are left largely implicit.

The reasons for this are quite apparent. The main focus of Collingwood's interest is civilization and the way of life appropriate to it. The essence of this is the mitigation of causes of quarrel so that, for example, bearers of grievances do not give up on justice and think themselves 'ill-used' (NL 40.37), as Collingwood puts it. A fear that social justice is not the state's business does much to explain Collingwood's reticence. Social justice is an idea which makes liberals nervous because it licenses a degree of compulsive public presence in private life which they do not want, although it also gives them hope since it promises to narrow the social and economic inequalities they oppose. In fact, Collingwood's description of social ills as incivilities shows us clearly where his priorities lie. Such was the speed of change wrought in Britain during the writing of *The New Leviathan* it is not surprising that the new articles of faith, later embodied in such documents as the Beveridge Report (1943), together with other similar manifestos of state sponsored social improvement, are encompassed, if at all, in Collingwood's work through an ideal which falls short of what they require. We might think of this not as a sign that Collingwood's hoped for rapprochement between philosophy and history had failed, but that for a short time in Britain, at a particular stage of its history, it was civility as the value basic to any liveable human society that needed defence. In fact, Collingwood was very aware that the track of ideas in history does not run smoothly. He gives an instance in *The New Leviathan* – 'Early Islam was a revolt against civilization only in the rather special sense that it was a revolt against something that had not yet happened; a revolt against the embryonic form that civilization had not yet quite taken, but was beginning to take' (NL 42.73). By taking this example as a model it should be perfectly possible to understand *The New Leviathan* (or at least sections of it) as a defence of social justice as a form of 'something that had not yet happened' but which it 'was beginning to take'. Collingwood, it might be argued, was sniffing the wind not, as he describes the early Islamists as doing, with the intention of mounting a pre-emptive attack, but to give an embryonic idea of social justice a little basic support. And yet my view remains cautionary. There is too much in *The New Leviathan* which treats the idea of social justice as unwarranted for this charitable interpretation to work completely. Collingwood's purpose was redemptive rather than reformatory. Whether or not the goods of civilization – social and economic well being, education, law and order – are considered as blessings or as tributes to the liberal way of life is a question that modern liberals usually refrain from answering, but it is one that in Collingwood's way of thinking retains a nagging influence. In any case the philosophical difficulty does not go away. Civility without social justice may leave many questions unanswered, but social justice without civility would scarcely be justice at all.

References

Addison, P. (1994), *The Road to 1945*, revised edition, London, Pimlico.
Amery, L. (1988), *The Empire at Bay, The Leo Amery Diaries 1929-1945*, edited by John Barnes and David Nicholson, foreword by Lord Stockton, London, Hutchinson.
Anonymous (1942), 'Review of R. G. Collingwood, *The New Leviathan*', *The Times Literary Supplement*, 11 July: 340.
Annan, N. (1990), *Our Age, Portrait of a Generation*, London, Hutchinson.
Arndt, H. W. (1940), 'The Social Outlook of the British Philosophers', *Science and Society*, 4, 4: 438-46.
Aster, S. (ed.) (2004), *Appeasement and All Souls, A Portrait with Documents 1937-1939*, Camden Society, Fifth Series, Volume 24, Cambridge, Cambridge University Press.
Ayer, A. J. (1977), *Part of My Life*, London, Collins.
Balfour, M. (1979), *Propaganda in War 1939-1945*, London, Routledge and Kegan Paul.
Ball, S. (ed.) (1999), *Parliament and Politics in the Age of Churchill and Attlee, The Headlam Diaries 1935-1951*, Cambridge, Cambridge University Press.
Barry, B. (1965), *Political Argument*, London, Routledge and Kegan Paul.
Barry, B. (1989), *Democracy, Power and Justice, Essays in Political Theory*, Oxford, Clarendon Press.
Barry, B. (1990), 'How Not To Defend Liberal Institutions', *British Journal of Political Science*, 20: 1-14.
Barry, B. (2005), *Why Social Justice Matters*, Cambridge, Polity.
Bassett, R. (1948), 'Telling the Truth to the People, the Myth of the Baldwin 'Confession', *Cambridge Journal*, II, 2: 84-95.
Batchelor, J. (2000), *John Ruskin, No Wealth but Life*, London, Chatto and Windus.
Bates, D. (1996), 'Rediscovering Collingwood's Spiritual History (in and out of context)', *History and Theory*, 35: 29-55.
Baynes, N. H. (1943), *A Short List of Books on National Socialism*, London, Historical Association.
Berlin, I. (1986), 'A Personal Tribute to Adam von Trott (Balliol 1931)', *Balliol College Annual Record*, 61-2.
Berlin, I. (2013), *Building, Letters 1960-1975*, edited by Henry Hardy and Mark Pottle, London, Chatto and Windus.
Berlin, I. (2015), *Affirming, Letters 1975-1997*, edited by Henry Hardy and Mark Pottle, London, Chatto and Windus.
Best, G. (2005), *Churchill and War*, London, Hambledon.

Bonney, R. (2009), *Confronting the Nazi War on Christianity, the Kulturkampf Newsletters 1936-1939*, Berne, Peter Lang, International Academic.
Bosanquet, B. (1917), *Social and International Ideals*, London, Macmillan.
Boucher, D. (1989), *The Social and Political Thought of R. G. Collingwood*, Cambridge, Cambridge University Press.
Boucher, D. (1992), 'Introduction', NL.
Boucher, D. (1995), 'The Principles of History and the Cosmology Conclusion to The Idea of Nature', *Collingwood Studies*, 2: 140-75.
Boucher, D. (1998), 'British Idealism and the Just Society', in David Boucher and Paul Joseph Kelly (eds), *Social Justice from Hume to Walzer* (1998), London, Routledge: 80-101.
Boucher, D. and Smith, T. 'Introduction: The Biography of *An Autobiography*', AWOW: xxi-xlix.
Boucher, D. 'Collingwood and European Liberalism', AWOW: 377-99.
Bowra, M. (1966), *Memories 1898-1939*, London, Weidenfeld and Nicolson.
Bradshaw, D. (1997), 'British Writers and Anti-Fascism in the 1930s, Part I: The Bray and Drone of Tortured Voices', *Woolf Studies Annual*, 3: 3-27.
Bradshaw, D. (1998), 'British Writers and Anti-Fascism in the 1930s, Part II: Under the Hawk's Wings', *Woolf Studies Annual*, 4: 41-66.
Brendon, P. (2000), *The Dark Valley, A Panorama of the 1930s*, London, Jonathan Cape.
Burke, E. (1982), *Reflections on the Revolution in France*, edited with an introduction by Connor Cruise O'Brien, Harmondsworth, Penguin.
Burridge, T. D. (1976), *British Labour and Hitler's War*, London, Andre Deutsch.
Cadogan, A. (1971), *The Diaries of Sir Alexander Cadogan 1938-1945*, edited by David Dilkes, London, Cassell.
Calder, A. (1992), *The People's War, Britain 1939-1945*, London, Pimlico.
Carritt, E. F. (1934), 'Dialectical Materialism', in Hyman Levy et al. (eds), *Aspects of Dialectical Materialism*, London, Watts: 123-46.
Charmley, J. (1993), *Churchill: The End of Glory*, London, Hodder and Stoughton, London.
Churchill, W. S. (1941), 'Be Ye Men of Valour', an address broadcast 19 May 1940, as reprinted in *Into Battle, Speeches by the Right Hon. Winston S. Churchill*, Compiled by Randolph S. Churchill, London, Cassell.
Churchill, W. S. (1949), *The Second World War*, Volume 1, *The Gathering Storm*, London, Cassell.
Churchill, W. S. (1951), *The Second World War*, Volume IV, *The Hinge of Fate*, London, Cassell.
Clarke, P. (2002), *The Cripps Version, The Life of Sir Stafford Cripps*, London, Allen Lane.
Cockin, F. A. (1945), *People Matter, Broadcast Talks*, London, SCM Press.
Cohen, G. A. (2000), *If You're an Egalitarian How Come You're So Rich?* Cambridge, MA, Harvard University Press.

Cohen, G. A. (2008), *Rescuing Justice and Equality*, Cambridge, MA, Harvard University Press.
Collini, S. (2006), *Absent Minds, Intellectuals in Britain*, Oxford, Oxford University Press.
Collini, S., and Williams, B. (2005), 'Collingwood, Robin George (1889–1943)', *Oxford Dictionary of National Biography*, Oxford, University Press.
Colls, R. (2013), *George Orwell, English Rebel*, Oxford, Oxford University Press.
Colville, J. (2005), *The Fringes of Power, Downing Street Diaries 1939–1955*, London, Phoenix.
Connelly, J. (2003), *Metaphysics, Method and Politics, The Political Philosophy of R. G. Collingwood*, Exeter, Imprint Academic.
Connelly, J. 'Collingwood Controversies', AWOW: 399–427.
Connelly, J., Johnson, P., and Leach, S. (2015), *R. G. Collingwood, A Research Companion*, London, Bloomsbury (hereafter referred to as RC).
Cowling, M. (1975), *The Impact of Hitler, British Politics and British Policy 1933–1940*, Cambridge, Cambridge University Press.
Cowling, M. (1980), *Religion and Public Doctrine in Modern England*, Cambridge, Cambridge University Press.
Crawford, S., Ulmschneider, K., and Elsner, J. (eds) (2017), *Ark of Civilization, Refugee Scholars and Oxford University 1930–1945*, Oxford, Oxford University Press.
Crick, B. (1964), 'Introduction to Dr. Brigitte Granzow', *A Mirror of Nazism, British Opinion and the Emergence of Hitler 1929–1933*, London, Victor Gollancz.
Crossman, R. H. (1958), 'When Lightning Struck the Ivory Tower: R. G. Collingwood', *New Statesman and Nation*, XVII, (1939), 222–3, as reprinted in Crossman, R. H. (1958), *The Charm of Politics*, London, Hamish Hamilton: 105–9.
Crowdy, T. (2008), *Deceiving Hitler, Double Cross and Deception in World War II*, Oxford, Osprey Publications.
Cruikshank, C. (1977), *The Fourth Arm, Psychological Warfare 1938–1945*, London, Davis-Poynter.
Dear, I. (1966), *Sabotage and Subversion, The SOE and the OSS at War*, London, Cassell.
Delmer, S. (1962), *Black Boomerang*, New York, Viking Press.
Dodds, E. R. (1977), *Missing Persons*, Oxford, Clarendon Press.
Doerr, P. W. (1998), *British Foreign Policy 1919–1939*, Manchester, Manchester University Press.
Donagan, A. (1962), *The Later Philosophy of R. G. Collingwood*, Oxford, Clarendon Press.
Dray, W. H. (1995), *History as Re-enactment, R. G. Collingwood's Idea of History*, Oxford, Clarendon Press.
Dubnov, A. M. (2012), *Isaiah Berlin The Journey of a Jewish Liberal*, New York, Palgrave Macmillan.
Dussen, W. J. van der. (1981), *History as a Science, The Philosophy of R. G. Collingwood*, The Hague, Martinus Nijhoff.

Dussen, Jan van der (1993), 'Introduction to R. G. Collingwood', *The Idea of History*, revised edition, Oxford, Clarendon Press.
Dussen, Jan van der. (2013), 'Collingwood's Philosophy of History in the Year of His an Autobiography', AWOW: 305–35.
Dutton, D. (2001), *Neville Chamberlain*, London, Arnold.
Eatwell, R. (1971), 'Munich, Public Opinion, and the Popular Front', *Journal of Contemporary History*, 6/4: 122–39.
Eisenstein, M. M. (1999), *Phenomenology of Civilization, Reason as a Regulative Principle in Collingwood and Husserl*, Lanham, University Press of America.
Ensor, R. C. K. (1939), *'Mein Kampf'*, Oxford Pamphlets on World Affairs, Oxford, Clarendon Press.
Evans, R. J. (2008), *The Third Reich at War*, London, Allen Lane.
Evans, R. J. (2015), *The Third Reich in History and Memory*, London, Little Brown.
Feiling, K. (1946), *The Life of Neville Chamberlain*, London, Macmillan.
Forster, J. (1874), *The Life of Charles Dickens: 1852–1870*, Volume 3, London, Chapman and Hall.
Furbank, P. N. (1978), *E. M. Forster, A Life*, Volume Two, *Polycrates' Ring 1914–1970*, London, Secker and Warburg.
Gardiner, J. (2004), *Wartime Britain 1939–1945*, London, Headline Book Publishing.
Garnett, D. (2002), *The Secret History of PWE The Political Warfare Executive 1939–1945*, with an introduction and notes by Andrew Roberts, London, St. Ermin's Press.
Gilbert, M. (1976), *Winston S. Churchill, Volume V, 1922–1939*, London, Heinemann.
Gilman, J. E. (1986), 'R. G. Collingwood and the Religious Sources of Nazism', *Journal of the American Academy of Religion*, LIV: 108–28.
Glasser, R. (1988), *Gorbals Boy at Oxford*, London, Chatto and Windus.
Glees, A. (1982), *Exile Politics during the Second World War, The German Social Democrats in Britain*, Oxford, Clarendon Press.
Glees, A. (1987), *The Secrets of the Service, British Intelligence and Communist Subversion 1939–51*, London, Jonathan Cape.
Glover, J. (1999), *Humanity, A Moral History of the Twentieth Century*, London, Jonathan Cape.
Goldman, A. (1979), 'Germans and Nazis: The Controversy Over 'Vansittartism' in Britain during the Second World War', *Journal of Contemporary History*, 14: 155–91.
Gooch, G. P. (1945), Foreword to *The German Mind and Outlook*, London, Chapman and Hall.
Green, S. J. D. (2011), 'Appeasers and Anti-Appeasers: All Souls and the International Crisis of the 1930s', in *All Souls and the Wider World, Statesmen, Scholars and Adventurers c.1850–1950*, edited by S. J. D. Green and P. Horden, Oxford, Oxford University Press: 223–63.
Guthrie, W. K. C. (1950), *The Greeks and Their Gods*, London, Methuen.
Haddock, B. A. (1995), 'Vico, Collingwood and the Character of a Historical Philosophy', in *Philosophy, History and Civilization, Interdisciplinary Perspectives on*

R. G. Collingwood, edited by David Boucher, James Connelly, and Tariq Modood, Cardiff, Wales University Press: 130–52.

Hannay, H. (1941), 'Review of R. G. Collingwood, *An Autobiography*', *International Journal of Ethics*, li: 369–70.

Harrison, B. (1994), 'Politics', in Brian Harrison (ed.), *The History of the University of Oxford, Volume VIII, The Twentieth Century*, Oxford, Clarendon Press: 377–413.

Harrison, B. (1991), 'Oxford and the Labour Movement', *Twentieth Century British History*, 2: 15–39.

Haslam, J. (1999), *The Vices of Integrity, E. H. Carr 1892–1982*, London, Verso.

Hastings, M. (2009), *Finest Years, Churchill as Warlord 1940–1945*, London, Harper Press.

Headlam, C. (1999), *Parliament and Politics in the Age of Churchill and Attlee, The Headlam Diaries 1935–1951*, edited by Stuart Ball, Camden Fifth Series, 14, Cambridge, Cambridge University Press.

Healey, D. (1989), *The Time of My Life*, London, Michael Joseph.

Hegel, G. W. F. (1967), *The Philosophy of Right*, translated with Notes by Thomas Malcolm Knox, Oxford, Clarendon Press.

Hill, C. (1971), 'A D Lindsay', Dictionary of National Biography 1951–60, Oxford, Oxford University Press: 641–4.

Hobbes, T. (1651), *Leviathan*, edited with an introduction by Michael Oakeshott, Oxford, Basil Blackwell, 1960.

Hogg, Q. (1984), 'Hindsight', in Hopkinson (1984), T. 30.

Holroyd, M. (1991), *Bernard Shaw, Volume 3: The Lure of Fantasy*, London, Chatto and Windus.

Hont, I., and Ignatieff, M. (1983), *Wealth and Virtue*, Cambridge, Cambridge University Press.

Hopkinson, T. (1953), *George Orwell*, Longman, Longmans, Green and Co.

Hopkinson, T. (1982), *Of This Our Time, A Journalist's Story 1905–1950*, London, Hutchinson.

Hopkinson, T. (1984), *Picture Post 1938–1950*, edited with an introduction and new foreword by Tom Hopkinson, London, Chatto and Windus.

Howard, A. (1990), *Crossman, The Pursuit of Power*, London, Jonathan Cape.

Howarth, T. E. B. (1978), *Cambridge Between Two Wars*, London, Collins.

Howe, E. (1982), *The Black Game British Subversive Operations against the Germans during the Second World War*, London, Michael Joseph.

Hughes-Warrington, M. (2003), *How Good an Historian Shall I Be? The Historical Imagination and Education*, Exeter, Imprint Academic.

Inglis, F. (2009), *History Man, The Life of R. G. Collingwood*, Princeton, Princeton University Press.

Johnson, P. (1995), 'Intention and Meaning in Collingwood's Autobiography', *Collingwood Studies*, 2, Perspectives, edited by David Boucher and Bruce Haddock:12–43.

Johnson, P. (2008), 'Talking with Yahoos: Collingwood's Case for Civility', *British Journal for the History of Philosophy*, 16, 3: 595–624 (This article formed the basis for Chapter 4).

Johnson, P. (2010), 'R. G. Collingwood on Civility and Economic Licentiousness', *International Journal of Social Economics*, 37, 11: 839–51. (This article formed the basis for Chapter 11.)

Johnson, P. (2012), *A Philosopher at the Admiralty*, Exeter, Imprint Academic.

Johnson, P. (2013), *A Philosopher and Appeasement*, Exeter, Imprint Academic.

Johnson, P. (2017), 'One Cheer for Marx: R. G. Collingwood's Defence of the "Fighting Philosopher"', *History of Political Thought*, XXXVIII, I: 134–66.

Johnston, W. M. (1967), *The Formative Years of R. G. Collingwood*, The Hague, Martinus Nijhoff.

Kennedy, P. (1975), 'Idealists and Realists: British Views of Germany, 1864–1939', *Royal Historical Society Transactions*, Fifth Series, 25: 137–56.

Kershaw, I. (2004), *Making Friends with Hitler, Lord Londonderry and Britain's Road to War*, London, Allen Lane.

Klemperer, Klemens von. (1988), *A Noble Combat, The Letters of Sheila Grant Duff and Adam von Trott zu Solz 1932–1939*, Oxford, Clarendon Press.

Klemperer, Klemens von. (1992), *German Resistance Against Hitler, The Search for Allies Abroad, 1938–1945*, Oxford, Clarendon Press.

Knox, T. M. (1951), 'R. G. Collingwood', *Dictionary of National Biography, 1941–1950*, Oxford, Oxford University Press.

Knox, T. M. (1969), 'Review of William M Johnston, The Formative Years of R. G. Collingwood, Martinus Nijhoff, The Hague, 1967' in *The Philosophical Quarterly*, XIX: 165–6.

Kramnick, I., and Sheerman, B. (1993), *Harold Laski: A Life on the Left*, London, Allen Lane.

Laski, H. J. (1940), 'The Decline of Liberalism', in *Hobhouse Memorial Lectures 1930–1940*, London, Oxford University Press, 1948.

Laski, H. J. (1942), 'Review of R. G. Collingwood, *The New Leviathan*', *The New Statesman*, XXIV: 97–8.

Lewis, J. (2010), *Shades of Greene, One Generation of an English Family*, London, Jonathan Cape.

London, L. (2000), *Whitehall and the Jews, British Immigration Policy and the Holocaust 1933–1948*, Cambridge, Cambridge University Press.

MacIntyre, A. (2007), *After Virtue*, Third edition, London, Duckworth.

Mackay, D. S. (1944), 'Review of R. G. Collingwood, The New Leviathan', *Journal of Political Economy*, December, 364–5.

Mackenzie, W. (2002), *The Secret History of S. O. E. Special Operations Executive 1940–1945*, with an introduction by M. R. D. Foot, London, St Ermin's Press.

Maiolo, J. (2010), *Cry Havoc, The Arms Race and the Second World War, 1931–1941*, London, John Murray.

Malcolm, N. (1958), *Ludwig Wittgenstein, A Memoir,* with a Biographical Sketch by Georg Henrik Von Wright, Oxford, Oxford University Press.
Manchester, W. (1988), *The Caged Lion, Winston Spencer Churchill 1932-1940*, London, Michael Joseph.
Martin, K. (1953), *Harold Laski (1893-1950) A Biographical Memoir*, London, Victor Gollancz.
Mazower, M. (2008), *Hitler's Empire, Nazi Rule in Occupied Europe*, London, Allen Lane.
McCallum, R. B. (1943), 'Robin George Collingwood, 1889-1943', *Proceedings of the British Academy*, 29: 463-8.
McIntyre, K. B. (1996), 'Collingwood, Oakeshott and the Social Contract', *Collingwood Studies*, III: 118-23.
McLean, I. (1973), 'Oxford and Bridgewater', in Chris Cook and John Ramsden (eds), *By-Elections in British Politics*, London, Macmillan.
Meehan, P. (1992), *The Unnecessary War*, London, Sinclair-Stevenson.
Middlemas, K., and Barnes, J. (1969), *Baldwin*, London, Weidenfeld and Nicolson.
Miller, D. (1976), *Social Justice*, Oxford, Clarendon Press.
Miller, D., and Walzer, M. (eds) (1995), *Pluralism, Justice and Equality*, Oxford, Oxford University Press.
Mink, L. O. (1969), *Mind, History and Dialectic, The Philosophy of R. G. Collingwood*, Bloomington, Indiana State University Press.
Mitchell, L. (2009), *Maurice Bowra A Life*, Oxford, Oxford University Press.
Mitchison, N. (1979), *You May Well Ask A Memoir 1920-1940*, London, Victor Gollancz.
Monk, R. (2000), *Bertrand Russell, The Ghost of Madness*, London, Jonathan Cape.
Monk, R. (2019), 'How the Untimely Death of RG Collingwood Changed the Course of Philosophy Forever', *Prospect Magazine*, 5 September 2019.
Montaigne, M. (1905), *Essays*, translated by Charles Cotton, London, George Bell.
Mowat, C. L. (1955), *Britain between the Wars 1918-1940*, London, Methuen.
Nagel, T. (1978), 'Ruthlessness in Public Life' in Stuart Hampshire (ed.), *Public and Private Morality*, Cambridge, Cambridge University Press: 75-91.
Newcourt-Nowodworski, S. (2005), *Black Propaganda in the Second World War*, Stroud, Sutton.
Newman, J. (1979), 'Two Theories of Civilization', *Philosophy*, 54: 473-83.
Nicholson, P. P. (1990), *The Political Philosophy of the British Idealists, Selected Studies*, Cambridge, Cambridge University Press.
Nicolaievsky, B., and Maenchen-Helfen, O. (1936), *Karl Marx: Man and Fighter,* Translated by Gwenda David and Eric Mosbacher, London, Methuen.
Oldfield, A. (1995), 'Metaphysics and History in Collingwood's Thought', *Philosophy, History and Civilization Interdisciplinary Perspectives on R. G. Collingwood*, edited by David Boucher, James Connelly, and Tariq Modood, Cardiff, University of Wales Press: 182-203.
Ollard, R. (1999), *A Man of Contradictions, A Life of A. L. Rowse*, London, Allen Lane.

Orwell, G. (1998), 'Politics vs. Literature: An Examination of Gulliver's Travels', in *The Complete Works of George Orwell*, edited by Peter Davison, Volume Eighteen, London, Secker and Warburg.

Overy, R. (2011), *The Ulrich von Hassell Diaries 1938–1944, The Story of the Forces against Hitler inside Germany*, Foreword by Agostino von Hassell, introduction by Overy, R. Translated by G. Brooks, London, Frontline Books.

Pakenham, F. (1953), *Born to Believe*, London, Jonathan Cape.

Palmier, J. M. (2006), *Weimar in Exile: the Anti-Fascist Emigration in Europe and America*, translated by David Fernbach, London, Verso.

Parker, R. A. C. (2000), *Churchill and Appeasement*, London, Macmillan.

Patrick, J. (1995), 'Fighting in the Daylight: the Penultimate Collingwood, 1937–1941', *Collingwood Studies*, 2: 73–88.

Patrick, J. (2013), 'The Oxford Man', in AWOW: 213–47.

Paylor, A. (2015), 'R. G. Collingwood's Critique of Nazism: Liberal, Marxist or Conservative?', *Politics, Religion and Ideology*, 16, 2–3: 54–172.

Paxton, R. O. (1972), *Vichy France, Old Guard and New Order 1940–1944*, London, Barrie and Jenkins.

Pether, J. (2011), *Black Propaganda*, Bletchley Park Trust, Report Number 12, new edition.

Phillips, D. G. (1983), *The British University reform Policy in Germany, 1945–1949*, Thesis presented for the Degree of Ph.D., Oxford, University of Oxford.

Pidgeon, G. (2003), *The Secret Wireless War, the story of MI6 Communications 1939–1945*, Sussex, Arundel Books.

Porter, R. (1988), *Gibbon*, New York, St. Martin's Press.

Rankin, N. (2008), *Churchill's Wizards, The British Genius for Deception 1914–1945*, London, Faber.

Rawls, J. (1973), *A Theory of Justice*, Oxford, Oxford University Press.

Rawls, J. (1980), 'Kantian Constructivism in Moral Theory', *Journal of Philosophy*, 77: 515–72.

Rawls, J. (1993), *Political Liberalism*, New York, Columbia University Press.

Rawls, J. (1999), *A Theory of Justice*, revised edition, Cambridge, Harvard University Press.

Rawls, J. (2000), *Lectures on the History of Moral Philosophy*, edited by Barbara Hermann, Cambridge, Harvard University Press.

Rawls, J. (2001), *Justice as Fairness, A Re-statement*, edited by Erin Kelly, Cambridge, Harvard University Press.

Rawls, J. (2009), *A Brief Inquiry into the Meaning of Sin and Faith*, edited by Thomas Nagel, London, Harvard University Press.

Ree, J. (1984), *Proletarian Philosophers, Problems in Socialist Culture in Britain 1900–1940*, Oxford, Oxford University Press.

Rees, G. (1971), *A Chapter of Accidents*, London, Chatto and Windus.

Reynolds, D. (1985), 'Churchill and the British 'Decision' to Fight on in 1940: Right Policy, Wrong Reasons', in Richard Langhorne (ed.), *Diplomacy and Intelligence during the Second World War, Essays in Honour of F H Hinsley*, Cambridge, Cambridge University Press: 147–68.

Reynolds, D. (2004), *In Command of History, Churchill Fighting and Writing the Second World War*, London, Allen Lane.

Roberts, A. (1991), *'The Holy Fox' A Biography of Lord Halifax*, London, Weidenfeld and Nicolson.

Roberts, A. (2006), *A History of the English-Speaking Peoples since 1900*, London, Weidenfeld and Nicolson.

Rogers, B. (1999), *A J Ayer, A Life*, London, Vintage.

Rose, N. (1978), *Vansittart, Study of a Diplomat*, London, Heinemann.

Scott, D. (1971), *A. D. Lindsay, A Biography*, Oxford, Basil Blackwell.

Self, R. (2006), *Neville Chamberlain, A Biography*, Aldershot, Ashgate.

Sell, A. P. F. (1995), *Philosophical Idealism and Christian Belief*, Cardiff, University of Wales Press.

Shirer, W. L. (1960), *The Rise and Fall of the Third Reich*, London, Secker and Warburg.

Shirer, W. L. (1985), *The Nightmare Years 1930–1940, A Memoir of the Life and the Times*, Volume II, Toronto, Bantam Books.

Shklar, J. (1984), *Ordinary Vices*, London, Harvard University Press.

Sisman, A. (2010), *Hugh Trevor-Roper, The Biography*, London, Weidenfeld and Nicolson, London.

Skidelsky, R. (1992), *John Maynard Keynes, The Economist as Saviour 1920–1937*, Volume Two, London, Macmillan.

Skidelsky, R. (2000), *John Maynard Keynes, Fighting for Britain 1937–1946*, Volume Three, London, Macmillan.

Smallwood, P. (2013), 'Collingwood's Autobiography as Literature', in AWOW: 427–49.

Smith, A. (1976), *The Theory of Moral Sentiments*, edited by D. D. Raphael and A. L. Macfie, Oxford, Clarendon Press.

Smyth, D. (1985), 'The Politics of Asylum, Juan Negrin and the British Government in 1940', in Richard Langhorne (ed.), *Diplomacy and Intelligence during the Second World War, Essays in Honour of F. H. Hinsley*, Cambridge, Cambridge University Press: 126–47.

Spender, S. (1951), *World within World*, London, Hamish Hamilton.

Susskind, J. (2011), *Karl Marx and British Intellectuals in the 1930s*, Burford, Davenant Press.

Sutcliffe, P. H. (1978), *The Oxford University Press, An Informal History*, Oxford, Oxford University Press.

Swann, B., and Aprahamian, F. (eds) (1999), *J. D. Bernal, A Life in Science and Politics*, London, Verso.

Swift, J. (2003), *Gulliver's Travels*, edited with an introduction and note by Robert Demaria, London, Penguin Books.

Taylor, A. J. P. (1983), *A Personal History*, London, Hamish Hamilton.
Thomas, E. M. (1965), *Orwell*, Edinburgh and London, Oliver and Boyd.
Thomas, K. (1965), 'The Social Origins of Hobbes' Political Thought', in *Hobbes Studies*, edited by Keith C. Brown, Oxford, Basil Blackwell: 185–236.
Todman, D. (2016), *Britain's War, Into Battle 1937–1941*, London, Allen Lane.
Trubowitz, and P., Harris, P. (2014), 'When States Appease: British Appeasement in the 1930s', *Review of International Studies*, 41: 289–311.
Vansittart, Sir Robert. (1941), *Black Record, Germans Past and Present*, London, Hamish Hamilton.
Vincent, A. (1995), 'Social Contract in Retrospect', *Collingwood Studies*, II: 134–45.
Waismann, F. (1968), *How I See Philosophy*, edited by Rom Harre, London, Macmillan.
Walker, P. G. (1991), *Political Diaries 1932–1971*, edited with an introduction by Robert Pearce, London, Historians' Press.
Walzer, M. (1977), *Just and Unjust Wars*, London, Allen Lane.
Werskey, G. (1978), *The Visible College*, London, Allen Lane.
West, W. J. (1987), *Truth Betrayed*, London, Duckworth.
Whiting, R. (1994), 'University and Locality', in Harrison, B. (1994), 543–76.
Wittgenstein, L. (1969), *On Certainty*, edited by Gertrude Elizabeth MargaretAnscombe and Georg Henrik von Wright, translated by Denis Paul and Gertrude Elizabeth Margaret Anscombe, Oxford, Basil Blackwell.
Wittgenstein, L. (2003), *Public and Private Occasions*, James Carl Klagge and Alfred Nordmann (eds), Lanham, Rowman and Littlefield.
Woolf, L. (1990), *The Letters of Leonard Woolf*, edited by Frederic Spotts, London, Weidenfeld and Nicolson.
Woolf, V. (1990), *A Moment's Liberty: The Shorter Diary*, edited by Anne Olivier Bell, introduction by QuentinBell, London, Hogarth Press.

Index

Anschluss 1–3, 6, 13–14
appeasement, British policy of 14–33, 37–53, 93, 96, 111–12, 121–3, 131–3, 143–6, 170
Aristotle 140, 214
Asquith, H. 37, 140, 180
Association of Writers for Intellectual Liberty (AWIL) 147
Attlee, C. 91–2
Austin, J. L. 19, 27–8
AWIL *see* Association of Writers for Intellectual Liberty (AWIL)
Ayer, A. J. 28–9

Baldwin, S. 132–4, 140, 143, 169
Barry, B. 79, 83, 178–82, 194
Battle of Britain 93, 99, 111, 123, 161
Battle of the Atlantic 99, 129
Bell, C. 4
Bell, Bishop George 164
Berlin, I. 6, 18, 161
Beveridge Report 5, 93, 221
Bevin, E. 128
Bosanquet, B. 190
Bowra, M. 162
Burke, E. 77–9

Cadogan, A. Sir 3
Carr, E. H. 37
Carritt, E. F. 43, 147
Chamberlain, N. 14–33, 37–41, 52–3, 68, 89, 120–1, 147–9, 157
 and the 'Other' Germany 107, 162
 and Vansittartism 147–9
China 168
Christianity 50, 53, 85, 94, 113, 184
Churchill, W. 8, 53, 91–3, 99, 102, 106, 111, 121–2, 129–30, 132, 134, 144, 148, 212
 letter to Laski 172
 and the 'Other' Germany 162, 167–9
 and Vansittartism 152

Cobban, A. 94
Cockin, F. A. 111, 124
Cole, G. D. H. 20, 26, 29
Collingwood, E. W. 24, 160, 165, 171
Collingwood, R. G. (works)
 An Autobiography 3, 13–15, 17, 21, 22, 25–7, 31, 33, 34, 37–9, 42, 46, 47, 58, 68, 79, 95, 125, 126, 128, 131, 132, 147, 148, 158, 160, 180, 190, 211
 'The Devil' 93
 'Draft Preface' to The New Leviathan (EPP 224-8) 116–19
 'Economics as a Philosophical Science' (EPP 58-77) 182–4, 188, 191, 192, 197
 An Essay on Metaphysics 5, 48, 50, 51, 56, 66
 The First Mate's Log 52, 58, 64, 214, 216
 'Fairy Tales' (PE 15-288) 5
 'Fascism and Nazism' (EPP 187-96) 90, 96, 107, 108, 111, 159, 160, 219
 'Goodness, Rightness, Utility' (NL 391-479) 6, 71, 140
 The Idea of History 45, 47–9, 51, 52, 67, 73, 81, 92, 123, 125, 213
 The Idea of Nature 45
 'Man Goes Mad' (PE 305-35) 43, 79, 144, 145, 215
 'Money and Morals' 191
 'The Nature and Aims of a Philosophy of History' (EPH 34-56) 50
 The New Leviathan (structure of) 115–25, 125–43
 'Outlines of a Philosophy of History' (IH 426-81) 4
 'The Place of Art in Education' (EPA 187-207) 214
 'The Present Need of a Philosophy' (EPP 166-70) 44
 The Principles of Art 48, 50, 74
 The Principles of History xi, 48, 66

'Political Action' (EPP 92-109) 77, 192, 206, 212
Speculum Mentis 25, 29, 47, 216
'Three Laws of Politics' (EPP 207-23) 17, 111, 160, 171, 214
'What Civilization Means' (NL 480-511) 76, 81, 123, 124, 208, 209
Collingwood, R. G. letters to
 The Clarendon Press 117-18, 141
 Collingwood, E. W. C. 24, 160, 165, 171
 Coulton, G. G. 124
 Gilpatric, C. 53, 116-18, 149
 Knox, T. M. 65, 68, 101, 110-1, 121, 128
 Leyden, W von 141
 Lindsay, A. D. 20
 Simpson, F. G. 4, 112, 147
 The Times 23, 100, 121, 149
 Trott, A von. 161
Coulton, G. G. 124
Cripps, S. 16, 17, 20, 39, 109, 159
Crossman, R. H. S. 18, 20, 29, 38, 108-9

Das Wahre Deutschland 70
de Ruggiero, G. 25, 96
Delmer, S. 108, 109
Dickens, C. 125, 140
Dodds, E. R. 29, 147
Dunkirk 99, 123

economic exchange 183, 187, 194, 205, 213
Eden, A. Sir 64, 102, 158, 159
Electra House 102
Ensor R. C. K. 99
eschatology 123

Finland 89, 107, 168
FIL *see* For Intellectual Liberty (FIL)
For Intellectual Liberty (FIL) 147-8
Forster, E. M. 124, 148
Fraenkel, H. 90
France x, 68, 94, 99, 102, 110-1, 121, 169
Freud, S. 163
Freudianism 152

German Freedom Party 102, 104, 105
Germany 12-18, 24, 26, 31, 34, 39, 45, 63-8, 89-92, 96-113, 121-33, 141, 156-8, 171, 217

Gibbon, E. 4
Gillies, W. 159, 166, 167
Gilpatric, C. 53, 116-18, 149
Glasser, R. 29
Gooch, G. P. 150
Gordon Walker, P. 18, 21-6, 28, 29
Grant Duff, S. 150, 156, 161
Greece 55, 58, 62, 129
Green, T. H. 17, 19, 25, 29, 41, 46, 171, 172, 190, 211
Guilty Men 120, 132-4

Haffner, S. 90
Halifax, Lord 24, 32, 96, 111, 161
Hassell, U. von 114
Hauser, H. 90
Headlam, C. Sir 4
Healey, D. 18, 19, 89
Heath, E. 19
Hegel, G. W. F. 3, 45, 57, 59, 80, 152
Hellenism 156
Hill, C. 21
Hitler, A. 1, 2, 4-7, 15, 16, 18, 30, 39-40, 67, 90, 93, 102-8, 111, 113, 120-1, 132, 136, 153, 158-61, 165, 168, 170-1
Hobbes, T. ix, 3, 6, 69-71, 74, 85-6, 115, 117, 122, 137, 143, 164, 178-9, 193, 203, 209-11, 215-16, 220
Hogg, Q. 17, 19, 21, 22, 24, 25
Hopkinson, T. 1, 22, 28, 33, 91, 92
Horace 207

ILP *see* Independent Labour Party (ILP)
Independent Labour Party (ILP) 15, 68, 146, 147
Islam 222
Italy 45, 64, 96, 108, 111, 160

Jacobstall, P. 105
Japan 111, 168
Joseph, H. W. B. 19
Judaism 67, 68
just war theory 6, 94, 135, 170

Kant, I. 130, 138, 153
Keynes, J. M. 30, 31, 33, 188

Knox, T. M. 15, 40, 65, 68, 101, 110, 111, 121, 128
Kristallnacht 66

Labour Party 15–28
Laski, H. 143–6, 148–53
Leyden, W. von 105, 141
Lindsay, A. D. 40, 121
   Collingwood's letter of support 20
   and Oxford by-election 17–30
   policies of rearmament 22–7, 31, 121
Lloyd George, D. 140

Macdonald J. R. 132
Machiavelli, N. 130, 143
MacIntyre, A. 139–40
Mackay, D. S. 106
Macmillan, H. 19
magic 48–55
The Manchester Guardian 69, 161
Marx, K. 37–55
Marxism 37–55
McCallum R. B. 40
Mill, J. S. 43, 79
Mitchison, N. 7
Momigliano, A. 105, 171
money 184, 188–91, 197–8, 201, 210, 214
Montaigne, M. de 78
Munich Agreement 13–15, 17, 21–40, 44, 66, 96, 124
Mussolini, B. 64, 132, 143, 148, 169

Narvik Debate 53
Nazi-Soviet Pact 66, 68, 89, 107, 111, 148
Negrin, J. 92
The New Statesman 4, 91, 122, 151
Nietzsche, F. 57, 153
Norway 53, 121
Nuremburg laws 67

Orwell, G. 5, 33, 64, 65, 68, 82, 83, 84, 146
Oxford by-election 16–30
The Oxford Mail 22
Oxford University Press 31, 37, 48

paganism 153
Pakenham, F. 19, 26
Paton, H. J. 27
Peace Ballot 169

Pearl Harbour 100, 130
Picture Post 92
Pink Lunch Club 29
Plato 63, 64, 130, 131, 143
political morality 77, 119, 129–40
Popular Front 14–68
Price, H. H. 27
Priestly, J. B. 4
Prussianism 39, 90, 153, 160

question and answer logic 45, 63, 96, 115, 117, 119–20, 126

Rassentheorie 67, 68
Rawls, J. 176–7, 180–1, 184, 193, 196–7, 201, 204, 207–8, 211
Rees, G. 38
Robinson, J. 42
Roosevelt, F. D. 89, 168
Rousseau, J.-J. 6
Rowse, A. L. 24, 39
Ruskin, J. 37, 91, 179, 201, 214, 216
Russell, B. 122, 168–9
Ryle, G. 19, 27

Saar plebiscite 161
Sandys, D. 41, 148
Scapegoatism 155, 157, 161
Sermon on the Mount 76, 82
Shaw, G. B. 67
Shirer, W. L. 153, 172
Shklar, J. 78
Simpson, F. G. 4, 112, 147
Sisam, K. 32–3, 118
Smith, A. 80, 186, 215
Smith, J. A. 19–20, 24
social justice 5, 8, 91–3, 97, 175–96, 199, 200–3, 218
Socrates 55, 58, 61, 62, 63
SOE *see* Special Operations Executive (SOE)
Soviet Union 65–6, 68, 93, 100, 107, 122, 130, 141, 152, 171
   see also Nazi-Soviet Pact
Spain 13, 15, 16, 22, 32, 33, 39, 40, 41, 92, 96, 111, 121
Spanish Civil War 92, 146
Special Operations Executive (SOE) 102–3

Spender, S. 13
Spiecker, C. 102–4, 107, 109
Spinoza, B. 80
Stalin, J. 27, 68, 102, 158
Stuart, C. Sir 102
Swift, J. 71–86

Tacitus 154
Temple, W. 219
Thucydides 60
The Times 1, 23, 26–7, 30, 34–5, 96, 100, 121, 149–50, 160
Trevelyan, G. M. 149
Trevor-Roper, H. 52

Trott, A. von 104, 105, 150, 155, 156, 159, 161, 162

United States of America 89–90, 93, 100, 112, 116, 122

Vansittart, R. Sir 106, 143–72
Vansittartism 4, 143–72

Waismann, F. 75
Wells, H. G. 13
Wittgenstein, L. 75, 82, 95
Woolf, L. 94, 159, 167
Woolf, V. 6

www.ingramcontent.com/pod-product-compliance
Lightning Source LLC
Chambersburg PA
CBHW072141290426
44111CB00012B/1938